VIRGIL

ALSO BY PETER LEVI

The Art of Poetry
Collected Poems 1955-75
Marko the Prince (Serbo-Croat translations)
The Noise Made by Poems
Yevtushenko's Poems (translations)
A History of Greek Literature
The Life and Times of William Shakespeare
Boris Pasternak: A Biography
Tennyson
Edward Lear
Eden Renewed: The Public and Private Life of John Milton
Horace: A Life

VIRGIL

HIS LIFE AND TIMES

PETER LEVI

St. Martin's Press ᨐ New York

Library of Congress Cataloging-in-Publication Data

Levi, Peter.
  Virgil: his life and times / Peter Levi.
    p.   cm.
  Originally published: London: Duckworth, 1998.
  Includes bibliographical references and index.
  ISBN 0-312-19352-1
    1. Virgil. 2. Rome—History—Augustus, 30 B.C.-14 A.D.—Biography.
3. Ovid, 43 B.C.-17 or 18 A.D.—Friends and associates. 4. Horace—
Friends and associates. 5. Virgil—Friends and associates. 6. Rome—
Intellectual life. 7. Poets, Latin—Biography. I. Title.
PA6825.L48   1999
871'.012—dc21   98-47718
                                                                      CIP

First published in Great Britain by Gerald Duckworth & Co. Ltd.

First U.S. Edition: February 1999

10 9 8 7 6 5 4 3 2 1

CONTENTS

FOR DEIRDRE
WITH MY LOVE

PREFACE

I have been reading Virgil for more than fifty years and for the last thirty of them I preferred early Virgil. But I have never found it easy to make up my mind about him until now. I had much help from standard editions, which have altered beyond recognition since the nineteen forties, and from the innumerable forest of books about him that continue to appear. Anne Kuttner's *Dynasty and Empire in the Age of Augustus*, Nicholas Horsfall's *Companion to the Study of Virgil*, Jasper Griffin's writings about the poet, and Colin Hardie's, have been important to me, and I am grateful to Anthony Hobson for the loan of J. B. Trapp's lecture to the Society for Renaissance Studies (1980), and to Thomas Clarke for the 1965 edition of W. F. Jackson Knight's *Roman Virgil*. I found Christopher Baswell's Virgil *in Medieval England* (1995) fascinating and deeply illuminating, and the *New Horizons Search for Ancient Rome* taught me things I had not known: for example the fact that the goddess Cybele was imported into Rome as a talisman against the Carthaginians before 200 BC in the form of a black, conical, aniconic stone. I learnt of sanctuaries of the nomads and crossroads and chapels like those in the Eclogues only on p. 603 of the *Western Greeks*, 1996. But readers can discover most references in the new *Oxford Classical Dictionary* and in Horsfall. All I can add is Bertha Tilley's *Antiquity* article of September 1945, 'Vergilian Cities of the Roman Campagna', which was to me a revelation. I have attempted in this book not to repeat things treated in my *Horace* (1997) or in my Introduction to the Folio Society's Dryden's *Aeneid* (1993). I have no serious quarrel with the Latin text of Virgil's Works established by Mynors, but the translation of the Georgics by Robert Wells has given me constant inspiration and personal pleasure, although I have not used it in this book.

INTRODUCTION

What do we owe to Virgil?

When I was a schoolboy Virgil was *the* Latin poet, in a sense that even children would question today. He was the embodiment of that vast, ballooning idea of Roman civilisation and its great power and impressive material culture. For better or worse, I have now lost that simple vision. But Virgil's stature as a poet has not in the least diminished for me. His poetry rises high above Rome and its Caesars, and his victory lies in the supreme merit of his work. It begins in the Eclogues, which must be the most astounding first book of poetry ever published. Not even Spenser for all his brilliance ever equalled them (if anyone ever did, in English, then Milton came close, and his friend Andrew Marvell as close or closer). And it was this supreme poet of the Eclogues who went on to write the Georgics, and in the end the Aeneid. What may still be defended today is Virgil's power as a poet and the freshness of his verse. The history of European literature is real and still an urgent subject. You cannot arrive at Ibsen or Pushkin without going back through Byron to the ancient writers and Virgil; and without mastering those writers you will not advance to an understanding of the modern world.

There is a pressing need to restore Virgil's poetry to the true, unglamorised history of his own times, and to the poet's private life as far as we can know it, and the process of analysis of Virgil against the background of his own world is among the motives of this book. Horace was the principal subject of his own poetry and took an ironic view of much contemporary history, but Virgil is a shy character, and his irony is subtler. His Aeneid in particular has had a glamorous and to my mind unpredictable success, and a majestic influence related to history and civilisation and all those mighty themes. Every success of that kind is almost bound to be based on a misunderstanding.

The trouble is that Virgil is to us still a classic and the Aeneid has been *the* classic of European poetry, as T.S. Eliot kept pointing out. We are (or we used to be) so soaked in a tradition that stems from Virgil that we can easily find in him all the qualities of a classic, because it is precisely from him that we learnt

1

them. In the same way we were taught that Virgil was a natural Christian: and we modified our idea of him and of Christianity to believe that was true.

It is the word classic that needs to be re-examined, as Frank Kermode argued in *The Classic* (1975). As he said there, in the very idea of the classic the central statement is terribly entangled with imperialism, with the Roman empire and its ghost the Catholic Church, sitting crowned upon the tomb thereof, in Rome. Eliot's idea of a mystical core of Europe fed by Virgil was fully stated in *What is a Classic?* (1944) and more vehemently in *Virgil and the Christian World* (1951); it was the time of the foundation of the London Virgil Society with Eliot as the first President. Yet Gareth Reeves[1] showed more than twenty years ago that Eliot's idea about Virgil dated from 1935, when he came across one of those heroes of anti-Nazism, Theodor Haecker, who worked for a Munich publisher and had just written his remarkable book, *Virgil, Father of the West*. Eliot published him in *Criterion*, and Haecker's Virgil book swiftly appeared in English. For Eliot and for Virgil scholars like Wilson Knight, that book was of central importance.[2] Haecker died in the last year of the war (he was twice imprisoned), he is not now much read.

If instead of a classic, or *the* classic, we speak of the classics and the classical languages, then we are at once discussing something much broader, something essential to a thousand years and more of our history. We would have to include not only Homer, but Aristophanes and Plato and the great tragedians. We would then be speaking of the severest and most deeply effective instrument of education the human race has so far come across. We would embark on a course of reading of great interest and on unexpected pleasures. Without wishing to turn back the clock, to ignore science or to neglect modern languages, we would find that a vast and illuminating programme awaited us. I cannot help adding, God help us if we neglect it.

What is a classic does not, in fact, depend on Virgil. He is not the central figure. We are now loose of any tie to Rome or its nasty heroics. The agrarian enthusiasm of the thirties that inspired Eliot and Haecker and Maurras and Chesterton and Belloc is dated now. There are fashions even in reaction, and that fashion is over. We do not find in the two or three famous lines about *amor* in the tenth Eclogue a link that can bind together an entire Roman society, still less an imperial one. The idea is gross, it is a bursted balloon, because what about the slaves? Horace owned at least a dozen, and Virgil probably more. In the Rome of the Caesars, slaves were terribly numerous and not well treated.

It is against this background that we must make a serious attempt to assess Virgil, and to notice what his achievements were and were not. Virgil was read all over the Empire. But the form in which the Aeneid was then known – for example in the mosaics from south Ham now at Taunton – is that of the merest erotic romance, as if the Aeneid were by a Virgil just as decadent as the great historian Mommsen thought he was. Aeneas with a golden bough, the Aeneid quoted by Juno at the rape of Europa, and the quotation of the Book 9 of the Aeneid (473) from Vindolando on Hadrian's Wall may be thought equally frivolous. Even Virgil enthroned among muses from Hadrumetarah in Africa does not dispel the romance in the Aeneid.

We will have to make up our mind where Virgil stands today. His influence in some ways works against him, because we see him through a haze of derivative writers. I am writing for readers without Latin, but I am not sure what are the best translations. I think the best is Dryden's, yet in the end Dryden said if he had the whole job to do again, he would try blank verse: no doubt he was thinking enviously of the verse style of Milton, and rightly.

The best complete modern translation of Virgil is by C. Day Lewis, done during the Second World War, but the first Aeneid ever published in Britain, which was in Scots dialect (1553), was better still. It was by Gavin Douglas, Archbishop of St Andrew's and he is reported to have finished his work in eighteen months. Between Douglas and Dryden the attempts are too numerous to catalogue here, but it is worth noticing that Dryden as a boy thought he had been brought up on the large and finely illustrated folio Virgil by John Ogilby, a self-educated adventurer who was later cartographer royal to Charles II. His Virgil is far better than you would think. I am bound to admit that apart from Dryden the nearest approach to the pleasures Virgil's Latin offers is what I have found in Salvatore Quasimodo.

He wrote the line *e le parole nate fra le vigne*, which is not Virgil. But, that line does raise the problem of Virgilian style. For Quasimodo – as it is for Dryden – it was mostly the same from the Eclogues to the end of the Aeneid. Indeed, it is not obviously very different from the style in which these poets translate Ovid.

Yet the differences ought to be enormous. At school we were taught to write Latin verse of our own, and Virgil was the most admired model. But he was impossible, since his linguistic resources, his playfulness and his sheer eccentricities make his poems at least as different from normal Latin as Milton is from normal modern English. Virgil has been so successful in his lifework that later Latin authors seem insipid to us, and many earlier Latin poets ridiculous by comparison.

There is a special blossoming, a kind of fresh excellence in Virgil which is a matter of his time – we have to say the same about the sonnets of Shakespeare. We know little enough about early Latin, but Latin literature and poetry represents a continuous attempt to follow the great achievements and even the circus tricks of the Greeks.

It is open to a Latinist to prefer early Latin, which sounds as if it was hand-carved on granite slabs, but in Virgil's time Latin as supple as Greek was a new invention. The narrative hexameters of Ennius (239 – 169 BC) are of a heaviness that is often comic. By the time of Ovid (43 BC – 17? AD) things had gone almost too far, he was rhetorical and too fluid. In the poet philosopher Lucretius (94? – 55 BC), Latin poetry as a medium is still crude and needs cultivation. In spite of his stunning talent one feels that he was born too early. It was the generations of Catullus (84 – 54 BC), who died young and of Virgil (70 – 19 BC) and Horace (65 – 8 BC) in which poetry of original genius most flourished in Latin. And Tibullus (50? – 19 BC) and Propertius (about 50 – before 2 BC) are enough to show that Virgil and his friends did not have a monopoly as poets.

After the death of Augustus, however, poetry hardly survived. All that Latin contributed later was the choking snarls of Juvenal and the bitter chronicles of Tacitus. Plutarch's Lives of the Roman Emperors could not have been written in Rome. We know, for example, from a most interesting and lucid study of the strikingly regional accents of poets like Lucretius and of Virgil, that he composed his poetry in a strong Northern accent, and was among the last to do so.[3] What went wrong with Roman poetry was Roman politics. Without certain minimal conditions, there can be no serious poetry, and after the satires of Juvenal there was none. The performances of Statius and the rest were pitiful. They were 'A song To keep a drowsy Emperor awake'. How lucky it is for us therefore that we have to deal with the spring season of Roman poetry, since it died in its first summer. Within that brief season there is about Virgil a kind of majesty.

In spite of attempts that have been made, we have no agreed image of Virgil's face. In the late Republic the Roman magistrates might put their faces on the coinage, with symbols of their august lineage. Indeed, in Asia they might accept divine honours. But from the time of Augustus on, it was the Emperors and their families and favourites who were commemorated in sculpture at Rome, while the status of poets was so low that Suetonius wrote in praise of an Emperor not how much he paid them but how much he paid for them.

Virgil is an intensely personal poet, yet he is anonymous. The lives that we have of him were written in late antiquity and are full of fantasies. We can learn more about him from Horace and the careers of Maecenas and Augustus, and the few scraps of Augustus's correspondence. We can notice the problems that must have preoccupied him and pay attention to the elegance of his solutions. But in this endeavour we must pick our way most carefully. We are like Aeneas in the woods at Cumae, but for us there will be no golden bough.

It is scarcely surprising that our own time has seen a wish in America and in England to shake off an influence so old, so pervasive, and so hard to understand. My aim is not so ambitious as to try and restore his prestige single-handed. It has simply been to try to understand him in his original context. Virgil's influence must take care of itself and fight its own battles. But it is curious how the large questions that arise from him (and cannot be ignored) can be pinned down to smaller questions that do have answers: Virgil's dream of the Roman empire, for example, compared with its reality, which in the century and a half since Mommsen first snuffled his way through Calabria for Roman remains we have become able to discuss with less prejudice.

There are comments we can make about Virgil's famous humanity too. Was the affair between Dido and Aeneas a myth or fiction? Did Virgil inherit the story or think it up? Those old-fashioned scholars who believed most devoutly in Virgil's consummate artistry preferred on the whole to think he did make it up.

R.G. Austin in the introduction to his edition of book one of the Aeneid (1971) is a good example. He notices that the model appears to be Homer's nymph Calypso who detains Odysseus for years in a cave, 'The parallel is evident, but it is superficial'.[4] Austin is almost as lordly with the possibility that the episode was invented by Naevius in an epic poem about the Roman war with Carthage. Naevius (about 260 – 201 BC) did describe the wanderings of Aeneas and the storm off Africa and the argument in heaven about Aeneas. He may perfectly well have used the passionate affair he imagined Aeneas had with Dido, and its result, to explain the feud between Carthage and Rome. Also, earlier recorders of the legend than Virgil say Dido killed herself on a bonfire to avoid rape by Iarbas King of Libya.

It is important to know how much Virgil freely invented, or to what degree he is patching up an old legend. Dido had a sister Anna, who has a mysterious importance. Virgil uses her as a confidante or attendant out of a scene in tragedy. But in Ovid she pops up later on to give Aeneas ritual absolution in Italy, so that he can become the god Juppiter Indiges – the god of the place. And the elderly antiquarian Varro, whom Virgil knew, declared it was Anna who jumped onto the bonfire and not Dido.

What makes the truth so interesting is that if Virgil had his hands tied by the myth, then his solution in the Aeneid, the reunion in the underworld, is humanly acceptable. Virgil's Aeneas fell for Dido, but the gods told him to leave her and Aeneas obeyed. Dido's furious behaviour in the underworld after her suicide is a consequence – and one may be sorry for them both.

Scholars sternly announced that Aeneas had to behave as he did because of religious duty to obey the gods (pietas). And Addison says he should never have taken shelter from bad weather in a cave, at least not with a girl like Dido. For many hundreds of years readers of the Aeneid took a view which fitted Christian rules of marriage with no divorce, and saints have wept over Dido and Aeneas.

5

But now his behaviour seems dire and his fate not worth having. If you are in love with a nice, generous, beautiful lady in the desert, you do not give it up and leave her to suicide, just to become the founder of Rome, do you? So I prefer to think Virgil got his plot from Naevius: that is at least highly probable. And I do not feel happy over Virgil inventing the divine touch on the rudder and Dido's suicide. In the underworld, I think the poet is on Dido's side. (This problem was given an airing by A.S. Pease in his edition (1935) of Book IV and one is free to choose one's point of view.)[5]

Protests against Virgil's version of the story were written in his time. One is a Greek epigram in the Palatine Anthology (16, 51)[6] which appears also in a Latin version attributed to Ausonius (epig.118) and in English in Walter Ralegh's *History of the World*. Ralegh says[7]

> I am that Dido which thou here dost see,
> Cunningly framed in beauteous Imagery.
> Like this I was, but had not such a soul
> As Maro feigned, incestuous and foul.
> Aeneas never with his Trojan host
> Beheld my face, or landed on this coast.
> But flying proud Iarbas' villainy,
> Not mov'd by furious love or jealousy
> I did with weapon chaste to save my fame,
> Make way for death untimely, ere it came.
> This was my end; but first I built a Town,
> Reveng'd my husband's death, lived with renown.
> Why didst thou stir up Virgil, envious Muse,
> Falsely my name and honour to abuse?
> Readers, believe Historians, and not those
> Which to the world Jove's thefts and vice expose.
> Poets are liars, and for verse's sake
> Will make the Gods of human crimes partake.

The last four lines are free composition by Ralegh, but his case is well argued. It is of course possible to accept Austin's view, that 'The tale of Dido, in the form which has stirred the human heart to pity for nearly two thousand years, was Virgil's own creation in a moment of intense poetic vision', but it is probably a question of what view you take of intense poetic vision. I must admit that I feel any critic who invokes it is about to attempt a conjuring trick.

I recently had the enjoyable task of searching through Gow and Page's edition of the *Garland of Philip*, a collection of poems in the Palatine Anthology, which contains many of those Greek epigrams written by poets Virgil knew, like his tutor Philodemos, and poets who may have been influences on him, among them Erucius, who is extremely hard to date precisely. The name Erucius is Roman, and he was born in Kalavryta in the north-west corner of Arcadia. Kalavryta was a Roman colony, and the source of much information and misinformation about that wild inland province which served as one of Virgil's greatest settings.

Erucius seems to have been a poet of about Virgil's own age, and he writes a dedication to Pan from Glaucon and Corydon, 'both Arcadians, both in the flower of their youth' (Eruc.1, Anth Pal 6, 96), names and phrases that recall Virgil's seventh Eclogue. Erucius has them herding cattle in the mountains, while Virgil has Daphnis in his scene sitting under an ilex where Thyrsis has brought his sheep and Corydon his goats. Only the fact that these two are both young, both Arcadians, ties Virgil and Erucius together. Arcadians enter the scene in Erucius because Pan is Arcadian, but in Virgil's poem the Arcadian scene-setting is gratuitous. Daphnis after all is usually a Sicilian in pastoral poetry, and the entry of Arcadia into the Eclogues seems to be Virgil's invention, borrowed from the Greek epigrams about Pan. Also, Glaucon is not a shepherd's name for Virgil.

So it does not look as if the greater poet is imitating the lesser one. This problem is small and no doubt insoluble. Probably they had the same source, which we have now lost, which considering the disorganisation of the poems of Theocritus, where genuine and spurious are jumbled together is not surprising. Virgil imitates both. In Virgil the line about the two Arcadians has more point, because they are going to sing antiphonally.

It is hard to put one's finger on just what Virgil drew from this huge ramification of small poems that have descended to us in the Palatine Anthology. To me it appears to be that he derived his basic instrument from the poems: the sharpest sensory contrast in words and the heaviest weight of implication in phrases. This is a matter of detail, and it is most obviously displayed in the Eclogues. Of course there are particular poems in the Anthology that remind one of Virgil, poems about the shade of a tree, the sweetness of honey, or one by Myrinos where Eros herds the animals and Thyrsis sleeps. But, even Cicero's aged friend Scaevola writes in Greek verse about Pan and his goats. Yet, it would be fair to say that most of what Virgil drew in from earlier poetry as a young man he found in Theocritus. This does not mean that Theocritus was the father of European pastoral poetry, but he was certainly the kind of poet from whom other poets can learn.

Virgil's own majestic influence came with the Aeneid and for reasons outside poetry. When Dante took Virgil for a guide – as Aeneas takes the Sibyl in the underworld – he followed the sixth book of the Aeneid in the lowest parts of his Inferno. It was probably Dante and not the piety of schoolmasters that bonded

Virgil so closely to Christianity in the Italian Renaissance. But, once the bonding had set hard, Virgil really did become *the* classic in Christian Europe as T.S. Eliot proclaimed him to be. This strange transformation had been all the easier in a world where scholars were seldom critics of any interest, and in which almost no one knew enough Greek. The Eclogues were more or less ignored, except by poets, who delighted in them from Spenser to Marvell.

The subsequent French controversy between the *anciens* and *modernes* (which reverberates in the introductory material to Dryden's *Virgil*) subsequently shook France rather than Europe. It left the English happily worshipping the idols of their schoolroom. The controversy centred on that curious anomaly, 'Christian epic', which those who wrote it felt to be far better than ancient epics. (Milton might have agreed with them.) The commotion had started in 1670 about whether the inscription on a new triumphal arch for Louis XIV should be in Latin or in French. Alas the authorities never finished building this monumental construction, so it never had an inscription, but the battle on this ground or others went on for fifty years.

Later the controversy shifted, in the inconsequent way it will, to translations of Homer, with the formidable and in my view admirable Madame Dacier batting for the *anciens* with more style than Nicholas Boileau, an early captain, had ever shown. The last shot in the war was probably Diderot on Homer or Iliad in the *Encyclopaedia*. He attacked the horrible cooking described in the Iliad, but pointed out that the ancient leaders in war did win battles, 'something that ours regrettably fail to do, though they invent sauces as fine as mayonnaise'.

It is hard to take the furious arguments seriously today, but a little can be said. The novel has told us things about ourselves and for example about women that Virgil did not consider. History itself looks very different now, so that Virgil's model for it, which was supreme until about 1670 and unmarked by the 'Christian epic', is now smashed.

At the cost of a further few lines it is worth noticing that John Dryden as a critic founded himself on Boileau, whom at times he gleefully robbed. The idea of refinement in English verse – with the heroic couplet as Dryden handled it the supreme achievement – comes from Boileau's *Art of Poetry*. Eliot puts it perfectly in a poem to Walter de la Mare (1958) as

> those deceptive cadences
> Wherewith the common measure is refined,
> By conscious art practised with natural ease ...

Refinement in Dryden's *Art of Poetry* is a whole system of progressive improvement in versification, through a list of names with himself as the climax, corresponding to Boileau as the inheritor from Malherbe. (These poets are not always exemplary characters, but it was in reviewing Mark Van Doren's book on Dryden that Eliot became a Dryden expert, making use then and later of Van Doren's quotations for *The Sacred Wood*. Small wonder then that Eliot should one day stand up for Virgil, just as Dryden did. He is not the only man of letters to have educated himself by anonymous reviewing, and although I have criticised his opinions I do not know anyone else who has so clearly, strongly and elegantly attempted an answer to that question.)

Yet it is essential to distinguish the history of a language from the progressive refinement of poetry. Civilisation is another matter, and most observers agree that it has its ups and downs – though whether the Roman empire was an up or a down is still a question that divides historians. Today the idea of perpetual and almost unavoidable progress is pinned in place by science, though scientific progress began rather recently, scarcely before Galileo. The basic fact that the world is round was forgotten for about a thousand years until the Renaissance, and the speculation that it was composed of atoms was not accepted until the seventeenth century, when it opened the path to atomic physics.

As for languages and forms of poetry, it is only Latin literature that shows such a progression and such a progressive refinement. In English Chaucer is as good as Byron, and as smart, and *Gawain and the Green Knight* is as talented and its language is as refined, as anything in modern English: and *Beowulf* and the Finnsburh fragment are arguably superior. Nothing since Shakespeare is fit to compare with him. And, as for the detail of Dryden's and of Boileau's couplets, it is like the slow perfection of the elegiac couplet in Latin: an illusion. Latin writers were so under the spell of the Greeks that their determination to do whatever Greek verse could do was unanimous.

Latin as a language, however, was already mature and supple and full of life in the days of Plautus (245? – 180 BC) and maybe earlier. The literature of Latin fell away and serious poetry came to an end, not because the poetry of the Augustan age was unsurpassable but for political reasons: because of the nature of the imperial government and the Roman state. If one looks at the evidence from inscriptions one can see that the severe, archaic style is in many ways preferable to the style adapted from Hellenistic epigrams which followed.

We have lost so much of Latin literature that one may find it hard to judge. Naevius is a marvellous poet, but lamentably fragmentary, and even Ennius, who in a way all but overshadows Virgil in the Aeneid, does not exist in great quantity. Certainly the crumbs that Edward Courtney has gathered in *The Fragmentary Latin Poets* (1993) are on the whole light in weight, and the few outstanding lines are those that are famous, like Porcius Licinus on the second Carthaginian war, when

9

the Muse wingfooted made her attack on the wild people of Romulus.

Porcius Licinus is hard to date but he is talking of the age of Naevius, the late third century BC.[8] It may have been a hundred years later than Naevius when he wrote a poem in Latin that perhaps holds its head up with anything in the *Garland of Philip*:

> Keepers of sheep and of the tender lambs
> Do you seek fire? Here is a man of fire.
> With a touch my finger will burn down the woods,
> And all your flocks, for all I see is fire.

Edward Courtney thinks this a clumsy poem, yet Ralegh or Wyatt might have liked it, though undoubtedly it is less perfect than Virgil.

The ideal that poetry should be metrically or technically always more and more refined, then, does not hold water even in Latin. Nothing analogous holds true for any of the arts in this last century of course. Music after Debussy and Ravel or Benjamin Britten and the Americans of his generation has offered us a precipitous decline, and painting since Picasso and Hockney no great improvement.

You can over-refine and whittle away poetry until nothing is left. You will end up writing verses like those of the Emperor Hadrian, to inscribe on a cherry-stone. A tradition must be ploughed, opened up and altered if it is to be fertile for long. The poetry of the French monarchy looks as if by Voltaire's time it has run into a dead end, though it was the monarchy itself that was a dead end – and the revolution was perhaps another one. It was only when modern French consciousness broke open that we were given the dazzling poetry of Baudelaire, to which the English conservatism and green gloom of Lord Tennyson could not aspire. The English clung to the wreckage of Virgil, but the French did not. Eliot was under an illusion in 1945.

What then has Virgil still to offer? First, he is extremely good. He is at least the laureate of laureates. He is one of those few poets who have almost too much to say, like Thomas Hardy and John Donne and unlike George Herbert. It is this pressure of serious thoughts that produces his abundance, his generosity of themes. Then, he was a true master of his language, as Racine was, and from that we can always learn however different our circumstances. Robert Lowell made an astounding attempt to translate Racine, and the result was a vigorous, energetic wrestling match: something new.

But Virgil is not a monument, he must be stalked and crept up on and studied sidelong as well as face to face. He is not a bland writer and must not be treated blandly. He is passionate but his passions are in reserve, he is an ironist but hardly in an obvious manner which scholarship can pin down, and he is a humourist, a man of many resources, who delights to cover his own tracks. What Dryden says in his dedication of the Georgics may very likely be true, that they are 'the best poem of the best poet'.

The history of our education is curious, and when I was young I was interested only in what he could do for me as a poet, being conscious of that vocation long before I had the capability. Now it seems possible and perhaps likely that European education from about 1500 to 1800 really was an attempt to train poets, and that its old purpose lingered on, at least in the sixth forms of old fashioned schools in England, until nearly our own times, persisting like the echoes of a siren voice. No doubt something analogous is true of America, where one of the first books ever translated, and perhaps the first poem ever written in our language, was a translation of Virgil by George Sandys, who published it on his return to England.

A time has come when so much stands between us and Virgil that we need to take a new and a close look at him. Much of the historical foliation that obscured him in the centuries after his death has now been cleared away, or it can be, which is due to the efforts of historians, and their struggles and controversies ever since Mommsen. One may notice that Mommsen was a contemporary of Karl Marx, with whom he shares some of the excitements of historical analysis: they are toxic and can still affect us in his history of the Roman republic, which ends with Caesar, and the watch-fires of the legions burning for the first time in the heart of the Roman capital.

At the end of the last war, English schoolteachers still believed as they had done for three hundred years that Virgil taught the responsibilities of empire. But it is the grave contributions of nearly two centuries of scholarship that have hacked away the nationalism and the racism and the nonsense from our ideas of Virgil and of Horace. They do not now appear distant or ghostly, but as two friendly human beings, two well-disposed and intelligent poets, such as one might meet.

I was also taught at school fifty years ago that Roman literature was no more than a footnote to Greek, and I still do not dare to dismiss that as an unfounded exaggeration. All the same we have much in Latin that we lack in the Greek form, and I prefer to think of Virgil in particular as the greatest writer of his time, though it happened that he wrote in Latin. Eduard Fraenkel says somewhere of Virgil's century that the deeper a Roman was, the more deeply he was penetrated by Greek and by the Greeks. I have certainly found that to be true of Virgil.

And then there is this too. In our time the planet appears to be shrinking, withering, and polluted, like an elderly apple on a windowsill. But in Virgil it is still green and strong, and that is something we need. Distant as he is in time, I can think of no poet we stand more in need of today: not for the contrivances of his 'epic', but for the texture and sap of all his verse: *e le parole nate fra le vigne.*

Yet it may be that in this chapter the question of what we owe to Virgil has not found an easy answer. That is because of a certain neglect of the obvious that has overcome the entire debate, though the problem is real, and as urgent as it has ever been. Few generations of genius have devoted such prolonged and deep study to what poetry is and can be as Virgil's did. Today we must probe the walls of his world both as they were and as he imagined them, in order to discover those of his art, who he was or what he was like as a poet in his own time. Our task is to think that from the mass of discarded furniture mostly in the imperial taste (first empire, third empire, nth empire) and decayed papers that fill the lumber-rooms of our minds, we inherit in some form the portrait of a poet who is unique. We inherit Virgil.

I

THE YOUTH OF VIRGIL

Virgil was born in 70 BC near Mantua, then Mantova, a Roman city which is still buried ten feet under the Piazza dell'Erbe, the Renaissance vegetable market. No one knows how old it was then, but the town was once Etruscan. By the time Virgil was born, it was part of the province called Cisalpine Gaul, which extended to the Alps and covered the Po valley where the god Silvanus, the Wood god, was very popular. The Alps were free and independent, though they were quite thoroughly explored and well-known to the Greeks as well as the Romans. Greek influence and Greek works of art had penetrated beyond Ancona and Rimini and far into the Alps long ago,[1] but in the early second century BC the Romans took over the entire region. Rimini (Ariminum) was founded in 268 BC as a Roman colony, a strong garrison town where disbanded legions of old soldiers were settled on the land, and in 225 BC the border had reached Milan, and in 219 the Romans put colonies at Piacenza and Cremona. Bologna, Mutina, Parma and Aquileia were colonised in the 80s BC; both Parma and Bologna are on the great military highway south of the Po, called the Via Aemilia, which heads for Milan, and Aquileia is the north-east point of Italy.

Quiet Mantua was on the richest part of the plain, in one of the wriggles of the river Mincio (Mincius), which runs down from Lake Garda to join greater rivers, *dove il Po discende per aver pace con seguaci sui*: where the Po runs down / Among his followers to find his peace. On the southernmost tip of the vast Lake Garda lies Sirmio where Catullus lived, though the impressive ruins still to be seen there are those of a grander and later building, probably an imperial palace. Not far east of Sirmio lies Verona (whose name is Celtic) which Catullus calls his town, but it appears to have been a dull place. Mantua was never huge and is now all but encircled by small lakes full of fish.

Beyond Mantua in the plain of the Po Virgil was born in a village called Andes. No one knows now where that was, though tradition puts it at Pietole (to the south-south-east), which Napoleon visited at midnight as a young officer, in awe of Virgil. The poet was named Publius Vergilius Maro – the English spelling Virgil is traditional. His middle name is not uncommon and his last name is Greek or Etruscan; his first is a mere Roman formality like 'Quintus' Horatius

13

Flaccus and 'Marcus' Tullius Cicero (106 – 43 BC). He was a middle-class child and a Roman citizen by birth. His mother's and his father's family held office as magistrates in Rome.

Virgil's father may even have been an *eques Romanus*, a Roman knight or squire;[2] but Miss Gordon (*JRS*, 1934) cleverly suggested he was the offspring of an Etruscan pottery family from Ligurian Hasta, and perhaps he dug clay from his muddy fields and made pots near Mantua. That would explain the story in Virgil's biography, that his father was an itinerant potter and a poor man who married his boss's daughter. That story is probably romantic moonshine all the same, invented hundreds of years after the poet's death to fill a gap left by ignorance; and the connection with Hasta is a guess.

Before we plunge into the morass of such traditions, we had better set out clearly what is known from history and from archaeological evidence. The name of a member of Virgil's family crops up much later as a grand priest whose office is recorded on stone, and when Virgil died he left money to his younger half-brother. He is also credited with two full brothers who died before him, but I do not believe they really existed at all. The money, half his wealth, was a large amount, but the brother mentioned in Virgil's will was the son of his mother Magia, who must have been born by 86 BC to bear Virgil in 70 BC, so by the laws of nature Magia is unlikely to have had another son after about 36 BC.

It happens that a poem in the *Catalepton* (the collection of short poems ascribed to Virgil) suggests that the poet's father was alive in the later forties BC, but this poem is a fantasy. It is the sentimental offering of some later schoolmaster, imagining Virgil welcoming his exiled family to his friend 'Siro's little villa and his poor plot' in the manner of Hellenistic epigrams. It need not detain us. So we should assume that the poet's father died at the normal age around 52 BC when his son was about eighteen, and his widow married again. Virgil looked after his half-brother, who was born about 50 BC, by leaving him money when he was thirty.

Yet we would like to know more about Virgil's father and mother, and his first youth, and to do so we must take a circuitous route. Mantua was Etruscan, as Virgil tells us in verse in the course of his amazing catalogue of the allies of Aeneas, in book ten of the Aeneid. Aeneas is at a meeting to get Etruscan allies through Evander, the old original Arcadian colonist of Rome. The allies set out in a half-magical fleet from the north of Italy and after the Clusians and the Ligurians and their mighty ship Centaur comes the curiously named Ocnus, son of Prophetic Manto and a Tuscan:

14

He gave you walls and gave his mother's name,
Mantua rich in blood, not one in race:
Three races, and four peoples under each
Head of the peoples, her strength Tuscan blood. (200-3)

Tuscan means Etruscan, and although commentaries suggest the names of three races (or tribes) they have no authority. Mantua according to Virgil was an ancient settlement of mixed race.

Mincius in a hat of the grey-green reeds of his father Benacus (Lake Garda) leads in his furious pine (ship) five hundred men that the legendary tyrant Mezentius armed against himself (204-6).

That does not tell us very much. Mincius was the river that snaked across the plains emptying the oceanic Lake Garda into the Po. And Mezentius may be fiction: in the Aeneid he fights on the wrong side and is killed. But the atmosphere reveals a good deal about Virgil's native place. Even the claim to a mere five hundred men from the margins of the world says something, and Ocnus is a Greek word for hesitancy, indolence or shrinking, that suits the endless windings of the Mantuan river. It is plain that we are speaking of the remotest of the Italian provinces.

This mixture of fantasy and mythology is confusing to modern readers, but it is worth noticing that Virgil insists on creating a part in the Aeneid for Mantua and the Ligurians. Furthermore, when Phaethon fell from heaven and his sisters lamented him inconsolably, they were turned into the amber-weeping poplar trees of the Po valley, and the crest-feathered Cunerus, Phaethon's brother, sang about him in their shadow to the stars until in white old age he was turned into the constellation Cycnus, the Swan (Aen. 10, 187b-f). Cycnus and Ocnus are similar words, and perhaps for Virgil Ocnus is the name of some fabulously beautiful and shy heron of the river Mincius or the Po.[3] On consideration I do not believe it has anything to do with the Oknos painted by Polygnotos, whose punishment in the underworld (Paus. 10, 29, 2) was to plait a rope perpetually chewed to pieces by a donkey.

Virgil loved Mantua passionately and mentioned it in all his books, but the mention in the Aeneid is the most intrusive and suggestive. As for the amber-weeping trees, amber is indeed the petrified gum of trees found in sea-sand: like gold and honey it glitters and lasts a very long time.

And as for the great river Po, the Romans identified it with the Greek mythical river Eridanos, where Phaethon fell and his sisters wept, as we have just seen. Virgil names a river in the happiest part of the underworld where the poets sing for ever the Eridanus (Aen. 6, 659). And in the first Georgic he is king of rivers, and the translator Ogilby (1649) likes him:

15

... Brasse in the Temples sweats: sad Ivorie weeps,
High woods *Eridanus* king of rivers sweeps
And on the plains with hostile billows falls,
Bearing with him the cattell and their stalls.

In the fourth Georgic, Ogilby says:

Golden Eridanus with a double horne,
Fac'd like a Bull, through fertile fields of corne:
Than whom none swifter of the Ocean's sons
Down to the purple Adriatick runs.

Virgil says no river rushes more violent to the purple sea. To this day the Po
has an alarming and uncontrollable appearance, and near Mantua, where the sea
is still a hundred miles away, this great river is more untamed than the Rhine or
the Rhone or the Loire or the Danube. But Mantua huddles in a bend of the
Mincius on a small hill among lakes. It is almost hidden, a defensive site.

The Romans came late to the vast region of the Po Valley which they called
Cisalpine Gaul (as opposed to Transalpine Gaul, Gaul on the other side of the
Alps) and when Virgil was born the Alps were still free and independent. The
Romans extended into northern Italy for strategic reasons as well as economic
greed, and the title of Cisalpine Gaul was used for political convenience as in
fact geographically the place and most of the people were Italian by race. The
Po valley was still a frontier region, and the Po itself was a barrier to the Romans
nearly as formidable as the Alps: both kept out the Celts.

For much of the second century BC the region was disputable ground, but the
Romans then swiftly advanced into the mining areas of the Alps. Little by little
they had become masters of the towns in the Po valley, including small Mantua.
Cremona lay fifty miles to the west and Parma on the Via Aemilia fifty south-
east: Verona the frontier town near Lake Garda was about forty north. Mantua
was about ten miles north of the Po, but a day's journey east or west from any
crossing, and a hundred miles from the formidable Po delta.

We first hear of Cisalpine Gaul as a Roman province with a governor or
military dictator appointed by Rome, not long before Virgil was born, though
its government as a province seems to date from about 100 BC. In 89 BC the
Roman consul was Pompey Strabo, or Pompey Squint-Eye, famous father of a
famous (or rather infamous) son, Pompey the Great. He made the place a Roman
military province, refusing at the same time to grant rights of Roman citizenship
because he despised its Gaulish inhabitants. Sallust and Tacitus bear witness to
this prejudice – which was of a type already causing trouble all over Italy. From

90 BC onwards all the Italians who were not Romans had demanded the rights of citizens. By 87 BC they almost all had these rights, only the territory north of the Po was unprivileged. The fighting was over by 89 BC, but Pompey Squint-Eye strengthened the northern frontier, colonising Comum and Verona and creating a society tied to himself and his family interests.

That is only one among many aspects of his settlement, but it is one that G.E.F. Chilver (1941) chose to emphasise, since as a result Caesar wooed this northern province by promoting universal Roman citizenship there. It finally happened towards the end of his life when he gave the citizenship to every town in Cisalpine Gaul. This left only those Alpine tribes which had already been 'attributed' to, or judged or deemed to come under their nearest Roman settlement, by Pompey Squint-Eye.

Most of these mountain border-towns had Latin rights, that is the rights of towns near Rome in Latium itself: only Cisalpine magistrates became citizens in 89 BC under Pompey Squint-Eye. (The reader may wonder whether a Roman colony might exist in foreign, tribal territory, beyond the boundaries of a Roman province. Certainly it might, since Eporedia was founded in 100 BC in the Val d'Aosta, in the territory of the Alpine Salassi. Rome was both extending her frontiers, sometimes with alarming speed, and consolidating her frontier territories.)

Virgil's father was affected by all this disturbance of course, but we do not know that he had any serious interest in politics. The vision of his generation was united Italy: an Italy of Roman citizens (although from the early eighties until Virgil's maturity the word 'Italy' was out of fashion). It is interesting that Cicero could not stand the Celtic accent in Latin – which seems to persist in Virgil's north-Italian accent.

Cisalpine Gaul was in several ways unlike the south. There seem to have been fewer slaves. And there were certainly fewer ex-slaves, except at Bologna, where they were numerous and left rich tombs. Tacitus thought the whole province full of 'remote and severe towns that still kept to the antique manners of old Italy' (Ann. 16, 5), and Chilver shares this view. They had never liked being governed as a province, and an orator under Augustus pleading a case at Milan might say with bitterness 'as if Italy were being reduced to the level of a province' (Suet. De Rhet. 6). Scholars have imagined that is what really happened for a time after the civil wars, but if it did (and I do not quite believe it) the matter need not concern us, because by then Virgil had left home and was settled in the south.

We know that the Po valley had many more woods or forests than it has now, but that Mantua was marshy. Later in history it had worse mosquitoes than anywhere else in Italy, and farming there is still a matter of clever draining. The farms were not extensive: the allotment of a Roman knight might be forty acres, but an ordinary citizen's (like an Elizabethan cottager's) was four acres if he was lucky. Knights were numerous, there were fifty in one town allotment.

Much of the wealth was in wool and wool-combing, and the animals climbed into the Alps in summer as they still do. In the ninth Eclogue Virgil's Moeris who has lost his farm cries out:

> Varus, if our own Mantua shall survive,
> Mantua too close to unhappy Cremona,
> Singing swans will take your name to the stars.

What interests me about this obscurely bitter complaint is the swans, because for Virgil they are a recurring theme. We have already seen the crest-feathers and Cycnus and Ocnus in the Aeneid. But in the second Georgic (198-9) we have

> Those meadows that unhappy Mantua lost
> Grazing on grass-green rivers swans of snow ...

and again in the third Georgic (12-15) he says

> I Mantua shall be the first with palms
> To place a white temple in green meadows,
> Beside the water where in his slow turns
> The mighty Mincius wanders and covers
> His bank with bending reeds ...

It will be seen that whenever Virgil has a piece of musical phrasing, or even an impression of colours that pleases him, he goes on working at it until he has it right. In the Aeneid twelve swans take off together from the fields and soar in circles; in the west of England, on the Severn near Berkeley Castle, one may still observe that, and Virgil learnt it and much else at Mantua.

Somewhere near Andes, the hamlet where Virgil's parents lived, a 'Virgil's ditch' and a 'Virgil's poplar' gave rise to the kind of nonsense that is often found in saints' lives and apocryphal lives of the early Christian era. The boldest is that of the Gonzaga family who decided that their renaissance stables for the breeding of horses a mile or so from Pietole, a few miles from Mantua, was the very spot the poet was born. The poplar begot a story of its swift growth, and the ditch became the birthplace. The poet's father became a 'merchant's traveller' to explain the ditch, and a potter of some kind, like a tinker in the Irish countryside a hundred years ago, a travelling man. Or was the potting to explain the boy's interest in legends? All these stories are charming and harmless enough,

18

but quite worthless. (Suetonius, of whose lost life of Virgil they were excretions, credited the child with a sweet new-born smile and a most fortunate horoscope, *genitura*. Virgil's father is supposed to have been first a traveller then a son-in-law of Magius, whose family did exist in the province, but the Virgils were not 'modest people'; the education of their son was conventional and expensive, and his command of Latin and of Greek amounted to mastery.)

The poet's boyhood is a blank to us. He observed the operations of agriculture – to what degree we shall see in the Georgics – and he learnt what there was to learn at Cremona, then at Milan, further and further west, before going south to Rome. The disturbance of the times continued, but Cremona was a bustling market town, visited by merchants from all over Italy, and Milan was noticeable not only as a powerful provincial capital, but for a certain sturdy republicanism. Virgil was resorting to the most Romanised centres of Cisalpine Gaul. This raises yet again the question what his father was doing in the fields around the river at Mantua. It is not impossible that he was sheep-farming or cattle-breeding. But, the idea that he was an old beekeeper is nonsense, based on the beekeeping stories in the fourth Georgic, which no real beekeeper's son would have written.

Young Virgil headed for Rome when he was about seventeen. That would be about a year after the early death of Catullus, who was born in 84 BC and died in 54 BC or so, and it is a great pity that they never met.

A number of poets who are marginal to our knowledge, to the life of Virgil, and to the history of Latin literature at this time, came from the north: Varro Atacinus from a village on the Aude in Provence, and Gallus of Fréjus (Forum Iuli), in Narbonne, were both from older Roman ground than Mantua. (Though in France, Provence and Narbonne were the two earliest Roman provinces.) Furius Bibaculus, who wrote humorous verse against Julius Caesar like Catullus and later against Augustus, both of whom ignored him, was born at Cremona (but we are not clear when, and the story of his writings is so disjointed there may be two of him). Valerius Cato was the most influential of these poets, the most honoured by the others, and perhaps their teacher, but the shadows swallow him and the circle has no centre. But he too was born and brought up in Cisalpine Gaul. So was Cinna, who was writing by the time Virgil was fourteen, and was famous for his death, torn to pieces by the mob in Shakespeare's Caesar, 'for his bad verses'.

There are a lot of these people, they are gleefully elegant followers of Alexandrian Greek poetry, epigrammatists and wits like Catullus, and 'chanters of Euphorion' whom Cicero thought boring. But as Yeats puts it 'That was no country for old men, the young / In one another's arms, birds in the trees'.

This raggle-taggle throng of mostly very minor poets, among whom Catullus of Verona circulates like a shark among minnows, are to us fragmentary, and, with one possible exception, scholarly labour has never made much of them or of other minor poets just before Virgil began to blossom: Q. Lutatius Catulus for example, who adapted Callimachus so badly and was personally acquainted with the awful Antipater of Sidon.

The possible exception lies in the *Appendix Vergiliana*, a thin collection of poems listed by those depraved sources, Servius and Donatus in late antiquity, and some of them known soon after Virgil's death in 19 BC. They are a bizarre collection, they all claim to be by Virgil or to be his youthful exercises, and it is not absolutely impossible that one or two could be genuine.

What is far more interesting about these poems is that they provide us with a museum of the inferior Latin poetry of the day. Robinson Ellis, a Professor of Latin with a formidable umbrella of learning who taught in Oxford a hundred years ago, thought the *Dirae* or Curses in the *Appendix* were by Valerius Cato, probably because they went with a piece to Lydia, one of the old grammarian's subjects. With you my Lydia plays, he says, *vobis mea Lydia ludit*. This pun is in bad taste, but there were tricks like it played at the time. We must withdraw from any serious attention and a few lines later, when the unhappy poet quotes the Georgics – 'O truly fortunate and happy fields / In which she plants her snowy feet ... (Geo. 2, 458) – he has become too bad, and cannot interest us. Vulgarities like these are not necessarily 'late antique', they are the real efforts of the untalented.[4]

The *Culex*, for a better example, is a poem 414-lines long of mind-boggling silliness about a mosquito, yet it was known to Lucian and to Statius. The mosquito saves a sleeping shepherd attacked by a snake, and the shepherd writes the mosquito's epitaph. It is no pleasure to me to sneer at bad poems, though I do think it my duty to go through all of them, rubbing their nose one by one in the dust. The *Ciris* has 541 lines and it is about Scylla and Nisus and metamorphosis (Ec. 6, 74), but the words hang heavy on the pen.

Moretum or The Salad is far better, being a short and gloomy poem about a farmer's life one early morning. It could be by Crabbe or some unknown English poet of the eighteenth century. But it is nowhere near Virgil alas. The farmer has only one slave, an African called Scybale, whose physique is described in detail (32-5). He owns a garden and a pair of oxen that he inherited. This little piece has an attraction of its own, it is only 124 lines long and we are lucky to have it, if only because it shows on how small a scale life could be lived. The *Copa Syrisca*, the Dancing Girl, is the most attractive of all. The poem is brief at 38 lines (19 elegiac couplets), but Wilamowitz's brilliant discovery that it is a versified advertisement for a wine-shop or afternoon drinking place adds greatly to the amusement of it. There is no reason at all to connect it with Virgil, so if the girl offers violet garlands of crocus flowers, who cares? Could they be autumn crocus?

This brings us to the *Catalepton*, the special list of little poems like epigrams in the *Appendix*. Three are to Priapus, and have all been translated by John Heath-Stubbs. One is so fresh it could almost be Virgil's work at twenty: it has that flicker of talent we must expect of him. Priapus was a god who came from Lampsacus after the Greek classical age was over. He was roughly cut out of any useless wood, fig or poplar, and he had a big phallus: he protected gardens, and Horace wrote about him (Sat. 1, 8). This version is the shortest of three ascribed here to Virgil, and the best.

> In spring I'm decked with roses, in autumn with apples,
> In the summer season with ears of corn:
> Winter alone for me is a frightful pest.
> I dread the cold – what's more I shouldn't wonder
> If I, being only a wooden god,
> End up furnishing firewood
> For some uncaring boors.

Still I do not stand by the attraction of this piece. It is two neat elegiac couplets, and they cannot be dated; it is only that they look like the work of an authentic poet, and the words '*ligneus ignem*' coming together suggest the fashion of a year not far from about 50 BC, when Virgil was twenty. All three are like pretty country pictures of the kind to be found painted on Roman walls.

Of the further poems in this list, one is a boring epigram to Plotius Tucca, who was a literary executor to Virgil, one a pedantic epigram about dialect, one is political but late in date. There is a silly love-verse to the Muse, and then quite suddenly comes number 5, the only one Eduard Fraenkel used to allow could be really Virgil's.

For a lifetime I have been seduced by it, and by him, though doubt of these verses has never died, indeed it is stronger today than ever. The wine-jars of rhetoric mean puffed cheeks, or they might refer to acoustics for which the jars were used in the theatre.

> Go, leave me empty pots of rhetoric
> Words puffed up with a dew that is not Greek,
> And you, Tarquitius, Varro, Selius,
> Tribe of tutors all dripping with fat,
> Go, leave me, empty cymbals of the young.
> And O Sextus Sabinus care of my cares,

Goodbye to you, goodbye to the beautiful.
I am setting my sails to the happy harbours,
To find the learned words of great Siro,
And a life free of all care of all kinds.
Leave me Muses, you too, goodbye to you,
Sweet Muses, because I will confess the truth,
Sweet you have been, and yet you could sometimes
Revisit my papers: decently: not often.

It is a charming self-portrait of a boy or young man, taking seriously to philosophy, precisely as Virgil did under Siro the Epicurean, just south of Naples, whose house he was one day to inherit. Philosophy to the entire Hellenistic world was a special and a dedicated subject, much as religion is for us. It was not taught at school or mixed with other subjects. The names of the people in this little poem do not matter, except Siro's. The poet is rather rude to Varro, though one may hope he did not mean Varro the antiquary, but only someone like Varro of Aude.

In Latin the poem is more musical and more moving than I can make it in translation, and it fits the metrical interest of the new poets of the North. There is a freshness of Greek influence about them that has not passed through Rome, and I believe that Virgil, if this is Virgil, has at least sipped from that. He is now fed up with schools, and giving up the tutors, the rhetoric, the disgusting devices. He is setting out for Naples like a novice, for a philosophy that he believes is a way of life and will make him happy. It seems to me fair to say that it did make him happy – and saved Roman poetry. Naples was his equivalent of a Japanese monastery; Epicurus appealed at this time particularly to aesthetes.

From this point alas the *Appendix* goes downhill until it lacks all credibility. There are quotations from and parodies of Catullus, there are allusions to Virgil (Catalept. 9, 18-20) in a poem to the great war-lord Messalla, and poems attached to other poems (which are also not genuine) by a word or a name; there is an epode (13) and a prayer to Venus that mentions Aeneas.

After the tailing off of the *Catalepton*, we get longer but equally absurd offerings: the poem *Est et Non* does not derive from the use of this odd phrase by St Paul (2 Cor. 1, 19). It is the work of some pedantic philosopher, long before Abelard who wrote *Sic et Non*, and perhaps arguably earlier than Paul, though quite worthless as poetry, and the same may be said of the *Vir Bonus*, 26 untalented lines. The last of these miserable treasures unhappily hoarded through the centuries is a pair of elegies crammed together as one poem, written to commemorate Virgil's patron Maecenas, who survived the poet by a number of years. They do have some interest in literary history, but none for a biography of Virgil.

If Virgil left any early works at all, they are either schoolboy verses like the epigram attributed to him in some ancient lives:

> Under this mound of stones, this heavy load,
> Cannon lies buried: go safe on your road.

Cannon (*Ballista*) was a school-master and highwayman, or at least that is the joke. This little verse is not in the *Appendix*. Anybody aged twelve might have written it.

When the poet was born, Julius Caesar was thirty. Caesar had helped Pompey restore the powers of tribunes and was intriguing actively north of the Po by offering them Roman citizenship. When Virgil was a tiny boy, Caesar's wife died and he married Sulla the dictator's grand-daughter. He also restored the trophies of Sulla's rival Marius at Rome. Marius and Sulla were both dead, but the republic on her own delirious death-bed proved an abundant mother of such violent and ruthless figures, of whom Caesar for all his unusual virtues was the last and most effective.

When Virgil was ten or eleven, Caesar had fought his way by tooth and nail to the consulship. He colonised Novum Comum at this time and became governor of the provinces of Cisalpine Gaul, Transalpine Gaul, and Illyria, with consequent command of their armies. From this time on he was in serious business as an empire builder. For the nine years when Virgil grew to be a teenager in a small town and then bigger towns in his province, and when he moved to Rome, Caesar was conquering Gaul, frightening the Germans, and invading Britain for the fun of it. But the senate was ruffled by Caesar and in January 49 BC, when Virgil was twenty (and a student of rhetoric under the man who taught Augustus) and Caesar was fifty, the senate withdrew his command, and civil war followed at once.

While Virgil let his twenties trickle slowly through his fingers among the charming philosophers of the Campanian coast, Caesar was beating Pompey and his successors out of Italy, then beating them in north Greece and in Egypt where Pompey was assassinated and Caesar had a quick son by Cleopatra, and then again beating them in Africa and in Pontus, and at last in Spain. The idiotic vanity of his career at this time was an exemplary lesson to any young man devoted to Epicurean philosophy.

Yet, from 48 BC Caesar ruled Rome like a province. He was dictator to oversee elections, consul, sole consul, dictator for life. He was king in all but name, with his head on the coinage and Mark Antony as priest of his cult. In 49 BC he gave Cisalpine Gaul universal Roman citizenship, as promised, though the slaves remained slaves. Perhaps out of fear of another slave war – Spartacus's rising (73-2 BC) was still well remembered – Caesar insisted that at least one out of every three herdsmen in Italy must be free. In early spring 44 BC, six months after adopting his great-nephew Octavian (Augustus) as heir, he was assassinated, and more appalling violence followed. In the two years 42-41 BC, a hundred-and-fifty senators and two-thousand *equites* died in the wars and purges.

Virgil took no part in all those wars, and no part that we know in politics or in Roman society. He had no ambition as a lawyer or as a senator. The Epicurean views about physics or cosmology or science that Lucretius so carefully lays out in detail were possibly of secondary importance to Virgil and to Siro. Their gods were a pleasing vision but they were deists, they did not believe the gods were worried by this distant world. These philosophers lived undisturbed and free from fear, at Pozzuoli (Puteoli) as they did in Athens, and both women and slaves might belong to their circle as equal members.

Puteoli was a little way south from Naples, towards Pompeii and Herculaneum where the house of Philodemos stood and some of his writings have been excavated from what may be his or Piso's house. Philodemos came to Rome in the wars with Mithridates the Great (88 -63 BC), probably as a refugee and he had been lucky enough to be taken up by the Piso family, one of whom, the consul of 58 BC, gave him his fine house at Herculaneum.

Philodemos appears to have been an Epicurean as Siro was, and is said to have influenced the Romans more widely than has ever seemed obvious to me. After the assassination of Caesar he apparently took up a strong view against Mark Antony, and Virgil and Horace have been cited among those he influenced: but Horace was abroad and the evidence in Virgil's case is mostly in the *Appendix*, which is negligible. A papyrus has been found at Piso's house, which has Virgil's name as one of the speakers in Philodemos's dialogue *On Flattery* (M. Gigante, SIFC, 1989). But, even without this lucky find, the mere fact of the two Greek sages of withdrawal living close to one another would suggest a way in which Virgil as he grew older may have become known to a wider world. Still, we do not know for certain when he first got to know those he addresses in his first book, his Eclogues.

They are a sign of something new in poetry, and it is only by hindsight that we appreciate their lively originality. Valerius Cato was a faded force in Roman poetry, his country house in Tuscany had been sold to pay debts, and by 40 BC when he was an old man he was dying in picturesque rustic poverty, caught in a few verses by his disciple Furius Bibaculus as precisely as a photographer from the Sunday papers. The old man had disciples but no patron. It is hard to know how these things happen: it was not only a change of fashion, yet it was also that. Its result was that a movement or something too cloudy to be called a movement had dried up before the death of Cicero, who identified them as these newfangled writers, the moderns, the *Neoterici*.

We are lucky that they aroused enough interest in later and sillier critics or theorists to furnish us with some idea of the literary culture in which Virgil grew up, just as Philip Larkin grew up when the ground was thick with late Georgians, and Yeats in the nineties had to fight his way out of the shadow of dying Tennyson, and Tennyson in his day out of the oppressive atmosphere of ladies' annuals under George IV.

Another Greek whom the Romans owed to their wars with Mithridates was Parthenius of Nicaea in Bithynia, who is said to have taught Virgil Greek. But Virgil must have learnt the elements of the language at home, where there were many Greeks, and we should conjecture that the influence of recent and obscure Greek poets like Euphorion (250? – 175 BC) and the late disciple of Theocritus, Moschos, and of epigram poets in their swarms was particularly powerful in Cisalpine Gaul, where the local culture was more Greek than Celtic. However that may be, Parthenius was sent to Italy in 73 BC and was there set free as a poet. Macrobius, a dignified and footling but not wholly inglorious man of letters in the fifth century AD, reports that Parthenius taught Virgil Greek in Naples.

Parthenius was a poet with a higher contemporary reputation than he deserved. He wrote in Greek prose a kind of encyclopaedic narrative of 'the passions of love', which has not been edited for nearly a century. As a very young student I used to read it hoping it would throw light on Virgil, but I do not remember that it ever did. It was a collection of myths, or 'just another' selection of them, on the way to being turned into novels.

Writers like him forty years ago were called *Scriptores Erotici*, and at Oxford you needed a note from your senior tutor to read them in the Bodleian. As the late Hellenistic writers, and to a lesser extent Virgil and Ovid, had a passion for the most unlikely erotic variations, our studies of Hellenistic Greek hardly got off the ground. Parthenius at least serves to fill out the picture we have of Greek influence south of Rome.

By this time the Greeks from the war with Mithridates were ageing. Philodemos had been a pupil of the Epicurean Zeno at Athens, but soon after 40 he was dead, and most of his relics are *vers de société*, frivolous or erotic or pathetic or playful epigrams. They are adroitly written but they smell of dust. Cicero attacked him without naming him, as an evil Greek influence on Piso against whom his onslaught was hell for leather (Pison. 68f). Still, Philodemos was a romantic of a kind, and original by the rules of his game. It is important not to make too much of him just because we happen to know his name, and it is very doubtful whether he was an influence on Horace, though Horace was strongly influenced on literary matters by Quintilius Varus who was Virgil's friend and fellow-pupil in Naples.

These Greeks were a network: there is a poem inviting Philodemos to dinner (Gow and Page, 22) which he is supposed to have written himself, and one of the other guests is Artemidorus, very likely the same son of Theopompos of Cnidos who warned Caesar about the Ides of March in 44 BC on his way to his assassination. (Would Virgil have taken the same side? In Caesar's four years of power, it had been possible for all Italians to hope, and the new settlement of Cisalpine Gaul must have confirmed Virgil in hopes.) At this self-invited dinner everyone is Greek, there are no Roman pupils.

> Artemidorus gave us cabbage, Aristarchus salted fish,
> Philodemos one small liver, Apollophanes some pork,
> Let's dine at four sharp: boy, I wish
> For garlands, slippers, scent, and talk.

In an invitation poem to Piso for an Epicurean anniversary, Philodemos mentions only luxuries not to expect, but we know at least that it was in these circles that Virgil spent his youth, and no doubt ruined his digestion.

Naples and Puteoli and Herculaneum were old Greek market towns, and had been so since Rome was a village. Naples was founded from Cumae about 600 BC and it had been the centre of the Greek Campanian coast. The Romans took it over in 327, but even though they finally colonised it, Naples remained loyal to the Romans, and so Greek was allowed to be spoken there and taught in the schools there until long after Virgil's time. Herculaneum was only five miles away: that was a small wealthy place, Hellenised by the shadow of Naples, though in the wars over the franchise just before Virgil was born the Romans had taken it over and Romanised it. Puteoli was founded by Samians in the sixth century BC, and taken over by Rome in the fourth. It was in Virgil's day the greatest Roman port for the Eastern trade, and second only to Delos as a market. Sulla had a house there, so had Cicero, and so later had Hadrian.

All these towns are within the small circle of Virgil's world as an Epicurean, but perhaps the best surviving example of what kind of world it was is Paestum, the Greek Poseidonia, where the temples are still standing and the roses in Virgil's day used to blossom twice in the year. That was founded about 600 BC from Sybaris in the south of Italy, but the local people, the Lucanians, took it in about 390 BC and held it until 273 BC, when it became a Roman colony. Since then the great pillars of the temples have stood a thousand years in the sea, but the sea has now receded, and when they were rediscovered in the eighteenth century they were sheds for water buffaloes. By Virgil's day Paestum must already have been plagued by mosquitos, in spite of its roses. The houses of his rich contemporaries with serious good taste were inland at places like Boscoreale.

The case of Cumae is the most extraordinary of all, since it was founded by about 750 BC by Chalcis and became the mother of many colonies, including Naples, Pozzuoli, and Messina (Messana) in Sicily. It was rich and powerful enough with Syracusan help to crush the Etruscans in Campania in 474 BC. Alas only fifty-three years later the Oscans took it, but then the Romans occupied it in their turn, and by 180 BC the people of Cumae were speaking Latin.

What excited Virgil at Cumae was the dramatic darkness of the Sibyl's cave. This prophetess had become entangled into Roman legend, and she was in a curious way central to Virgil's plan for the Aeneid, just as Cumae itself must have influenced his thoughts on Roman Italy, Greek Italy, complex and united Italy. Cumae is not very far from Naples, but of course we do not know how far south he ventured. Northerners used to say Italy ends at Rome and ends badly – though my own feeling is that it begins at Rome and begins well. To Virgil Cumae was wonderfully impressive in its antiquity and doubtless he climbed to its impregnable acropolis.

In the cave no doubt Virgil heard 'the echoes bellowing in the hollow rocı (Aen. 6, 99, *antroque remugit*). As a decent Epicurean and a modern poet he did not believe in things like the Sibyl, though he was greatly interested, as an Epicurean should be, in the nature of sense perception. Virgil had certainly read Lucretius. He gives evidence of believing, as Lucretius does, that perception is infallible but inference from it misleads us. Lucretius's *On the Nature of Things* was published posthumously and had required editing. So the poem would first have been available when Virgil was about eighteen, edited by Cicero it seems. Virgil was the right age for it then, and old-fashioned, or even wonderfully curmudgeonly as the poem was, it influenced him deeply. The study of Lucretius is alarmingly pitted with elephant-traps, we do not know whether he was an aristocrat or an ex-slave, whether he was poisoned by a love-philtre – it is a wonder that did not happen more often – which may be a false inference from his inveighing against passions.

Lucretius's patron Memmius was in politics, and patron to Catullus and to Cinna, and we are told to Parthenius. He took them all to Bithynia where he was governor when Virgil was in his teens. Parthenius is a slippery figure for literary historians. He made a disgusting attack on Homer, but as he is said to have outlived Augustus there may well have been two of him: anyway, his circumstances leave it open to us to hope another Parthenius was to blame, not Virgil's tutor. Memmius was a man of influence married to Sulla's daughter who stood as consul with Caesar's support in 54 BC, but a scandal undid him and he died in exile in Athens before 46 BC. He bought the old house of Epicurus, and to Cicero's alarm thought of redeveloping it.

Neither Memmius's patronage nor any other in that generation is to be taken very seriously, except maybe Piso's. Old Archias of Antioch used to compose Greek verse impromptu and wrote entire epics in praise of Roman leaders, and when his Roman citizenship was contested he attracted the patronage of Cicero, who successfully defended him in a speech as delicious and light as a wine made of the elderflower, but they did not stay friends. Archias was born in the second century, though he was still alive when Caesar fell. In July 61 BC, a year after his speech, Cicero was already writing to Atticus in Athens, 'Thyillus has forsaken me, and Archias has written nothing about me' (Ad Att. 1, 15). No doubt Archias preferred the great family of the Metelli, and may be they looked after him. Things were not as bad for mediocre Greek poets as they were to become by Juvenal's time, but men like Archias had a sort of street wisdom that even Cicero lacked.

We are now to deal with a different atmosphere and another matter. What emerges from all this tattered information and clouded judgement is that alarming phenomenon, a great book of poetry that two thousand years have not in any way lessened. Virgil's Eclogues were Spenser's and Milton's starting-point in poetry, and Shakespeare in his comedies constantly returned to them. The problems of their date and the order of their composition are comparatively small, but much about Virgil's life both now and later hangs on a rigorously exact account of his patrons in these poems.

The Eclogues were presented to the world we are told in 37 or 36 BC and they swiftly became an enormous popular success. Tacitus records (Dialog. 12) that they were performed in the public theatre at Rome and the Romans stood to applaud Virgil. Nothing like it is remembered of any earlier Roman poet. From the first words of the first Eclogue, 'Tityre, tu ... ' he was victorious, or that lazy, self-echoing musical phrase was victorious.

Throughout these poems the musical phrases and tones of the verse do deliberately echo themselves, and the first word, Tityre which he uses as a name, is also a Greek word for a shepherd's pipe: a tityrist is a piper, but tityros can mean a bird and it comes from the word for the cheeping or the warbling of young birds. As a name Tityros can mean a Satyr (but only in the late writer

28

Aelian), a he-goat, or a bell-wether, or just the reed. It appears to be a Sicilian Doric word, though Theocritus who invented this kind of poetry never uses it.

The noise of a self-echoing flute or self-echoing bird has been re-invented many times in the half rhymes and internal rhymes of poetry, in Persian and in Welsh, and in English in William Barnes and his modern followers, but in Virgil's Latin sparingly and with a fastidious perfection in the Eclogues. The fact that Latin metre was by long and short syllables and not by accent (like English poems down to Kipling) slightly muffles the bird-twitter or fluting effect, but does not abolish it. Virgil's phrasing in the Eclogues has a peculiar, dandified beauty which is vernacular. If it imitates Greek then it imitates a dialect pronunciation of Theocritus which we cannot now imagine. Such things alter, and we do not know what exact stage Italian Greek had reached in Virgil's lifetime.

Since this subject has interested me for so many years, perhaps the reader will forgive me a short diversion on its later history. Virgil's bird-noises delighted the naive ears of medieval poets, and the imitated noises of lark-song in particular are enshrined in fifteenth-century French and English: 'Tirra Lirra by the river' sang Lord Tennyson. The bird-noises, which are to be found in the *Oxford English Dictionary*, survived into the age of sobriety as nonsense verse, as I found in Herbert Read's 1939 anthology *Knapsack*: Tirlery lorpin, the laverock sang, / And merrily pipes the sparrow.

The best example is one I scribbled once in an old notebook[5] from *Shepherds' Gowns* (1923) called The Singing of Birds. The lines turn out to be by Charles d'Orléans, but I do not know whether he wrote then as a prisoner in England, for twenty years after Agincourt, or in France.

> *La gentille alouette, avec son tire-à-lire*
> *Et tire-lire-à-lire, tirelirant tire,*
> *Vers la voute du ciel, puis s'en vol vers ce lieu*
> *Vire et désir dire Adieu Dieu, Adieu Dieu*

Virgil tells us that his patron's commands led him to write his Eclogues, which are a rather single-minded adaptation of the *Idylls* of Theocritus. Virgil's statement is in the dedication of the eighth Eclogue, where the patron is given the grandest praise but is not named. As a young man I despaired of these lines, since it was commonly taught then that the patron was G. Asinius Pollio, which made very little sense. But I now gratefully accept Wendell Clausen's clear account in his commentary (1994), which is based on a suggestion by Bowersock (1971) that Virgil's patron was Augustus, no less. Augustus is not named in the first Eclogue either, but it is obvious that he is referred to as the young man old

Tityrus goes to Rome to see, and that the star, Caesar's comet or 'hairy star' (88) as Suetonius calls it, which had appeared on the coinage by 38 BC, refers to Augustus as well as Caesar (Ec. 9, 47).

When Caesar died in 44 BC, Augustus was not yet twenty and a student on the west coast of Greece. In November 43 BC after some tough skirmishing Augustus had himself made consul, and with Antony and Lepidus formed the triumvirate for state. In the year 42 BC when Antony defeated Cassius and Brutus at Philippi and they committed suicide, Agrippa (Augustus's fellow-student) Maecenas (his grey eminence) and Salvidienus Rufus (who did not last) were Augustus's friends and allies. That same year, in October, the treaty of Brindisi (Brundisium) entailed the marriage of Antony with Octavia, Augustus's sister, which Virgil apparently celebrated in his fourth Eclogue. The Eclogue is about Pollio's consulship (which was at that time) and about the birth of a son and the new golden age.

Either at Brindisi or at Taranto (Tarentum) three years later, Maecenas, travelling south on a diplomatic errand to meet Antony, again took Virgil and Horace with him (Hor. Sat. 1, 5). Maecenas was the literary patron through whom Augustus worked. He was a Roman Knight, an Etruscan nobleman, and like Julius Caesar the descendant of many kings. There is much about the politics and the wars of these times I have no appetite to re-enter here, since I wrote about them recently in my Horace (1997), Horace being more enmeshed by the times than Virgil was: while Horace fought and ran at Philippi, Virgil lived in retirement near Naples.

Virgil was not blind to Roman affairs, and he writes that he 'sang of Kings and battles, till the god / Tugged at my ear' (Ec. 6, 3). The phrase is conventional, almost proverbial among poets: the god said to him 'Tityrus, graze fat sheep, but sing thin song'. It is not inconceivable that Virgil was already playing as a young man with myth and legend, before his patrons were startled by his perfect adaptations of the true tone of Theocritus, by his truth of tone. Maecenas became a close friend of Horace, and their friendship was lifelong: he was already a friend of Virgil, and it must have been through Maecenas that Virgil aimed his Eclogues at Augustus, whom it is perfectly possible he had never actually met.

Pollio's position, greatly as he was praised in the third and fourth Eclogue – and he was not alone in exciting the praise of Virgil in the Eclogues – was lesser and came later. It is only about Augustus that there hang such claustrophobic veils of tact – and even there with striking exceptions in the Emperor's private letters, which Suetonius as an imperial secretary in his own later day can quote. It seems possible Augustus would not want to be acknowledged as the patron of a war of such patent homosexual sensibility.

Pollio was born in 76 BC or earlier, praetor in 45 BC and consul in 40 BC, he had a triumph in 39 BC, and built a public library at Rome with his loot. He retired from public life, became a historian and a man of letters, and trod the maze of literature delicately enough to die aged eighty in 4 AD. After his praetorship in 45 BC, he went to Spain as a military governor, was recruited there by Antony, and may have served as Mark Antony's governor of Cisalpine Gaul before he returned to Rome in 41 BC and became consul.

It has been said that Pollio was a supporter of Mark Antony who was converted by Maecenas to be an Augustan, say in 42 BC. But this involves us in unpalatable difficulties. He would have to be Virgil's patron as a mere praetor in 45 BC before he went to Spain, and Augustus would not be the young man Tityrus went to see in Rome, and Caesar's star would burn with only an ambivalent fire. The truth seems to be that Pollio was an Antonian as Caesar's follower, naturally and by chance, and became an Augustan on the earliest opportunity. He then retired from politics and wrote modern history down to Philippi, which he seems to have done severely and well.

Once we have removed Pollio from the dedication of the eighth Eclogue (in which neither he nor any one else is named), he is only a person complimented in the third and the fourth Eclogues.

The fourth is an astonishing performance which rings up the curtain on the golden age (3 and 11-14), and Pollio is a consul under Augustus and the third is in the same mood:

> Our Muse is rustic, Pollio loves our Muse:
> Heliconian Muses graze a calf for him.
> Pollio makes his fresh songs: graze a bull,
> Who tosses horns and his feet scatter dust.
> Who loves you Pollio, let him come where you love,
> Let honey run for him and thorn bear balm.
> Who don't hate Bavius, let him love Maevius's songs,
> Let him yoke foxes, let him milk he-goats. (84-91)

The reference is undoubtedly literary, and Horace (*Epod.* 10) follows it. The first coincidence of Horace's and Virgil's works is thought to be the sixteenth Epode with the fourth Eclogue, where they share a Sibylline prophetic point of view but take quite different views of the future of Rome. In the period 44-40 BC different views were possible certainly, and one might even like Pollio change one's side. But the business of these hated literary men, Bavius and Maevius, clearly unites the two poets. Bavius died in Cappadocia, where he was a supporter of Antony. There was a wicked rhyme about this pair among the fragments of Suetonius:

> Bavius's brother possessed all things
>   In common, one lad with the other lad:
> Lands, house and money as they say, what stings
>   Is one soul in twin bodies they had.
> One had a wife with whom the other slept,
>   So friendship came to an end:
> It all dissolved in anger and accusation
>   Of fraud, and new alliances in the end.

The rhyme is by a minor poet, but the peculiar venom of this clash, which is in Virgil's life rather unique, suggests (pleasantly to my mind) that if Virgil was involved in a dispute, Horace weighed in.

We are told Pollio had governed Cisalpine Gaul, and the commentaries on Virgil tell us that Virgil's father's land there was confiscated, as so much land was, for the resettlement of troops after Philippi. Virgil became swiftly so famous that history was built around him. Now we know (and I have explained at great length in *Horace*) that land tenure in that age was essentially fragile and mutable. It is therefore certain that the peasants, let alone the shepherds, viewed these sudden alterations of ownership with extreme alarm. It must surely have been an ordinary staple of their conversation, and it appears to me that Virgil reflects this and little more. In the Eclogues, old Tityrus is not young Virgil, and the antique commentaries which have built up an entire fabric from the imagination that he was, have done a disservice to history. Appian tells us that the redivision of land in Cisalpine Gaul was kept by Augustus in his own hands. But from false inferences from what Virgil himself tells us, the commentaries have built a construction that looks as if it depended on separate evidence.

The famous tale of Virgil's three friends, Pollio and Gallus and Alfenus Varus, having been appointed commissioners for the redistribution of land, and Virgil's land being confiscated and then excepted and returned to him, is just rubbish. The *Appendix* Epigram 8 is also nonsense. Pollio was governor, and he was particularly tough on the Paduans, as Macrobius (1, 2, 22) tells us, late in the day but probably rightly. Gallus is supposed to have collected money from towns that had not contributed land, but this mission of his is attested only by the commentary on the sixth Eclogue (64) where Gallus has suddenly appeared 'wandering by the Permessus', which is the river on Helicon where Hesiod's Muses used to sing (Theog. 5). What worries the commentator is how Gallus got into the Eclogues at all. Alfenus Varus is praised in the sixth Eclogue (6-7), though he does not seem to have had any hand in land deals in the Po valley. He was Augustus's deputy as a consul in 39 BC, but not a heroic or a martial character (Horace mocks a financial manipulator with a similar name, Alfino, who thinks he loves the country (*Epod*. 2) but prefers money).

What did happen then? Virgil was living at the far end of Italy. He had already left Mantua where, if his family were on the wrong side, they will surely have lost their land. Virgil, like everybody else, knows plenty about the misery that swept across the countryside, and he knows Mantua lost land to Cremona. That is all.

We would like to know when Pollio and when Alfenus Varus were his friends, and the answer appears to be 40 and 39 BC when they were consuls. Why not? Pollio had taste and retired after his triumph in 39 BC: that is when he formed his circle of friends. But by then Virgil already belonged to the circle of the friends of Maecenas. That is why Pollio appears so cheerily in the eighth Eclogue just as a fellow-poet. Gallus appears near the end of the book in the same way. As for the estate – if it was one – near Mantua, we had better give up the chase. The loss of it, and a shared distaste for Antony and his civil war, may well have influenced Siro in leaving his own villa to Virgil.

Gallus was perhaps a year younger than Virgil and was born at Fréjus in Provence. When he was forty years old and a military engineer, he did rather well in Egypt, but success went to his head, he was recalled and disgraced and killed himself in 26 BC. The obelisk that stands in St Peter's Square in Rome carries some of his boasts, as nearly every ancient monument did that he came across.

We have very little evidence of his ability as a poet. That clown the commentator Servius maintains that Virgil had intended to close the Georgics with his elegy, but there is no evidence that he ever entertained so preposterous an idea. In the Eclogues Virgil associates him with the passion of love, and that is all we know of their relationship. His girl was called Lycoris, who was a *poule de luxe* and later Antony's mistress. The dullness of Gallus's few surviving lines is very sad:

> Then Caesar will my fate be sweet
> When you are the biggest thing in our history,
> And many temples of the gods
> Shall be the richer for spoils that all may see ...

The small literary tricks of this kind of verse, at which Gallus is adept, make it somehow all the worse. Indeed it is true of this whole school except Catullus that technique outruns sense, something one very seldom feels in Virgil, though the 'then ... when' trick does occur in the dedication of the eighth Eclogue.

But the worst is to come. Cinna the father of this flock wrote a poem of good wishes for the young Asinius Pollio setting out on a journey to the Greek east, they say in 56 BC, a *propemptikon*, as such poems were called.

You shall not marvel so much at the mighty piles
That the unnumbered ages have heaped up,
Ever since Danaus and the year of birth
Of the city of Cecrops, and since Tyrian Cadmus.

This poem got attention from grammarians in the lifetime of Augustus, and small wonder maybe. Cinna is talking about Argos, Athens and Thebes, but it does not matter. Cinna is also supposed to have written a *Moretum*, The Salad, in Greek, and we would rather see that (unless it is only a confusion). At least he deserves to be remembered for his poem, *Zmyrna*, which he took nine years to write; it was about incest. Of all the longer poems of the *Appendix*, the only two Fraenkel singled out for real merit are the Salad, *Moretum*, and the Curses, *Dirae*.

Yet it is undeniable that Virgil grew up under the influence of these people, as he did under that of his river, the soft mud and the crown of reeds. The boys who swam and net-fished in the lakes of Mantua forty years ago were the same kind as the ones he knew in his brief childhood.

Virgil may have known Pollio before Pollio's brief six years of politics. Pollio came from Chieti and his rise under Augustus was at first through the army and – being six years older than Virgil – he was a tribune of soldiers, then a legate, under Caesar in 49 BC, under Curio in Sicily, and then in Africa, and in 46-5 BC legate in Africa and Spain. His foothold in politics was secured as tribune of the people in 47 BC at the age of thirty-one.

We know that Pollio's appetite for literature and truth eventually overcame his taste for public life. But it may also have preceded it. Cinna's idiotic *propemptikon* must surely date from Pollio's twenties, otherwise it would be even more patronising than it is. By the year 50 BC, when Virgil was twenty, and Pollio was attracted to Caesar (with whom he crossed the Rubicon), Pollio must have put aside poetry at the age of twenty-six. That is the right age surely for adventure.

If then, as it appears, he had been a poet and a friend of Cinna and of Virgil in his twenties, they were friends in Rome, before Virgil withdrew to Naples and Pollio to the army. Cinna by the way came from Brescia: 'through the Celtic willow-groves, / Dwarf ponies hurry my French cart along' (fr. 9, Courtney). He must have been born in the eighties, and been as much older than Pollio as Pollio was older than Virgil. No doubt it was in Rome that all three of them encountered one another.

Virgil complained of a weak stomach on the journey to Brindisi he took with Maecenas and Horace three years after the treaty, but he was a tall, well built

34

man with a healthy country countenance and a dark colour. And yet even here one must hesitate, because this pleasing picture may come from a painting, which may well reflect in turn the shepherds and goat-herds of the bucolic world of the Eclogues. Let us settle for it that at least in his youth he was a tall, big-built fellow with a dark face who lived in Naples.

The Po valley is not the landscape of the Eclogues, which contain only small touches observed from nature. Though I grew up believing that Theocritus was vague about time – it was all misted into a golden age, like that wonderful golden dust or ground-mist in the cattle paintings of Cuyp – I think now that he was quite clear about when he set his scenes. Yet with Virgil both the when and the where are eccentric. We know exactly the kind of landscape where Bianor's tomb is (Ec. 9, 60): we have seen such places in Sicily between Agrigento and the sea. But Virgil is inventing as he goes along like a painter of stage scenery, or of those frescoes of just this period that Vitruvius discusses.

I have maintained that Virgil took a long time over his Eclogues. The early lives allow him only three years, but I have stretched it out even further than Colin Hardie because I think it would take a long time, particularly for a young poet under thirty, to attain such perfection of tone in adapting a line of verse from another language. The Georgics are better still, but I cannot think that they would take as long as these complex little poems. He never refers again to the 'Kings and battles' (Ec. 6, 3) of his very first attempts and they may not be real.

Virgil was clearly the master of those tiny, tinkling phrases that are so charming and in the end so deadly in the Greek Anacreontics of his time and their Latin offspring. He had paid a closer attention than any critic or poet whose work has survived to the texture of verse, to what elements in a line of verse make it work, give it an enchantment. If there is an exception then the other such master was Horace. Their old friend and critic was Quintilius Varus, whom Horace commemorates with Virgil towards the end of his Ars Poetica. But Quintilius has left us nothing in writing. What is far worse, because it plunges us into a chasm of loss, is the fact that Augustan Latin is no longer a spoken language, and there must be things about it in the Eclogues that elude us, and lines where we blunder.

The Eclogue that is easiest to date is the fourth. It is in a style that is like no other and can hardly be the style he used to sing of Kings and battles. The earliest example of his style for Theocritean scenes is probably the song sung by Alphesiboeus in the eighth Eclogue (64-109), which O. N. Nilsson first noticed in 1960 is metrically close to the second and third, while the song of Damon is not. The style seems early but the matching of the dissimilar pair in a single Eclogue would be among the latest of the whole collection, and be close in time to the first Eclogue, which is late. That, as Clausen points out with satisfaction gives us two and three and the song to bring back Daphnis from the city as early, and one and eight, both in praise of Augustus, both late.

The biographers and scholars of late Roman times say Virgil began his book in 42 BC at the age of twenty-eight and finished it in 39 BC. But when I was a student Hardie was already allowing the poems eight years from 45 to 37 BC. Their order was thought thirty years ago to have been 2, 7, 3, 4, 9, 1, 4, 6, 8, 10, in which list 7 could be put later. They had been re-arranged by Virgil to give the effect of alternating poems of different kinds. Whatever else is true, they have clearly been much revised and it is now impossible to be certain of so precise a list. Servius already admitted this.

The model for the song at 64 in the eighth Eclogue is Theocritus (2, 1-63), where the faithless lover is Delphis not Daphnis, and the setting is not at all rustic. It is Virgil who introduces lynxes stupefied (because they loved music) and rivers quiet and their courses altered, as they were for Orpheus. It was also Virgil who introduced the dew on the early pastures (15) and the Arcadian theme (21), when this piece was finally put together (in 35 BC but no earlier, if we are right in taking the dedication to refer to Augustus himself).

When would Augustus have commanded Virgil to write Eclogues? It is not probable before the war, before the siege of Modena (Mutina) in Cisalpine Gaul in 43 BC, the campaign of Philippi and the suicide of Brutus in 42 BC,* or the siege of Perugia (Perusia) and the defeat of Antony's brother in 41 BC. Yet the date of the fourth Eclogue, Pollio's consulship in 40 BC, is extremely likely. That wonderful and wonderfully ambiguous poem seems to me to mark an arrangement with Maecenas, who emerges into our sight for the first time only at the siege of Perugia.

Whether Virgil had begun the second and third Eclogues a short or a long time before we cannot know, or whether the song of Alphesiboeus was his first attempt at Theocritus, we have no way of being certain.

Nor are the compliment to Gallus (Ec. 6, 64-73) and the loss of his girl in the tenth Eclogue easy to date, since Gallus had lost the girl long ago to Antony and his public career only begins in 30 BC. The extravagant compliments Virgil pays in the Eclogues are not paid to the powerful, and they are not a sign of weakness, only maybe a sign of youth. The same symptoms are revealed in the lyric poetry of Horace, whose close friend he now became and remained for life. They did not settle down to milk the republic or the Roman state or the new aristocracy of the empire, but they had both made their peace with life.

In Virgil one may notice a certain vehemence on the subject of Italy, which

* Brutus defeated Augustus in the first battle and Antony defeated Brutus in the second battle at Philippi.

did not cease. Maecenas built him at some time a house inside or overlooking his own gardens on the Esquiline hill, not far from where the Arch of Gallienus once marked the point in the Republican wall of Rome where the Esquiline Gate used to stand. We have said whatever we could about the great lakes that run down from the Alps, which of course are seriously high mountains, and about the multitude of rivers that fall into the Po, and make its plain and its huge delta the richest and wettest land in Italy. But the one thing about Virgil we should make clearest is that he was a Roman. He was born a Roman citizen, put on the toga at about fifteen, and records in his first Eclogue (19-25) where white-haired Tityrus has been to Rome,

> I thought the city called Rome, Meliboeus,
> Was like this one of ours, fool that I am,
> Where shepherds often take their sheep's offsprings.
> As puppies have the look of dogs and kids
> The look of nannies, I compared small with great,
> But she lifts up her head among cities
> As the wild cypress does above the ditch-rose.

When the other shepherd asks him why he went there, Tityrus answers as Horace's father would have done, in a ringing word of three long syllables: *libertas*, liberty. This may be a story about an invented character, but I find it very moving. Virgil must have known many for whom it would have been real.

II

COUNTRY SINGING

Virgil's Eclogues have no obvious plot, but they do offer sub-plots and allusions, many of them lost to us because they involve us in dead or in lost poetry, or in Greek poets who themselves offer quite equal difficulties. The Muses and the gods are shadowy and still-footed. But the green woods and the loud noises of birds and even the pipes of shepherds can arouse us with an insistent freshness. The habit of alternate, impromptu song in the countryside has been recorded in eastern Europe by A.L. Lloyd, and I have heard it in Afghanistan. The songs are brief and competitive, maybe only a line or two, and shepherds sing from hill to hill in the mountains: Have you seen the bus go by? / No, but the shadows are lengthening.

The competition in remembered and repeated songs is longer, of course, and these as it were folk-songs do not exist now in a recognisably Virgilian form. But Virgil is intensely literary, and adapts his hero Theocritus, as well as Bion and Moschos, and he pillages the brief poems of the Greek Anthology unblushingly. In the Eclogues he is the poet of the phrase, of the dying, melodious phrases of the Greek, and of the line or brief run of lines, like his own shepherds.

What holds the Eclogues together then? Crispness, and variation, and the subtext: the world that is never fully stated, only hinted at, the life-stories that must be imagined. One can return to the Eclogues for a life-time, and they draw one in, they hook one's curiosity: not just about their mysterious feats of balance and near-balance as Wendell Clausen shows, but the sheer ambivalence of shadows and of woods.

First Eclogue (Meliboeus, Tityrus)

The first Eclogue has two principal characters. There is no title and they are not necessarily named. The poem is a conversation like the dialogues of Plato, and we are told little at first about where it takes place. But we are shown at once that Virgil will not continue unless he chooses with a single model in Theocritus: although he begins with the natural music echoed in self-echoing words that overwhelms readers of Theocritus's first Idyll, he shifts at once to the seventh (88-9) and to an undertone that may recall Epicurean philosophy 'at rest in its

39

gardens, where it likes and, lying on the grass, softly and delicately calls us away from public life' (Cic. *De Or.* 3, 63). The forest music is like the lonely country music of the cicada in a Greek poem, and Clausen may be right to see a link between this line and one in the sixth Eclogue, and also between Caesar here and in the fifth Eclogue and Gallus in the sixth and the tenth. This division and the link (1 and 5, 6 and 10) are taken up by Horace in the first book of Satires.

But if we pursue these elaborate patterns too fervently they will infuriate and bewilder us, nor do they add to meaning, so we shall on the whole ignore them. They are a phenomenon of revision and of a kind of frantic over-writing. Virgil is best read a phrase at a time and a poem at a time, while the woods echo and re-echo with 'Amaryllis'. The name is Theocritean (Id. 3) like most of Virgil's names, but the musical oat-straw (2, *avena*) maybe means a reed (as it is in the sixth Eclogue) and like Amaryllis may be here for euphony? Clausen takes the old British view that you cannot make music out of an oat-straw, but I would not bet on his being right. What is the scrannel-pipe in Lycidas (Theoc. Id. 7)?

In the opening of this Eclogue Dryden plays a full and rich music, but re-orders the lines; Ogilby is thinner yet fine in his way.

> Mel.   Under the spreading beech, at ease from cares,
>   Thou (Tit'rus) playest on tender reeds soft airs ...

The old man lies at his ease under the broad beech and on his thin oaten pipe meditates the Muse. We leave our country and sweet fields, while you Tityrus, lazy in the shade, teach the forest to re-echo Amaryllis (3-4). The task of translating into prose or verse is laborious and unrewarding, since this Eclogue is as subtly musical as the opening of Milton's Lycidas. At least the plot is simple. Meliboeus, whose name means cow-herd, has to leave his dear native soil, while Tityrus lazes in the woods.

Tityrus replies at once. A god gave him this happy idleness (another word with a strong Epicurean ring to it). He will be a god to me for ever, I will sacrifice lambs to him, he has let my cattle wander and let me play what music I choose on my rustic reed (6-10).

I am not envious, says Meliboeus, just amazed when there is such disturbance in the countryside (11-12). It is already apparent that the 'god' might stand for someone with power. Meliboeus and his goats are suffering, as he recalls the blasted oak trees prophesied. Who was the god? Tityrus has been to Rome. Whatever for?

Freedom, which came at last, though slow to come. (27)

II. Country Singing

Tityrus has saved up money (as a shepherd could) because he was allowed to look after a few sheep of his own among the flock. John Aubrey notices that in the seventeenth century that was still in southern England the only way that shepherds were paid: Aubrey was delighted to discover the same custom in Roman times, in Plautus's *Asinaria*, which he quotes (Green, 1993). The money a shepherd saved was called his *peculium*, which derives from *pecus*, his herd. There is a problem here, stirred up by Sir Ronald Syme in his *Roman Revolution*, where his remarks on the political use of *libertas* (freedom) as a slogan of Caesar's party confuse the issue of slavery with lesser civil rights. Meliboeus had his own farm, he was a free landholder whose land was confiscated. But old Tityrus had only his ruinous place and his money, which he wasted on Galatea, until Amaryllis took him over, white-haired as he was.

When Tityrus was set free he went to Rome to know how such landless ex-slaves were to live. Augustus told them all to live as they had lived, which of course was on common lands and in forests.

> For thee the bubbling Springs appear'd to mourn,
> And whisp'ring Pines made vows for thy return.

Tityrus first met the divine young man in Rome, to whom twelve times a year his altars smoke (42-3). The god heard him. His grounds were restored and he could feed his flocks. The Hellenistic ruler's birthday was once a month, and this must be worship of Augustus,[1] not of the family Lar, since Tityrus had not got one. So we may be in autumn of 36 BC when the worship of Augustus swept across all Italy: though an example does exist in Theocritus on Ptolemy (17, 126-7).

Augustus assured the anxious crowd of petitioners, 'Pasture your oxen boys, and breed your bulls' (45). To this Meliboeus replies:

> Happy old man, your country will remain,
> And big enough for you, though naked stone
> And marsh and muddy reedbeds block the field. (46-8)

This surely is the borderland of town lands, the untamed wilderness or common, where Tityrus is a squatter. Meliboeus had more to lose, and he must go into exile who knows where? Flocks herded by slaves went a little earlier all over the Mediterranean, but in Italy things were now more organised and at least one herdsman in three must be free. The laments that follow are gross exaggeration, like those in the tenth Eclogue.

The speech of Meliboeus (46f.) introduces one of Virgil's great themes of the Georgics:

> Happy old man, here among known waters
> And holy springs you drink shady and cold. (51-2)

Here the bees will buzz for him and persuade sleep with their light murmur, and under the high rock the pruner will sing to the breeze, the throaty pigeons you look after and the wood-dove will lament high in the elm (57-8). It is of course the imagery as well as the phrasing. It is the sudden hint of cold, the sudden heat in which the pruner sings to the breeze, and the mild, dangerous buzz of the bees that make the poem grip. It is not a landscape or a vignette, whatever Tennyson made of it, but it is do-it-yourself poetry, in which the reader is persuaded to imagine the sting of the bee, the cold of the water, and the pains of love, without their ever being mentioned. Dryden's

> Stock-doves and Turtles tell their Am'rous pain,
> And from the lofty Elms of Love complain.

But in Virgil the turtle just moans ceaselessly from the airy tree (58): 'Nor Turtles cease to groan from elmy bows', as Ogilby puts it.

Tityrus now introduces a series of impossibilities: Deer will graze in skies ... before I forget him. Meliboeus in foreseeing his own fate seems to take up this extravagance of language. Shall he ever see his cottage again? The ghastly soldiery has his fields, that is what civil war leads to. Graft your pears Meliboeus, put vines in rank (73). Are these perhaps the orders of the new master, to contrast with Augustus's few words to Tityrus? Meliboeus will never lie in rock-shade again to see his goats hanging in the mountain air. I will sing no more songs (77).

Dryden has dropped sweet apples from Tityrus's evening invitation, and he muffles the Alpine shadows falling bigger from the high mountains.

> This Night, at least, with me forget your Care;
> Chestnuts and Curds and Cream shall be your fare:
> The Carpet-ground shall be with Leaves o'erspread,
> And Boughs shall weave a Cov'ring for your Head.
> For see yon sunny Hill the Shade extends
> And curling Smoke from Cottages ascends.

They will sleep like that in the forest where they met and where they still are, somewhere on the edge of the woods maybe. Having passed the night with its innocent supper, they will separate and Meliboeus will begin a lifetime of wandering, perhaps as far as the British islands, who knows? He is now a true nomad, and the Roman Empire does not set limits to his wanderings. He will not cross the Alps or the Danube all the same. Now some will go to the thirsting Africans, / Some to Scythia and the chalky Oxus / Some to the Britons, a whole world away (64-6). He does not know really where these places are: scholars are equally at a loss about the chalky Oxus. Did Virgil think it was chalky, or only Meliboeus? Questions like that can never be answered in the Eclogues. It is like the question about the oat-pipe, whether it was a joke or a children's toy.

Second Eclogue (Corydon)

In the second Eclogue Corydon is in love with Alexis, a slave-boy who is loved by his master, and that is that. Only among the dense beeches, the shady crests, he often came alone and flung these artless words to the mountains and forests (3-4). It is like Virgil that he gives us the essential circumstances in a line and a half, then the shaded place and the lonely lover, who will have this poem to himself. The names of Corydon and Alexis and the twin fires and harvest time occur in an Anthology epigram.

The early biographers say Virgil was homosexual, and loved a slave-boy that Maecenas or someone similar gave him, and it seems to be true. Yet this Eclogue is as much fantasy as the others. It is a contrast of coolness and heat: now even the flocks look for shadows and the cold, now bramble bushes hide the green lizards. Bits of this are from the Greek love poetry of the last generations, but the green lizard 'sleeping in stone walls at noon' has here been given a bramble bush and his colour and Thestylis, who pounds up magic herbs in Theocritus, is just 'pounding up garlic and thyme, smelly herbs for harvesters weary of the roasting heat' (10-11). Its strong taste suits the blazing heat.

But while I trace your steps, the bushes under the punishing sun re-echo with cicadas (12-13). The poem is a rigmarole, as it were, altering subject as it chooses, but always returning to the heat and to the pains of love. Was it not more than enough to suffer the anger and scorn of Amaryllis? And Menalcas, though he was black and you were white (14-15)?

Suddenly the forest is full of characters, like a Shakespearean Forest of Arden, but the names do not necessarily mean the same character as figures with the same name in another poem, or even someone of the same name in Theocritus. If this indicates a world, then the world is dream-like.

> O lovely boy don't put your faith in colour,
> White box falls, dusky cranberries are picked. (17-18)

You despise me Alexis, you don't want to know who I am, how rich in sheep, how overflowing in snowy milk. I have a thousand ewes in the Sicilian mountains, summer or winter I don't lack fresh milk (19-21).

So are we in Sicily? No more in this poem perhaps than in another, though since this Eclogue is supposed to be early, perhaps Virgil still follows an imaginary setting out of Theocritus (but the shepherds in Virgil are a race apart, wanderers like the gypsies). Clausen compares a Theocritean boast from Polyphemus, and suspects irony, but R. Coleman (1977) dismissed that as preposterous. It sounds like a lie, but why not? The reference to Theocritus is confirmed by what follows, yet from line after line there drifts towards us a scent of Anthology epigrams, the same state of mind, the same flowers. The length of these exquisite poems is set by Theocritus of course, and so is the jumble of characters like figures glimpsed in a landscape as that also shifts.

The boasting gets stranger still. I sing the same song Amphion used to sing (23), and then a line of four exotic names: Dircaean Amphion in Actaean Aracynthus. The sound pattern is Homeric but adapted by Hellenistic poets, as Oscar Wilde adapted the painted carnation. Dirce is a spring at Thebes, and Amphion built the walls with his flute, but Actaean means Attic, and Aracynthus was the pretty name of an obscure ridge in the Parnes range: the entire line may well have been the transliteration of a Greek verse.

Corydon having got to this climax says he saw himself naked reflected in the calm sea, and Daphnis is not more beautiful. This comes from a joke about the Cyclops, but here it is not a joke. Daphnis and the Cyclops both still insinuate Sicily, and the scene is surely influenced by a painting like Agrippa's from Bosco Trecase, of which Clausen's cover offers a photograph painted it seems in dark pea-soup. To compound the difficulty for scholars of these charming lines, they contain a syntactic echo of the idiot engineer Gallus (Courtney, 1993). Nisbet saves the day by pointing out that Gallus was copying Virgil (*ibid.*). So early in Virgil's career a complexity of confusion is possible, and one may prefer to stick to Dryden:

> Nor am I so deform'd, for late I stood
> Upon the Margin of the briny Flood:
> The Winds were still, and if the Glass be true,
> With Daphnis I may vie, though judg'd by you.

Corydon wants Alexis to live with him in a humble cottage, to hunt the deer and entertain the goats with music. He praises Pan as the first piper and assures Alexis that Amyntas longed to learn piping, and Damoetas left Corydon his seven-jointed pipe when he died. Amyntas liked the kiss, the roughness of the pipe on the lip. Amyntas's name is that of a King of Armenia but in pastoral poetry he is a slave-boy and Damoetas is a Theocritean singer (Id. 6) who imitates the Cyclops.

Corydon offers two kids for playthings, 'fleck'd black and white, the true Arcadian strain' (40-1), that Thestylis has her eye on, and ends with a wonderful few lines of flower poetry, flowers of the garden like lilies that the water-nymphs will bring in baskets:

> Pale violets and poppies' topmost heads,
> Narcissus and the sweet scented anise
> With Daphne, weaving in sweet herbs to paint
> Soft bluebells with the yellow marigold. (47-50)

It is hard to be quite accurate, since the flower-names are not all securely identified, and ancient writers did not bother much about seasons so noticeable in the north. The poor Cyclops offers 'snowdrops and poppies' in Theocritus, which unless the poppies are anemones would never bloom together. The violets are pale if they are white violets or dying; the bluebells might as easily be cranberries, and no doubt that thought introduces the textures of fruit, the white downy quince, the chestnuts, waxen plums, and the laurel and myrtle to mix their scent. The whole list is vivid and intoxicating, made for senses that are surely sharper than ours: it is only ten lines (45-55), and left Milton in the beginning of *Lycidas* in some confusion, which he took a number of versions to correct.

Corydon knows his long outburst has been fantasy, and that the boy's master Iollas can outdo his gifts. But he comforts himself that the gods themselves have lived in the forest, and so has Trojan Paris. Let Athene cultivate her cities, we prefer the woods (61-2): another phrase that will re-echo from this poem as late as the Georgics. The lioness goes for the wolf, the wolf for the kid, the wanton kid for flowering moonclover (which is a plant unknown to us) and Corydon's Alexis goes for you: and every creature is pulled to his pleasure (63-5). The word *voluptas* is stronger than pleasure or delight, its pull is magnetic and central to the Epicurean system and to Lucretius (1, 1; cf. 2, 258). It will reappear as 'love' in the last Eclogue.

Suddenly this poem closes, like Marvell's Severn fishermen with coracles on their heads, with the oxen bringing home the ploughs upside down: and the shadows grow double as the sun departs. But I burn with love, love has no measure. Corydon, you are mad (66-9).

> Your vine in leaf hangs in the elm half-pruned:
> Do at least something that is needed now,
> Weave willow, interweave it with soft reeds. (70-2)

VIRGIL: HIS LIFE AND TIMES

The touch of pain and heat is smothered in the coolness of cheese-making, of the willow and the reed. You will find another Alexis if this one despises you (73). The poem descends into the most mundane comfort.

Third Eclogue (Menalcas, Damoetas, Palaemon)

The third Eclogue is another early attempt. It has another real person in it, Pollio, but the reference to him is undatable, because his switch from Antony to Augustus is hard to trace. This praise of him may be added later, or equally it may date from his poetical youth, as I imagine it does.

This Eclogue includes a snatch of real song, and the singer knows the songs of two famous performers. It represents surely a truth about shepherds in Virgil's day, and I have long suspected that their most exaggerated flights owe something to the naive decorations of real popular songs: but we have not enough material in the remains of popular lyrics from Alexandria either to prove this or to disprove it. We do know that Theocritus like Virgil was fascinated by the contrast of rival singers in close competition, and by the solemnity of their judges and their prizes.

One feels at once a quarrel that has roots unknown to us, and those also occur in Theocritus. Professor Merkelbach has prudently warned us that real herdsmen's songs can never have been composed in hexameters. My own feeling is that they were always composed in a beating kind of rhythm, lengthened and transformed by the pipes. What today we call ballad-rhythm (two lines of which treated as a single line make up the long line of medieval Greek popular poetry, a metre that swept across Europe in the thirteenth century AD, probably starting with the Hungarians) may well have had features in common with the lost songs that Theocritus had heard, and probably Virgil also knew, whether from the South Italian Greeks, the Sabine herdsmen who were in Campania, or nearer home. Once again we begin with clarity about the circumstances.

Whose is that flock, Damoetas? Is it Meliboeus's? (1) No, Aegon's ... (2) Unfortunate fellow, unfortunate flocks: he's mad about Neaera and jealous of me, and meanwhile here's this stranger shepherd milking twice in an hour: he takes the juice out of the flock, and the milk away from the lambs (3-6).

These two characters Damoetas and Menalcas are competitive singers in Theocritus, whose fourth Idyll opens in more or less the same exchange. But in his Greek poem, Milon the owner has gone off to Olympia, where (the whole world knows) he became a great champion. That dates the poem long ago, of course, and so Virgil will not follow suit. His Damoetas replies to Menalcas with some heavy sexual innuendo:

II. COUNTRY SINGING

Good words, young Catamite, at least to Men:
We know who did your Business, how, and when,
And in what Chappel too you plaid your prize
And what the Goats observ'd with leering Eyes:
The Nymphs were kind, and laught, and there your safety lies.

Dryden is more explicit only in the word Catamite, which is implied but not expressed by Virgil, who is funnier. The Chapel is in the Latin but it means a rustic grotto where there is a shrine and luckily some privacy.

The insults become hotter as they turn to theft and malicious injury to someone's vines and the bow and arrows of Daphnis, which the boy had won, and Menalcas 'but for mischief, would have died of spite' (15).

What should masters do when thieves are so audacious? Didn't I see you steal Damon's goat while Wolf the dog barked and barked; and when I shouted 'Tityrus, guard the flock, where is he off to?' you were hiding behind the sedge (16-20). Well, and had he given me the goat I won from him with my pipe? That was my goat if you want to know, and Damon admitted as much, but he said he couldn't give it to me (21-4). *You* beat *him* at singing (25)? And so on, and the interest has swung back to the central subject of poetry itself.

Meanwhile Virgil has shown us another side of his rustics. The sexual joke is lightly sketched (7-9) and does not recur – though it has drawn an alarming weight of donnish commentary. The dishonesty illuminates a landscape and a way of life. It is not possible to think what simple, innocent rogues these are. They are spiteful and passionate, and the expression of passion in art is the only solution (for Epicureans, I suppose).

As the match is set up, we learn more. Damoetas used to play at crossroads, but now he bets a calf. Menalcas can make no offer from his flock because his father and his stepmother count the sheep twice a day, and the other one counts the goats. (This need set us no problems about Menalcas and his social status because either years have passed or it may not be the same Menalcas as in the first Eclogue.)

Menalcas decides to hazard beechwood cups by Alcimedon, carved with a vine and ivy. 'Alcimedon' is invented, and the cups sound like South Italian painted pottery. As for the central designs in the bottom, one is by Conon (nonsense) and the other he can't remember who by, showing the seasons. Damoetas has two of Alcimedon's cups as well, one with the woods running after Orpheus as he plays. The elaborate descriptions of these elaborate and unlikely objects is a foolish whim of Hellenistic taste – based on Homer – which may be found in Theocritus. It seems to me a joke, though perhaps one seriously intended. It does not represent contemporary taste, but it may be intended for the hideous things rustics would treasure. There are worse objects about a hundred years old in the Worcester porcelain museum of which people are still proud.

At this moment, when they are close to blows over the value of the prizes, old Palaemon luckily passes by, and agrees to be judge.

> Sing then; the Shade affords a proper place,
> The Trees are cloath'd with Leaves, the Fields with Grass,
> The Blossoms blow, the Birds on bushes sing,
> And Nature has accomplish'd all the Spring.

It is only here that we notice no one until now has mentioned the weather, or the joys of nature. As a narrative the poem proceeds seamlessly, yet the change bridges a deeper alteration and in a way an unsuspected deepening of theme. Here it enters a long duet in which any variation is competitively introduced, every score is melodious, and the conversation is created by two voices compelled into harmony. I think that this does reflect the way Cretan *mantinades* or Spanish *coplas* can work impromptu to this day, but here at a level of art that no exhibition of folksong can match. The most amazing aspect is that Virgil, never mind Theocritus, can capture something of the true freshness: as Shakespeare might have done if he had such a tradition to delve into.

> Pal.   Begin Damoetas, and Menalcas follow:
>   Sing in replies, the Muses love replies. (58-9)

Just as they love echoes in the woods, and the self-echoing songs of birds, and just as the echoes of shepherds' pipes in the mountains suffer metamorphosis into the piping of Pan: Virgil like Lucretius is a good Epicurean.

> Dam.   Music begins with Zeus, all's full of Zeus,
>   he forms the earth, he's shepherd of my songs.
> Men.   Apollo loves me, all his gifts are mine ... (60-2)

But here I must defer to Ogilby, who finds himself faced with a sweetly reddening hyacinth, and produces a couplet of strange beauty:

> Dam.   With Jove begin: all things are full of Jove,
>   He keeps our fields, and doth my verses love.
> Men.   And Phoebus me: and I have for him still
>   His own Bay, and sweet blushing Daffadill.

> Dam.   Light Galatea me with fruit would win,
>   Then flies to th' willows: but would first be seen.
> Men.   My flame Amyntas courts me oft alone ...

(So that is who was with Menalcas in the Chapel.) Damoetas knows where to find pigeons for his girl, but Menalcas has sent his boy ten apples. The boys and the girls in these poems are very innocent, like the girl Ezra Pound took from Propertius, 'happy, selling poor loves for cheap apples'. If ever Ogilby is truly a poet it is here: where Virgil is universal because he is dreaming about adolescence. Menalcas asks what is the point of Amyntas secretly not scorning him, if Amyntas hunts the boar while Menalcas keeps the net. It appears to me Menalcas has the best of all these exchanges – but that is not Palaemon's view – and I have always disliked Damoetas.

The praise of Pollio (84f.) leads to the hatred of Bavius and Maevius (90) which as I have said Horace echoes in an Epode, and a splendid array of hot and cold and similar-dissimilar textures follows:

> Dam.   Fly, who cull Flow'rs, and earth-born Strawberries,
>   For in the grass a cold Snake hidden lies.

Menalcas counters by warning sheep from the river-bank where the ram fell in and is shaking his fleece dry (94-5). Damoetas calls Tityrus, still a slave one assumes, to bring his kids to be washed in a spring. The fact that all these sharp sense-perceptions are in deliberate contrast between one couplet and the next is our only proof that Virgil could write verse with a precision in which he has had few followers. But in his development as a poet, these are early days.

The end of the contest is the most childish of riddles: Damoetas asks: in what country is all heaven six feet wide? Menalcas asks: in what country are flowers written with the names of kings? The answers are not given, but the first is a well in Egypt or surely a grave at Mantua, the second is the flower that blossomed where Aias (Ajax) died at Troy, or where Hyacinthus died in Sparta (the hyacinth with its first two letters in Greek like a drawing of the flower, so they say).

The last word is Palaemon's. Ogilby makes him like the epilogue to a comedy, which is a just observation, but a sadly interesting one in 1649.

> 'Tis not in us this difference to compose:
> You both deserve the praise, and each who knows
> Or fears sweet love, or hath the bitter try'd.
> Swains shut your Springs, the Meads are satisfied.

His 'Springs' are irrigation channels opening from the Mincius as they do to this day, and as channels do in Sicily where water is brought a distance. They work much like a mill-leat, which is opened when the miller needs a force of water.

Fourth Eclogue

The fourth Eclogue, because of its glorious prophecies and its Sibylline tone, and because it foresaw the birth of a divine child, was swiftly adopted by Christians. They clung to it through thick and thin until about 1900 as a prophecy of the coming of Christ. This view is not intellectually respectable, but it goes back to Constantine and Eusebius, and to the allegorization of Virgil by such venerable characters as Fulgentius and the same Eusebius.[2]

We used to be reminded in church of Sibylline powers by the *Dies Irae*, which begins

> The day of wrath that dreadful day
> Shall the whole world in ashes lay,
> As David and the Sibyl say.

Unluckily the surviving writings of those cave-dwelling and hysterical ladies the Sibyls are late Jewish imitations, often anti-Roman and prophesying only the fall of the city – as the Book of Revelation at one point does. A.D. Nock has taken a cool look or two at this sort of literature, and his comments are still valuable. Augustus as Emperor naturally disapproved, and burnt as many prophetic books as he could get his hands on; considering the use Horace (*Epod.* 16, 2) made of one and the catastrophic irony of the fourth Eclogue from this point of view, this is hardly surprising. It is more pleasant to record that among a long stream of devout scholars, only the Jesuit La Cerda (1617) stands out as paying the merest lip-service to the Christian interpretation. The Christian misinterpretation is most fully and most credibly stated by Lactantius, a serious Latinist (*Divin. Inst.* 7, 24) if not a serious theologian.

Virgil's restoration of the lost golden age of Hesiod and the mysterious galaxy of the Virgin in Aratus (who revisits mankind in their dreams) through the birth of a child in the consulship of Pollio in 40 BC, is a daring stroke, particularly if Pollio was Antony's man and not Augustus's (Syme, 1939). But the child was born to Octavia, Augustus's sister, by Antony anyway. It is notorious that this attempt to stick the split-world of Augustus and Antony together with a marriage did not work, and their child was a girl. Had Antony's and Octavia's child been a boy, he could have claimed descent from Venus on his mother's side, and Hercules on his father's, and Hercules is referred to here (14-17).

The poem is coloured from Hellenistic ideas, undoubtedly, but it is not Theocritean (though Theocritus praised princes) nor Callimachean. Virgil has taken a leap into a language of his own which no surviving prophetic text can have originated. He is original in the same way as William Blake, and with the same admixture of an audacious simplicity. Only the ending of this Eclogue has Greek origins.

The golden age is to come, as Communism was under Stalin, and in the age of a man the seasons will turn to perpetual autumn, 'the oaks will sweat a dew of honey' (30). Many of the images will recur, particularly the honey on the oak tree and the 'grapes reddening in the bramble bushes' (29). The scene is a pantomime transformation scene, but it has likely enough been altered between its conception in 40 BC and its publication about the time of Antony's death and Cleopatra's suicide in 30 BC.

No one has ever been able to conjecture how it once stood, and it is an ironic thought that Antony if questioned would have answered, Virgil? You mean the poet who wrote a hymn for my wedding to Octavia? I don't remember him. We met at Brindisi? Ah, I was thinking of other things.

This Eclogue and Horace's sixteenth Epode have a good deal in common, though they take very different views. Most scholars think Virgil wrote first but I am not convinced either poem is an answer to the other. Nor can I see, now that I reconsider the matter, how Horace's so deep despair was possible between 40 BC and the battle of Actium in 31 BC, when Augustus defeated Antony. The truth is one may sort out the poems and date them as one chooses. Pollio's consulship in 40 BC is only two years after the suicide of Brutus at Philippi, but it is in those two I would expect Horace also to feel suicidal.

The poem suits Dryden as a translator and Clausen as an interpreter. Sicilian Muse begin a loftier strain! / ... Sicilian Muse prepare / To make the vocal woods deserve a Consul's care (1-3). Sicilian not just because it is Theocritean, but because Sicily is near enough to Brindisi (which has no Muses?). Virgil calls the Muses *Sicelides*, daughters of Sicily, which appears to be original but scarcely significant. Yet, the thrilling announcement in line 4 flings the Muses on the rubbish-heap of poetry where they belong: The last age of Cumaean song begins (4). Dryden is content to call it 'foretold by sacred Rhymes', because he needs the rhyming word:

> The last great Age, foretold by sacred Rhymes,
> Renews its finish'd Course, Saturnian times
> Rowl round again, and mighty years, begun
> From their first Orb, in radiant Circles run

What Virgil says, to put it with less of a mantic flourish, is that the great order of the ages begins again from the beginning. Now the Virgin returns, Saturn's kingdom returns, now a new offspring is sent down from high heaven. Chaste Lucina, now your Apollo reigns, favour the new-born boy, through whom the age of iron first ends, and all over the world a golden people shall arise (5-7). The likeness of all this to Christianity is striking and remarkable until we come to Lucina, the birth-goddess. Dryden, who was by then a Catholic, was frightened to put in the Virgin, who, as Norden pointed out in the wonderfully strange *Birth of the Child* (1924), is essential to the whole complex of ideas.

The boy, sufficient glory of the age,

> Shall Pollio's Consulship and Triumph grace;
> Majestic Months set out with him to their appointed Race ...

They will set us free of the last traces of our crime, perpetual fear (the crime being civil war), and he will lead the life of the gods, will see the heroes mingle and be seen by them. Virgil's doctrine is Homeric (*Od.* 7, 221) like Horace's: 'by this art Pollux and wandering Hercules climbed the citadels of fire'. The child shall rule the world his father's virtues have tamed (17): the virtues are those of Augustus or Julius Caesar rather than Hercules or Antony.

> Unbidden Earth shall wreathing Ivy bring,
> And fragrant Herbs (the promises of Spring)
> As her first Off'rings to her Infant King.

Dryden discreetly evades the Indian lotus and Egyptian thorn, but he can manage the goats coming home with swollen udders (Hor. *Epod.* 16, 49-50) and the great herds in no fear of lions.

The cradle will blossom and the serpent and the deceiving poisonous weed will die: Syrian spices will grow everywhere. When he can read the praise of heroes and the deeds of his ancestors, and is able to know true virtue and what it is, the meadows will grow yellow with soft corn and the grape blush on the natural wild bramble, and the hard oaks will sweat dews of honey. A few traces of our old dishonesty will survive, to bid us tempt the sea in ships, ring towns with walls and set furrows in earth. Another Tiphys (the helmsman) and another Argo shall carry chosen heroes: there will be wars again and great Achilles shall be sent to Troy again (24-36).

This threatening passage seems to mean war in the wealthy east, as much as it means a new heroic age. It is confined to the newborn child's adolescence, because as soon as he is a man ships and trade by sea shall cease and the whole earth will bear everything; no more ploughs or sickles and the oxen will be loosed from their yokes. Dyed wool shall not lie about its colour, the ram in the meadows shall turn his own fleece deep purple or crocus yellow, and crimson will clothe the lambs (39-44). This remarkable fantasy is a memorable challenge to translators – there is a sense in which verse translators are the only serious readers of Latin poetry left. Ogilby is neat and fine enough, but Dryden is grander.

> But the luxurious Father of the Fold,
> With native Purple, or unborrow'd Gold,
> Beneath his pompous Fleece shall proudly sweat:
> And under Tyrian Robes the Lamb shall bleat.

No doubt this extraordinary vision is still hidden in the future, lambs like a field of fritillaries and rams richer than velvet, but may we live to see it. Having got to this climax, Virgil brings into play the Fates out of Catullus, and pays his final, most grandiose compliments.

> O of Celestial Seed! O foster Son of Jove!
> See, lab'ring Nature calls thee to sustain
> The nodding Frame of Heav'n, and Earth, and Main:
> See to their Base restor'd, Earth, Sea, and Air,
> And joyful Ages from behind, in crowding Ranks appear.

Inspired, no bard and not even Pan would outdo Virgil on such a theme. He calls on the infant to smile and recognise his mother, who deserves it after the discomfort of pregnancy. No god blesses the board, no goddess blesses the bed, of an unsmiling child (63).

The entire performance is only 63 lines long, so it is the shortest Eclogue. Several words of its exotic colouring occur in this poem for the first time in Latin. It is written I think, at least as we have it, from a prudently Augustan point of view. It is not lavish about Antony, still less about Cleopatra (it is an exercise of imagination to consider what such a poem written for Antony would have been like).

Virgil's golden age is no more than an embellished Italy. It is Italy that he passionately loves, from the Alps to the Greek ruins. He venerates the Sibyl of Cumae for her antiquity, not the Sibyl of Tibur. He has concentrated his remarkable powers of language, of imagery, and of controlled fantasy, in praise of a human child who was never to be born. Octavia had two daughters in the end by Antony, but his sons were by other women. The Eclogue is sufficiently confused or mysterious, and has surely been altered to make it more so, that scholars grasp at other identifications of the child, each unlikelier than the one before. (Scribonia married Augustus as her third husband in 40 BC, a political act to bring in young Pompey as an ally. Their child Julia had a tragic life.) But the occasion of this Eclogue was surely the short-lived alliance with Antony, any positive trace of which has been removed.

Fifth Eclogue (Menalcas, Mopsus)

The fifth Eclogue, the end of part one of the Eclogues as we have them, is a dialogue 90 lines long between Menalcas and Mopsus (referring back in its closure to the second and third Eclogues), and has two long centre-pieces about 25 lines long. Since the two of us are together, says Menalcas, why don't you play the pipes while I tell some verses (1-2)? You are older than me, says Mopsus, so it is up to you to say whether we settle where the Zephyrs keep moving the unstable shadows, or go into a cave (4-7).

> Or will you to the cooler Cave succeed,
> Whose mouth the curling Vines have overspread?

After a little more of this foreplay, in which the praise of Alcon, the death of Phyllis, and the fury of Codrus are suggested as themes, Mopsus decides to sing about Daphnis. But he has called it 'the sad Verse, / Which on the Beech's bark I lately writ' (perhaps Virgil is unable to imagine true folksong or its oral transmission). The lament of course was still among the commonest and most popular kinds of folksong while folksong survived.

Mopsus has been a little nettled to be told Amyntas rivals him (8), but now that is forgotten as he begins.

> The Nymphs about the breathless Body wait
> Of Daphnis, and lament his cruel Fate.
> The Trees and Floods were witness to their Tears ...

The entry into his subject is immediate and sudden as we are assumed to remember the lament in the first Idyll of Theocritus. Virgil must not seem to challenge or weakly to imitate it. The Theocritean names in this Eclogue are from the seventh Idyll, not the first. The mother of Daphnis is a new character altogether. We are told by learned men that she was a nymph or a muse, Calliope, but Virgil neither knows nor cares, and the 'evidence' is only an anthology epigram. Her calling on the gods and cruel stars is quite conventional. In a real country lament it would be she and not Mopsus who was singing.

On those days, Daphnis, none took the cattle to the cold rivers, no beast sipped at the brook or touched the growing grass. African lions howled at your death, Daphnis, and the wild mountains and the forests uttered. Daphnis taught how to harness Armenian tigers and to bring in the revels of Bacchus (24-30). The lions should have warned us that we were entering a wonderland of mythology, though it was visually familiar to the Romans, and the contrast of hot and cold and that of colours operates here as brilliantly as ever.

The line on Bacchus is followed by 'And weave the bending spears in the soft leaves' (31), as if the riot and the tigers had dissolved away.

> Vines ornament the trees and grapes the vine
> And bulls the herd and crops the fertile ground ... (32-3)

Daphnis is all beauty to his own. When the fates took him, (divine) Pales and Apollo deserted the fields. You set fine grain in the furrows and darnel and wild oats come up (34-7). It is not unfair to remark that, considering the impurity of ancient seed, they might as easily come up anywhere as wheat.

For the soft violet, for bright narcissus, the thistle and sharp thorn (38).

> Come Shepherds, come, and strow with Leaves the Plain;
> Such Funeral Rites your Daphnis did ordain.
> With Cypress Boughs the Crystal Fountains hide,
> And softly let the running Waters glide;
> A lasting Monument to Daphnis raise
> With this Inscription to record his Praise,
> Daphnis, the Fields Delight, the Shepherds Love,
> Renown'd on Earth and deify'd above:
> Whose flock excell'd the fairest on the Plains,
> But less than he himself surpass'd the Swains.

It is a curious combination of poetry, concern for the earth, the rags and tags of religious poetry in Greek, and that strange piece of nonsense, the verse epitaph. We have seen the same tricks worse played by Virgil's contemporaries. Even so, this dirge is less than moving, and the theme of 'universal nature did lament' is somehow less convincing here. But the verse, the substance of Virgil's poetry, still glides as softly as the running waters.

Divine poet, says Menalcas, your song comes over me like sleep in the grass to a weary man: like quenching one's thirst from a leaping spring of sweet water in the heat. Not only your piping but your voice equals the master. Happy boy, you will succeed him. I must say my bit anyway and raise Daphnis to the stars, because he loved me too (45-52). Mopsus other has heard of the song from Stimichon (55), and we are off: Menalcas sings, White Daphnis wonders at the floor of heaven / To see the clouds and stars below his feet. / Therefore keen pleasure fills the country woods (56-8).

> For this with cheerful Cries the Woods resound,
> The Purple Spring arrays the various ground:
> The Nymphs and Shepherds dance, and Pan himself is Crown'd.

The wolves are kind to the flocks, no nets are set for deer: good Daphnis (like Epicurus, whose *voluptas* possesses the woods) loves idleness (*otium*). The unbarbered mountains fling their voices to the stars, and the banks and bushes sing, He is a god, Menalcas. Be kind and happy to your own! Here are four altars, two for Daphnis and two for Apollo, I will give two cups foaming with new milk every year, and two urns of rich olive oil (61-8). This last provision is peculiar because the oil is in mixing urns for wine and water, but he takes the Greek word from Theocritus who offers a great urn of white milk to the Nymphs, and one of sweet oil. We must assume that Theocritus knew what he meant (Id. 5, 53-4), but that Virgil did not care. He just felt the strong attraction of the Greek.

Menalcas then proposes a feast with wine, 'in frost by hearthside at harvest in shade' (70), of Ariusian nectar (Chian wine) drunk in tumblers: Cretan Aegon and Damoetas will sing, Alphesiboeus will dance like the Satyrs (or the Fratres Arvales, who performed annually in Rome an antique and thumping kind of rustic dance). This shall be yours whenever we pay our dues to the Nymphs or walk in procession round the fields (71-5).

> While savage Boars delight in shady Woods
> And finny Fish inhabit in the Floods,
> While Bees on Thime, and Locusts feed on Dew,
> Thy grateful Swains these Honours shall renew.

This almost ecstatic song of country pleasures ends with a prayer to Bacchus and Ceres and a bow to Daphnis as a god.

Mopsus is thrilled and cannot think what present or prize to give: not the whistle of the rising wind nor the sea beating on the shore, nor rivers that run down the stony vales give him such pleasure (83-4). Menalcas overwhelms him by the present of his old hemlock pipe on which he composed the second and third Eclogues (so much for the oat-straw mentioned in the first Eclogue) so Mopsus offers his shepherd's crook, which Antigenes used to envy: its hook is bronze, 'the Knobs in equal range' (90). That ends the first part of the Eclogues.

The Sixth Eclogue (Silenus)

The second part of the Eclogues contains some unexpected developments because the 'Eclogue' is not a form with rules. It is a process; it alters as Virgil alters. The sixth Eclogue is remarkable. Two boys called Chromis and Mnasyllus (Blacky and Forgetmenot?) come across Silenus sleeping off a drink, so they tie him up and demand a song long promised. All kinds of Fauns, Satyrs and animals crowd to listen, and first of all the nymph Aegle comes (who left her name to Eglantine). The wicked old god who finds she has painted his face purple with wild berries (a colour or mask that denotes divinity) remarks: the Nymph shall be rewarded in her way (26).

The trees dance to Silenus's song.

> Not by Haemonian Hills the Thracian Bard, (Orpheus)
> Nor awful Phoebus was on Pindus heard,
> With deeper silence, or with more regard.

We are 30 lines into the poem, but this first scene is so exactly painted that we ought to linger over it. It is all but static, like a painting, and it could possibly depend on one, but not on one we know. Silenus, the Pappasilenos of Greek painting, was an important figure in the Satyr-plays of classical Athens, which were regularly played after three tragedies. We have fragments of one by Aeschylus, and one whole play, *The Cyclops* of Euripides. This scene may well derive from one: they were imitated in the South of Italy, and those imitations were often painted on pots, a few of which have survived.

The song of Silenus all the same seems to derive from the Orphic cosmogony, not the early version in *The Birds* of Aristophanes but a late version by Apollonius of Rhodes (1, 496f.), and of all unlikely roles Silenus transforms himself to a literary critic. The whole epilogue of this poem is addressed to Varus and concludes with praise of Gallus. It is a manifesto for the new school of poetry.

Varus worried the ancient scholars. Servius thought he was the general defeated in Germany (too young), and Donatus thought Alfenus Varus, who was never distinguished as a soldier.

So why not Quintilius Varus (whom Servius might well confuse with P. Quinctilius Varus, a soldier favoured by Augustus)? Quintilius Varus was from Verona. He was a friend of Virgil and a fellow philosopher named with Virgil as a critic by Horace. We are briskly told he was never a soldier at all, but who knows? He could perfectly well have been a military tribune as Horace was, a young man appointed to the staff for the sake of his conversation. That is the likeliest solution, and I do not see why no one has adopted it. What is more, the dedication of this Eclogue is baroque:

> My muse was first to play in Syracusan verse,
> And not to blush to live in the wild woods:
> I sang of kings and battles when Apollo
> Plucked at my ear and told me 'Tityrus
> Shepherds should graze fat sheep and sing thin songs'. (1-5)

This is a reference to the ancient Greek poet Callimachus, and suitable to address a critic like Quintilius Varus. But 'there will always be enough poets longing to tell your praises and deal with unhappy wars Varus' (6,7) takes us into an unknown. Was Virgil in youth prepared to knock up an epic like Archias? It is in the highest degree unlikely. 'I on my thin reed muse a country song' reflects Theocritus in the first Idyll, and dismissing epic praises of warlords is only meant to lead up to that.

I sing commanded, but if anyone reads and loves this, of you Varus my tamarisks and all the grove will sing. No page pleases Apollo more than one that bears the name of Varus (9-12). My translation is awkward but more or less accurate (the 'tamarisk' is not alas our seaside tree; it is unknown). At line 13 Virgil says 'Buck up my Muses', and the poem proper begins.

The fact that Quintilius Varus is an unforgettable figure we owe not to this baroque prelude, but to Horace (*Ars Poet*. 438f.). It might seem Virgil's enthusiasm for him was a quirk were it not for that neglected poem. But given that Quintilius Varus presides over the opening of this Eclogue, the end of it addressed to Gallus falls into place.

When Silenus began (31),

> He sung the secret Seeds of Nature's Frame;
> How Seas, and Earth, and Air, and active Flame
> Fell through the mighty Void; and in their fall
> Were blindly gather'd in this goodly Ball.
> The tender Soil then stiffning by degrees,
> Shut from the bounded Earth the bounding Seas.
> Then Earth and Ocean various Forms disclose,
> And a new Sun to a new World arose.

Virgil gives his wonderful Epicurean cosmogony (it is not a creation) 10 lines, and he dives into metamorphosis, and the stones that become men, the golden age, the fate of Prometheus, the death of Hylas and the rape of Pasiphae by a bull: Who on soft hyacinth leaned his snowy side, / Chewing pale grass under a black ilex (53-4)

> But ah! perhaps my Passion he disdains,
> And courts the milky Mothers of the Plains ...

I do not think any poet has ever more sharply communicated what it might feel like to be a girl passionately in love with a bull, not even in Greek. We are to think of Calvus's *Io*, but we have nearly none of it.

Scholarly speculation runs wild among the densely packed and rather obscure allusions of Virgil's poem: the daughters of Proitos who believed they were cows, and were cured by a magician in the remotest cave in all Arcadia, and the sisters of Phaethon who turned to alders by the Po. In the Aeneid (10, 190) Virgil reverted to poplars, but here the strangeness is a large part of the poetry.

Suddenly (64) we come upon Gallus wandering beside a river on Helicon:

> Then sung, how Gallus by a Muse's hand
> Was led and welcom'd to the sacred Strand:

and the chorus of Muses stood for Apollo's man; the mythical bard Linus crowned with flowers and bitter celery was their spokesman, who gave him the pipes from the Muses that were once Hesiod's. Gallus is to sing about Apollo's famous grove in Asia Minor, the 'Grynean' grove (72).

Virgil goes on with hardly a pause from this to Scylla, to Tereus and Philomela: All that Apollo mused and the blessed Eurotas heard and bade his laurels learn (82-3).

> Silenus sung: the Vales his Voice rebound
> And carry to the Skies the sacred Sound,
> And now the setting Sun had warn'd the Swain
> To call his counted Cattle from the Plain.

Suddenly it was night and the star Vesper came out from unwilling heaven (86), which ends the sixth Eclogue. In no poem is Virgil more gleefully disregardful of rules, more dense in images and literary allusions, and he proves here triumphantly that this does not matter in the least. I now think I understand every nuance and every allusion of the sixth Eclogue, but when I was young and understood none of it I enjoyed it just as much. It is a virtuoso piece, a young man's poem.

Seventh Eclogue (Meliboeus, Corydon, Thyrsis)

The next Eclogue is another dialogue: the god Daphnis sat under an ilex, and Corydon and Thyrsis brought their goats and their sheep, says Meliboeus,

> Both in the flower of youth, Arcadians both,
> Ready to sing and answer in their songs. (4-5)

Here while I was protecting tender myrtles from the cold, the father of my flock the old billy himself had wandered, and I spotted Daphnis. 'Come quickly Meliboeus', he said, 'your billy and your kids are safe; if you have a minute, rest here in the shade. Even the cattle will come here across the meadows to drink, here Mincius has covered his green banks with bending reeds and swarms of bees echo from the holy oak' (6-13).

The introduction is pleasantly casual, and the country conversation is rather real than idyllic. Yet how much Virgil insinuates without saying it: the heat of the day, the shadow of the ilex, the herds everywhere, and suddenly the Mincius, although the herdsmen are Arcadian and Daphnis is a god. These are not conundrums, they are only vague because memory is vague and nothing is explained. If the myrtles would be hurt by frost Meliboeus would protect them. The Mincius with the mists of the Alps would fit that while Arcadia would not fit so easily.

What was I to do? I had neither Alcippe nor Phyllis to lock up my lambs at home, so I put my serious jobs below their game, and they began to compete in alternate verses (14-18).

Corydon's first offering is a little pompous and obscure, Thyrsis's is more direct and charming. Then Corydon sings an epigram (29-32): These branches of a Stag, this tusky Boar Young Micon offers – which does recall Erucius (30, *ramosa cornua*). Thyrsis replies with a simpler bid:

> This Bowl of Milk, these Cakes (our Country Fare),
> For thee Priapus yearly we prepare:
> Because a little Garden is thy care.
> But if the falling Lambs increase my Fold,
> Thy Marble Statue shall be turn'd to Gold.

This is a ridiculous fantasy of course, a piece of rustic exaggeration. Corydon counters strongly:

> Fair Galathea, with thy silver Feet,
> O whiter than the Swan, and more than Hybla sweet;
> Tall as a Poplar, taper as the Bole,
> Come charm thy Shepherd, and restore my Soul.
> Come when my lated Sheep at night return;
> And crown the silent Hours, and stop the rosy Morn.

Thyrsis is less impressive, but they are beginning to catch at each other's verses, as Corydon's silver caught at the gold, and his white is turned by Thyrsis's black sea-weed.

Corydon calls on mossy springs and shady trees, so Thyrsis answers with winter fires, Corydon loves Alexis and Thyrsis loves Phyllis. The correspondences between stanzas are multiple and perhaps intuitive.

Meliboeus remembers this poetry, and now Corydon is unrivalled. Yet we notice Daphnis has simply evaporated: who was the judge? Was the beginning stuck to the body of the poetry later? Is this why the Mincius is graced by two Arcadians? Was that part just patched together at a late stage, and did Virgil (as I suspect) not think it mattered? But it is possible or even likely that Virgil thought of this introduction with its casual narrative to be an advance, like that of Plato's Republic. (There is in fact some evidence that Plato's introductions were written independently of his dialogues, since one lacks an introduction altogether.)

Eighth Eclogue (Damon, Alphesiboeus)

The next dialogue, the eighth Eclogue, is patched together even more strangely. First the circumstantial introduction, then a long and stately dedication to a person unnamed, and finally two long songs in competition or in contrast, but with no judge and no decision. I have agreed earlier with Clausen's view that this poem patches or matches an old piece with a new one, in which case Maenalus, an Arcadian hill, is a late element. More doubtfully (but with envious admiration) I agreed that the poem must be meant for Augustus. There are consequences of this view we must go into here, and it should be stressed to outsiders that studying Roman history in its details at this period is like playing patience with a defective pack of cards.

Damon and Alphesiboeus at whose music the heifer forgot the grass, lynxes were stunned, and rivers altered courses and were still, let us speak of their music

61

(1-5). This introduction tells us very little (and I suppose it is late). The dedication (6-13) follows at once, and after it we get 3 more lines.

The cold shadows of night had scarcely left heaven, the time when dew on young grass is most delicious to the flock: Damon settled to the smooth olivewood and began like this (14-16). The importance of dewfall and dawn grazing in Mediterranean countries can hardly be over-estimated, but the touch of realism that surprises is a pipe carved from olive-wood: it is just possible that Virgil means only leaning on a smooth olive tree, and if it is possible it must be preferable here.

The dedication is carefully not put at the beginning, as in the first and sixth Eclogues, and there is something unfinished about it, as if Augustus did not want it. (Line 6 reverses the view that it is Pollio who is coming home to Rome, since it is to someone moving in the opposite direction. The rocks of Timavus are beyond Aquileia and the boundary of Italy; looking across Timavus one sees mountains, and those must be the rocks: there are none in the sea near the estuary.) Or even if you are skirting the Illyrian shore follows.

When shall I be allowed to speak of your deeds? Shall I be able to tell the whole world of your songs worthy of Sophocles? (6-10) This is not Pollio, not Varus, not Gallus. Is it Augustus? We know Augustus attempted an *Ajax*; he used to write it in the bath and, when asked about it, said his play had fallen on his sponge. The rest of the dedication does sound like Augustus. You are my beginning with you I shall end: take these songs begun by your command let this ivy wind around your brows among the conquering laurels (11-13).

If that is not Augustus, who is it? It is too grand for Maecenas, who was no tragedian. No doubt the dedication will always have puzzling implications, but at least Augustus makes sense, and Pollio does not. The poem can now be dated to the Dalmatian (Illyrian) campaign of Augustus in 35 BC.

Can the dedication be a mixture of fragments to fit Augustus with a fragment about, for example, Varus? Though I do not think Virgil was quite so careless, he does recycle fragments. His use of quotations is like Eliot's: he even quotes himself. It is apparent that how to fit allusions together is for Virgil in youth a great part of the skill of a Roman poet: it is like Basho's skill in connected *haiku*. As he gets older Virgil will become more seamless, and even in the Eclogues one must remember that to him poetry is about idleness and music, both with some degree of sexual edge to pleasure. The dazzling succession of Silenus's themes in the sixth Eclogue has a strong sexual content. They are not a string of literary quiz-questions. In the end after the worst nightmare (the story of Tereus, 78f.) we are left with the poetry or the music of the nightingale. There is something about that bird that fits Virgil. Edward Lear's Greek servant Giorgis said it must have more brain than the other birds, because it never sang exactly the same song twice.

Damon impersonates an unhappy man whose wife (18) has left him. His lamenting self-expression is neatly divided into stanzas with the repeated line: Begin my pipe a song of Maenalios (21 etc.). The word *tibia* used for the pipe in the context of these lines makes one think it could be of olive wood? But as before, every strange or new device is taken from Theocritus. He sings to the pine forest on Maenalus that knows all about love-song from listening to Pan.

> Who suffered not the Reeds to rise in vain:
> Begin with me my Flute the sweet Maenalian strain.

Nysa has been wedded now to Mopsus (see Ec. 6), but their names are of no account, they are false trails.

> Scatter thy Nuts among the scrambling Boys,
> Thine is the Night; and thine the Nuptial Joys.
> For thee the Sun declines: O happy Swain!
> Begin with me my Flute the sweet Maenalian Strain.

He remembered his first sight of her and how he gave her dewy apples: like the grass the flock eats, no doubt. The first down was then on the poor fellow's chin. He was twelve then and she was with her mother (38). Love is the child of tigers, it was Love that made the mother (Medea?) murder her children. 'Old doting Nature, change thy Course anew', says Dryden indignantly.

Now let the wolves run from the sheep, let hard oaks bear golden apples, and the narcissus blossom on the alder, let tamarisk sweat rich amber from his bark, let the owl rival the swan, let Tityrus be, Orpheus in woods, Arion among dolphins (52-6). One would think amber was magical but the only mystery was where it came from (the Baltic mostly); the Greeks and the Romans used it for sculpture. The line about Tityrus sounds like a joke: can he represent a real and long remembered farm servant? His name makes it unlikely.

The lover jumps into the sea, which finishes his poem, and the next one starts at once. So Damon; what Alphesiboeus replied / Tell Muses, we cannot all do everything (62-3).

Alphesiboeus's song about Daphnis is from Theocritus's second Idyll, but Virgil has rusticated it. He has observed the ritual in Theocritus, not in low life as perhaps Horace did for the *Epodes*. We have no real models to compare it with in Latin, only in Greek. But in pondering the Greek Virgil has lingered on details that attract him.

63

Bring water from the house and tie a soft ribbon round the altar, burn rich twigs and masculine incense (64-5). The incense is tiny balls with a swell to them, after 'rich' or fat boughs and the soft ribbon. Virgil's scene is wonderfully more exotic than the Greek. Nothing more is needed but chants, that can bring the moon out of the sky, and split open the cold snake in the fields. Splitting snakes open by chanting to them was a speciality of the Marsians, whose ancestor Circe Virgil invokes; Lucilius recorded this kind of magic, which is genuinely Latin: H.V. Morton thirty years ago claimed the Marsians were still at it in 1969.

Now the woman, who only wants her husband, Daphnis, home (66), takes the three-coloured triple thread three times round the altar and the doll three times around, then Amaryllis is called on to knot it three times three and cry out 'I tie the bonds of Venus' (78). It is a realistically boring bit of ritual, like that lovely song,

> Go toss these oaken ashes in the air,
> And sit three times in yon enchanter's chair,
> And tie up three times three this true love's knot,
> And say she loves me, or she loves me not'.

She says in her less innocent version: As this mud hardens and as this wax melts with one and the same fire, so may Daphnis for my love. She sprinkles flour and burns breakable bay-leaves and bitumen. Daphnis burns me, I burn him in this bay (80-3). It is as real as the power of poetry can make it, but a million miles from Horace's nastier charms: even the fire is no more than a crackling bonfire.

> As when the raging Heyfar through the Grove
> Stung with Desire pursues her wand'ring Love,
> Faint at the last she seeks the weedy Pools,
> To quench her Thirst, and on the Rushes Rowls

The cow is too distracted to go home at night, like a hound after an aged doe in a poem by Varius Rufus on death (Courtney 273, fr. 4, line 6). The doe 'thought not to run for home at nightfall', that is all. But no doubt the single line Virgil quotes was a compliment to his friend and fellow Epicurean. Varius was a literary executor of Virgil and he and Plotius Tucca edited the Aeneid: and Varius and Virgil introduced Horace to Maecenas we are told. It is interesting in so close a friend that Varius vigorously attacked Antony for confiscating the land of Roman citizens (Courtney fr. 1).

The lady in the Eclogue now digs her few souvenirs of Daphnis into the earth.

Moeris has given her poison from Pontus, she knows Moeris can become a wolf or bring souls out of sepulchres or move crops from field to field. Amaryllis must fling ashes over her head: Daphnis does not care for gods or chants.

But suddenly the ashes burst into flame on the altar, and here comes Daphnis:

> ... no more, my Charms;
> He comes, he runs, he leaps to my desiring Arms.

We are lucky to have Horace as well as Virgil, and to know what a dark underworld Virgil was playing with. One could wish we also had the memoirs of Moeris, articles on lycanthropy are no substitute. Moving crops by chanting was forbidden under the most ancient and severest Roman law.

Ninth Eclogue (Lycidas, Moeris)

The ninth Eclogue is an outburst of suppressed feeling, even after all this. It is also earlier than the first, here again one must agree with Clausen. The poem is tightly interwoven with the realities of the land crisis at Mantua, and needs careful reading. As the name Lycidas indicates, Virgil is drawing on that masterpiece, the seventh Idyll of Theocritus. Moeris here is not the character we met in the eighth Eclogue.

Where are you off to, to the city, as the road goes? (1) O, Lycidas, I have come to this in my lifetime, that a stranger should own my land (I never expected it!) and say 'This is mine, away with you'. Now we're beaten and unhappy, because chance overturns everything, and I'm sending him these goats, curse him (2-6).

Lycidas: I had heard your friend Menalcas and his songs had saved all the land from where the hills slope down and flatten out as far as the water and the stag-headed beeches? (7-10).

Moeris: So you heard, and that was the rumour, Lycidas, but our songs are worth no more in a world of weapons than doves when an eagle comes. If I hadn't heard of new conflicts coming from a raven on the hollow ilex on the left, your friend Moeris would be dead and so would Menalcas (11-16). The narrative is of course fantastical, yet the country is the same. It seems to lie towards Valezzio, just visible from Mantua.

Lycidas is horrified to hear about Menalcas: if he died,

> Who then should sing the Nymphs, or who rehears
> The waters gliding in a smoother Verse
> Or Amaryllis praise? – that heavenly lay ...

He then calmly quotes three lines, neatly translated, from Theocritus (Id. 3, 3-5).

If it was not clear already it must now be quite clear that Menalcas is not Virgil. We have to deal with a convincing and indignant piece of fiction. The lines of Theocritus do come from the poem beginning 'I'll sing to Amaryllis and my goats Graze on the hill, Tityrus guides them'. It goes on in more or less the same words as Virgil: 'Tityrus my darling, graze my nannies, Take them to the spring Tityrus, mind the billy, That tawny Libyan, or he may butt'. He is quite as loving to Amaryllis as he is to Tityrus.

The confusion of quoting Greek while telling his Roman story leads Moeris to 'the song he sang to Varus unfinished'. But this is plainly by Virgil.

> Your name Varus if Mantua survives
> Mantua too near unhappy Cremona
> Shall be borne to the sky by singing swans. (27-9)

Lycidas is pleased with this. May your bees avoid Corsican yews, and the udders of your cow swell with clover (30-2), he says. One must admit this poem is very rich even when it seems over-rich. The shepherds call me a poet too, though I don't believe them, he goes on. I can't yet sing anything worthy of Varius and Cinna, I am a goose among swans (32-6). The commentators know of a poet supporting Antony whose name was *anser*, Goose or Gosling. Ovid mentions him.

Moeris now tries to remember a song that escapes him:

> Come, Galatea, come, the Seas forsake:
> What pleasures can the Tides with their hoarse Murmurs make?
> See, on the Shore inhabits purple Spring,
> Where Nightingales their Lovesick Ditty sing:
> See, Meads with purling Streams, with Flowers the Ground,
> The Grottoes cool with shady Poplars crown'd,
> And creeping Vines on Arbours weav'd around.
> Come then and leave the Waves tumultuous roar,
> Let the wild Surges vainly beat the Shore.

Dryden as usual goes too far, but this is only as it were an Anthology epigram, another study in variation of style, and in Dryden – as in Virgil – complete in itself. Lycidas recalls a different song, of which he knows the tune but not the words.

II. COUNTRY SINGING

'Daphnis why observe the ancient rises of constellations?
Look where the star of Caesar son of Venus comes.
A star to bring the crops to their ripeness
And paint grape colour on the sunny hills.
Graft pears Daphnis, the fruit your children's children will pick'. (46-50)

Moeris answers with a change of mood.

The rest I have forgot, for Cares and Time
Change all things, and untune my Soul to Rhime:
I could have once sung down a Summer's Sun,
But now the Chime of Poetry is done.
My Voice grows hoarse, I feel the Notes decay …

Perhaps Menalcas will supply the rest? (55)
But 'now the Waves rowl silent to the Shore', and they are at Bianor's tomb, they might have a rest. Lycidas is as friendly as a dog: they can sit in shelter if it rains, or he can take his friend's load. Moeris says: No more now boy, let's do our job: we'll sing songs better when Menalcas comes (67).

So the Eclogue ends; it was one of the shortest, but deft and intricate. Nothing more has been said about the attack on Menalcas since line 17. The last person to say anything serious about politics was the raven in the hollow oak (15). The bits and pieces of song were only epigrams and, although Caesar's star shines on 2 or 3 of the most beautiful lines in any of the Eclogues, disturbances and hard times are normal, land tenure is never as secure as one thinks, fortune turns things upside down and time takes everything, even the soul. Virgil's sadness in these poems is not only the sadness of every aesthete because the sun will go down. It arises from a country-learnt wisdom even more than it does from philosophy.

Tenth Eclogue

The tenth Eclogue has a 10-line conclusion for the whole book, so is not perhaps as short as it was meant to be. It sets off briskly enough with a line to the Sicilian spring Arethusa which the ancient world supposed travelled by magic underwater from the Peloponnese, and which is still to be seen in Syracuse below that Cathedral with Doric columns that was once a temple of Athene. The poem is dedicated to Gallus and his lost Lycoris, who was lost to Antony in 49 BC at a time when Gallus was only twenty-one (if not so early, his affair was after 45

BC). This Eclogue is written probably in the later forties since the girl was Antony's mistress from 49 to 45 BC.

Lycoris is quite unreal, she is a figure of fantasy, and so is her despairing, dying Gallus. This gives an air of allegory or unreality to the poem which mingles with its other mysteries. Yet, when it is first encountered and simply read, it is great poetry and I think uniquely memorable.

The first few lines to Gallus, offering the spring an inviolate crossing of the straits unviolated by the bitter waves and then settling to sing of Gallus and his troubled loves 'while the kids eat away at tender shoots' (7), are ordinary Hellenistic verse. 'We sing not to the deaf, the woods reply' (8) transmutes to the famous lines of Theocritus that Milton used: 'Where were ye Nymphs?'

> Not steepy Pindus could retard your Course,
> Nor cleft Parnassus ...
> ... For him the lofty Laurel stands in Tears;
> And hung with humid Pearls the lowly Shrub appears.
> Maenalian pines the Godlike Swain bemoan
> When spread beneath a Rock he sighed alone,
> And cold Lycaeus wept from every dropping Stone.

It is not surprising that Dryden is below Virgil, but it is curious that Virgil has an intensity even Theocritus lacks.

The under-theme is Gallus's conversion to bucolic poetry (17-18). By rivers lovely Adonis shepherded, now the shepherds and the swineherds come, and Menalcas wet from mashing winter acorns. Apollo and the others want to know what ails Gallus, assuring him Lycoris has gone to sea with his rival. Silvanus comes, the favourite god of the lower Po and of Illyria, a wild figure here 'shaking great lilies and the hemlock flowers' (25), a line of unexpected sensory power.

> Pan the Arcadian god, whom we have seen
> Bloodred with elderberry and minium (26-7).

Pan is Lucretian, but Virgil's personal claim to have seen him goes against Lucretius and against Epicurus. Yet the 'I' or the 'we' who saw this vision of him in the wilderness may not mean Virgil himself. The red face of the god is rustic Roman belief, and well explained at some length by Weinstock in his *Divus Julius* (1971). Lucretius (4, 587) has Pan 'shaking the pines on his half animal head': the point is that he is a vision in the wilderness. Had Virgil seen him as a child?

We cannot claim even to guess, but we note that Horace as a lyric poet made equally startling claims.

Gallus replies: Sing this to your mountains Arcadians. Only Arcadians can sing. I wish I were one of you, a shepherd or vine-keeper of ripe grapes. Phyllis or Amyntas (what does it matter if he is dark? Violets and bilberries are dark) would lie between the willows under vines, and Phyllis gather garlands, Amyntas sing. Here are cold springs, soft meadows, Lycoris (30-42). He wails that her soft feet tread the Alpine snow and the Rhine frosts without him.

I shall take my songs written as elegies, and tune them to the Sicilian shepherd's oat (50-2). The strange oat is not a joke, and the line deliberately recalls the second line of the first Eclogue. Gallus is a convert to Virgil's poetry. He will carve his name on trees and run around Pan's mountains in north-east Arcadia. His songs please him no more, and whether he dies in the north or the south, grazing Ethiopian sheep under Scorpion. Love conquers all, so let us yield to love (69). This is the most powerful and surely the central moral statement of Virgil's book of poems.

But in what sense yield to love? He recalls line 33: O how softly may my bones rest, if your flute ever tells my loves; and line 43: Here may I waste away an age with you. He is not frantic in this line, only despairing, and it is the last line of the Eclogue proper. It is not quite death or suicide, which in Theocritus (Id. 1) it is, but it carries undertones of unplumbed intensity.

That is enough for your poet to have sung Muses, while he sits weaving a cheese-basket with thin hibiscus. You will make these songs great for Gallus, my love for him grows by the hour like the bending alder. Let us go, the shade is heavy for singers: juniper shade is heavy, shadows lie heavy on the crops. Home goats, you are full, here comes the evening star (70-7). This is a mere unwinding, though it is not without a few unexpected stings.

Why is Virgil so keen on Gallus, whom he has not seen for years? Gallus has frozen like a figure in ice, but he is loved as a colleague and an equal at the end, in spite of being invested with the Apolline grandeur becoming to a patron. What happened in Cisalpine Gaul is befogged, one hears only the munching of the pigs in the acorn mush, and as for the future, it is wholly unforeseen.

This poem, like the entire book of poems, is among other things a sort of photograph album from disturbed times. Virgil is truthful about the background, but the idea in ancient commentaries that one Milienus Toro (*primipilarius* of a legion) threw him off his farm, or one Arrius chased him into a river, or that his farm was first confiscated, then given back, then retaken and then returned to him again, is pure fantasy. It is on a level with the local legend at Sulmone, that Ovid and Cicero toured for seven years in search of wisdom, but Ovid learnt twice as much because he could read through the soles of his feet (as you can see in the market square where his statue is standing on a book).

Some of the critics of Virgil were probably near-contemporary schoolmasters, but since they attacked the Eclogues they had better be dealt with here. Some of them barracked at his public readings, but most of these attacks, which Horace indignantly refutes, are on specific words, because they are Greek, or novel, or ordinary but in new combinations. The point to grasp about this is that criticism centred on diction because there were no dictionaries, there was no historical dictionary of good or normal Latin, so schoolmasters argued about diction in the poems of their betters like the waves of the sea.

But if we choose nowadays to enquire into any word or phrase in Latin, we can do so easily, and find at once all the evidence that survives, which is often amazingly full. The verbal criticism of ancient scholars may now appropriately be abandoned by normal readers. Anyone interested will find a discussion by Nettleship (1881) in the fourth edition of Conington's *Virgil*, which is intended for historians of the Latin language. The most memorable criticism of Virgil was Agrippa's, who thought he had invented a new kind of affectation in his magical-seeming combinations of ordinary words. That of course is what we mean by poetry.

III

VIRGIL'S ITALY

Much of the Eclogues are a vision of Virgil's own youth, whether literary or real one can seldom quite tell. Something similar is true to this day of many early books of poems: not because the poet is young who produces them, but because now the stopper is out of the bottle. As a study in style, the Eclogues are puzzling, and all the more so as a self-portrait, but one senses that to Virgil the question or choice or attainment of style is all-important.

In the Georgics this concern with style hardly exists. They seem to be written with absolute assurance, and one has to peer closely to see the working of his mind and it is useful to observe the reworking of lines and of themes from the Eclogues. Virgil was at least thirty-five or thirty-six when his Eclogues were such a success, but his new plan was a bold one. It is said that the Eclogues took three years and the Georgics seven or eight, but these are the highly unreliable and speculative estimates of antique scholars. But it does look as if Augustus read them complete by about 29 or 28 BC, when all his battles were over, Antony and Cleopatra were dead, and Italy had at last begun to settle down.

My own generation had looked forward since we were undergraduates in the fifties to a commentary on the Eclogues and the Georgics by Roger Mynors, but the immense burden was ready for publication, or virtually so, only in 1989 when he died at the age of eigthy-six. In 1972, at about seventy, he had given up the enjoyable but testing project of the Eclogues, and suggested to Wendell Clausen that he should take it up, and twenty years later when Mynors was dead it was published. Mynors on the Georgics appeared in 1990, and there has now been time to digest it. All that is lacking is the unifying essay on the Georgics which would have made fuller sense of the complete work: but that sense is communicated in comment after comment, as well as in the brief quotations Nisbet offers 'quoted from Mynors's drafts'.

Strange that Virgil's Georgics, as heartfelt a poem as ever was written, should rest in a way on a foundation of make believe. A keen eye for nature, for light and shade, mountain and river, beast and bird and tree; a mind which found the work of earlier poets as rich a source of stimuli as things seen and felt; a passionate love of country and hope for its future,

71

not untinged with deeper questions about what we might call the values and destiny of the individual – *how did those things assume the mask (which proves to be no mask but an essential element in the result) of a didactic poem about agriculture with a Greek title which might have been intended to mislead?* (my italics)

The quotation in Nisbet's preface to Mynor's commentary (1990) continues, but this is the crucial question.

The naive answer is as we were taught, that scholars are always quite happy with anything that occurs twice, and this occurs three times: Bucolics or Eclogues, and Georgics, and Aeneid, are all Greek words, and their choice by Virgil is the mark of a proper respect. But a didactic poem? In spite of what anthropologists have sometimes maintained, I do not think poetry is ever genuinely didactic. As early as Hesiod poetry brings traditional wisdom together, makes it memorable and even proverbial, but it is not how one in practice learns agriculture. Certainly Hesiod like Virgil infuses natural process and human work with a special magic by which morality seems to arise with or from agriculture and to be crucially linked to it. That link is common to primitive stages of society, and it has persisted in Europe until living memory. Why are you shooting your gun? Jevons of Cambridge asked his neighbour one Easter at Athens. Because if Christ did not rise from the dead, came the answer, how would the corn grow?

That is an extreme example, but we shall see how Virgil insists that Roman morality and religion and agriculture are closely linked. Therefore, the restoration of all three go together.

In this Virgil is an Augustan: after dizzy generations of civil war, the last arguably the worst, Italy is now to settle and to revive, and religion and morality with it. A unified and Roman Italy is fundamental to his hopes. The original sin must now be wiped away from memory and the new world is to be Epicurean. Not uninterestingly, Virgil thinks the sin was Laomedon's, when as king of Troy he defrauded labourers of their wages, Neptune who built his walls and Apollo who looked after his cattle. There are other versions of these events, and other sins, and like most theological arguments, they have some relevance for those who advance them, however far-fetched they appear from a distance.

The end of the first Georgic expresses the anxieties of the campaign of Actium (31 BC); the events of 31 and 30 BC seem to underlie the praises of Italy in the second Georgic; and the epilogue at the end of the fourth Georgic indicates early 29 BC when Augustus returns to Rome from Syria and has pacified the world. But Virgil does not go back over the Georgics so that they all fit the feelings of one particular date.[1] He had not corrected the Eclogues in that way either, so there is often a puzzle to determine the dramatic or the real date of those poems.

It is at least clear that the Georgics were written during the great climactic civil war which ended the disturbed period since the murder of Caesar in March 44 BC and the battle of Philippi in 42 BC.

I am not sure that to live through so catastrophic a period either destroys poetry or makes it flourish, but one can watch Virgil's and Horace's poetry putting down its tough roots in the history of their own times. When Virgil undertook the Georgics they were commissioned as a triumph of Italy and of agriculture, but we shall see at the end of the first Georgic how near that scheme was to becoming a disaster that irony could not have redeemed. The four Georgics together are 2,186 lines long, each of them being between 514 and 566 lines. The Eclogues taken together are on my count 889 lines. The new commission was therefore most serious, and imposed at once on Virgil a kind of winged speed which must be variable and interweave themes and subjects, as any writer of a whole book must do.

First Georgic

Virgil found his inspiration not far away from Theocritus, in the *Phainomena* of Aratus, an Asian Greek of the same generation who had written by 274 BC. It used to be thought when the first commentaries were written about Virgil's time that the famous poet Aratus was perhaps the same friend and colleague of Theocritus to whom the sixth Idyll is dedicated, and to whose love life part of the seventh Idyll is dedicated: a proto-Gallus in fact. This is now thought unlikely, but that does not mean Virgil did not suppose it (Gow 2, 118-19).

In the first Georgic Virgil exhausts much of the Appearances, both the astronomy and the advice about the movements of birds and changes in the weather. This brings him to the climax he wants, in the disturbance of nature at the time of Caesar's assassination. In that dramatic scene by the way, his baroque description of the Po in flood does not suggest that he was an eye-witness or in any way personally involved in whatever happened in Cisalpine Gaul. He was in Naples, and it is likely that Maecenas asked him for the Georgics and Augustus showed how his own wishes stood while Virgil was still writing Eclogues.

Hence perhaps the air of haste in the final stages of that book. Ancient publication was not at all like having a book printed. A copy was sold to a publisher like the brothers Sosius, and copied and resold by them. But the manuscript was circulated and read aloud in public by the author before it was finished. We know of cases when Virgil's audience yelled out rather rudely or humorously, always to question the use of a word or a phrase.

Plough naked – 'And you'll catch your death of cold'.
Whose flock is that? – 'Not Latin for a start'.*

The patron to whom a book might be dedicated would know it long before
it was complete, as Maecenas knew the *Epodes*, and as I believe Augustus knew
the Eclogues. It is an important point that Virgil was five years older than
Horace, and seven older than Augustus. Virgil was in his early thirties and a
famous poet at the height of his powers when Augustus was in politics still a
novice, lucky to have survived so long.

Aratus was many times translated into Latin verse: the heavenly bodies added
to the solid worth of science a particular respectability of their own, with which
Virgil was pleased for a time. Cicero produced a version stiff with solemnity, and
the Julian prince Germanicus, who was born soon after Virgil's death, produced
a much more exciting one. Virgil makes what use he chooses, and where he once
has reason to mention the zones of the orb of Earth he takes a few lines from the
scientific poet Eratosthenes, who was one generation later than Aratus and
Theocritus.

Virgil begins the first Georgic, after the dedication to Maecenas and the
contents, with an address to the lights of heaven and to the twelve gods of the
Romans (5-6) just as Varro did. Cato before Varro had written about agriculture,
in magnificent prose, and luckily they both survive: indeed Milton put Varro on
his syllabus for schools.

The difficulty arises at once however that although the Greeks and then the
Romans knew that they believed in twelve gods, it was never finally decided who
these gods might be, and who should be excluded, so Varro's list included Flora
and Robigo, Blossom and Mildew, Flora who stopped fruit blossom from
appearing too early and being nipped by frost, and Robigo who rotted the corn.
One could see why these two negative powers would not suit Virgil in the
Georgics.

Virgil's opening is architecturally grand, like that of Lucretius, and it serves
for all four Georgics, though each book as it follows has a tour de force for an
introduction of its own. The first words seem to recall Lucretius, 'heaven's
undersliding signs'; here it is

O most clear lights of the world,
Who lead the year that slides around heaven.

---

* *Cuium pecus? anne latinum?* The word *cuium* for 'whose' was archaic but it survived
in dialect.

Virgil must mean the Sun and Moon, and not the signs of the Zodiac. Sun and Moon come second in Varro, after Jove and Earth: Bacchus and Ceres follow, who come third in Varro. Then we have the Fauns and Dryads, Neptune who struck the ground with his trident to produce the horse, and more obscurely Aristaeus, who is not named. Why is Apollo not named either? Study of the Athenian Festivals would have revealed him as agricultural, and so would study of the Homeric hymns. Is he somehow subsumed in Aristaeus? The forests and the flocks require Aristaeus, and of course Pan (16-18), with whom Virgil couples Athene (Minerva), inventor of olive oil, and the boy Triptolemus who invented the plough. Last of the twelve comes the Cisalpine favourite Silvanus, holding an uprooted young cypress, which maybe he will plant? But there is no room for his Illyrian companion, or rather epithet Saxanus who I suppose was the god of masons and quarrymen working in wild, rocky places.[2] We cannot have everybody alas, and the list ends in Socratic style with 'all ye other gods and goddesses'.

The matter is not closed. Virgil prays to the gods of seeds not sown by men and those who send abundant rainfall, and to Caesar. At this name (25) the poem suddenly opens out into all the provinces of life over which he might rule, the seasons or the oceans, or July and August, 'Betwixt the Scorpion and the Maid.' The calendar was in a muddle, and it would in fact be Augustus who would regulate it by adding July for Julius and August for himself.

> The Scorpion ready to receive thy Laws
> Yields half his Region, and contracts his Claws.

The only way to attain a thorough understanding of what the ancient world believed – and Virgil reflected about the heavenly bodies – is to study the obscure writer Manilius, who was brilliantly edited by A.E. Housman.[3] Now it so happens that the blazing star Arcturus is in the poisonous Scorpion, and there, as Manilius says, Mars burns. In a few years' time Augustus was to proclaim his son 'the second Mars', but the connection did not appeal to Virgil. Indeed it is even to me a little reminiscent of 'And thou Dalhousie the great god of War, Lieutenant-General to the Earl of Mar.' Mynors answers the elementary questions neatly, but he does not spread himself among heavenly influences or their earthly resonance.

Julius is not to be a god of the underworld or hell's prisoner, Virgil goes on, but (40-2) let him give help to farmers. Cultivation is our subject. In alternate years, the poet assumes the farmer must let his ground lie fallow, while the sheep crop any weeds it grows. Activity begins not with autumn ploughing but with late winter (in English terms), or Italian spring.

75

> While yet the Spring is young, while Earth unbinds
> Her frozen Bosom to the Western Winds;
> While Mountain Snows dissolve against the Sun,
> And Streams, yet new, from Precipices run ...

The farmer must bring out his plough 'even in this early dawning of the year', which for the Romans begins with March. Different soils grow different crops:

> A fourth with Grass unbidden decks the Ground:
> Thus Tmolus is with yellow Saffron crowned:
> India black Ebon and white Ivory bears:
> And soft Idume weeps her odorous Tears.

Virgil has not seen these crops, but he is varying colours and textures just as he did in the Eclogues, and just as the Greek poets did with the colours of their smaller, wilder world. Dryden's line about Idume is a half-line of Virgil saying 'the soft Sabaeans send their incenses.'

The naked Chalybes, a race of miners in the east mythical since Aeschylus, send iron, Pontus castor oil from beavers' balls, which had a use in medicine, and Epirus Olympic champion racehorses. The list of all these places is like a mad, toppling tower (56-9), yet they are briefly contained, and the noise is impressive. The closeness of the naked Chalybes to the beaver-balls of toxic Pontus is scarcely unintentional: the Olympic games also were naked, and bring us back to the toughness of primitive man, born from the stones scattered by Deucalion after the flood.

But the most ordinary processes of agriculture yield a wonderful music to Virgil (73-8) in the burning of the fields. You must remove 'the fragile reeds and sounding forest' of pulses and tares and lupine, because a crop of oats and poppies steeped in deathly sleep will burn the ground, which must be rested. Virgil is less concerned with precise instruction than he is with the beauty of nature, in which I include 'burning the light straw in the crackling flame' (85).

> So earth conceives rich foods and secret powers,
> Whether all vice is burned out through the fire
> Or useless damps and humours sweated off.

There speaks the Po valley farmer, one feels.

The verse paragraphs, the sustained passages of the first Georgic seldom seem to be longer than 10 or 20 lines, and are often much less, but they are well woven together as poetry if not as rational discourse. There is a similar problem with the longer poems of Horace: where to mark the verse paragraphs can be a matter of some skill. The use of fire is a longer section in the Latin text than Dryden allows. The truth is that Virgil comes back and back to the same subject until he has exhausted it, with an air of constant enthusiasm and renewed pleasure, and with much variation of structure, which only the very best Hellenistic poets show.

No doubt all these divisions of the poem, which are for the ease of the reader, are modern. In the Latin Georgics they are confusing and insufficient: even Mynors marks subdivisions more clearly in his commentary than in his text.

The prayer for a wet solstice and a quiet winter is clearly a proverbial beginning for a new paragraph (100), but the old and quasi-proverbial charm was for 'Dusty winter, Muddy spring and a big harvest', yet Virgil's wet solstice must be Christmas, not mid-summer where Mynors says it ought to be. Virgil has been studying astronomy, he knows there are two solstices and has confused the folklore no doubt. The crops, he says, are most happy with a dusty winter. But this leads into another considerable digression.

> For Winter drout rewards the Peasant's Pain,
> And broods indulgent on the bury'd Grain.
> Hence Mysia boasts her Harvests, and the tops
> Of Gargarus admire their happy Crops.

The crops are in north-west Asia and I do not know enough about the effect of monthly rainfall on the crops to comment further; nor I suspect did Virgil. What he knew was the gossip of the corn exchange.

The Roman farmer, having sown his land, must cover the grain with his hoe or plough-boards, he must then weed and water and drain: Virgil puts aside the weeding (until 155) simplifies the rest, and dramatises the procedures, which of course suits Dryden.

> The wary Ploughman on the Mountain's Brow
> Undams his watry Stores, huge Torrents flow;
> And ratling down the Rocks, large moisture yield
> Temp'ring the thirsty Fever of the Field ...

The whole process sounds most hazardous, he sends in his flock to crop the young shoots for fear the heads should be unwieldy 'And drains the standing Waters, when they yield / Too large a Bev'rage to the drunken Field.' It is in autumn and spring he must fear water and marshy mud, and the enormous flocks of migrating geese and cranes.

Jove deliberately made us work hard. 'Before his day everything was in common and abundance was natural' (128). 'Jove gave poison to the snakes and hunger to the wolves',

> And shook from Oaken Leaves the liquid Gold:
> Remov'd from Humane reach the cheerful Fire,
> And from the Rivers bade the Wine retire,
> That studious need might useful Arts explore.

That prehistoric moment was the first closing time in the gardens of the west: the age of Saturn was the golden age, and Jove's arrangements govern modern times. 'Then first on Seas the hollow'd Alder swam' (he is still thinking of the Po), and traps and hounds were perfected and stars charted, and in Dryden 'Baits were hung on Hooks' (but Virgil is innocent of that skill, he knows only net-fishing). Ceres helped by inventing agriculture, but mildew (Robigo, one of Varro's negative gods) and thistles rapidly altered the balance back against mankind, and we get a splendid line or two about weeds (153-5) which one must admit that Virgil likes, and so do most of us whose business is not the earth. He warns us to do plenty of bird-scaring and pruning away of shade and pray for rain; otherwise we must envy others their crops, and go to the forest,

> And shake for Food the long abandon'd Oak.

This brings us to the tools and instruments, as laid down by Hesiod some seven hundred years earlier (160-75). Here Virgil contrives that his verse will still smell of the earth. His big excitement is the plough, which is completely wooden: only the oldest readers today will remember how their teachers strained over this brutal object, and with what curious diagrams they tried to match Virgil's words to reality. I well remember the joy of Mynors one year when a Spanish pupil reassured him that a plough such as he had described was still in use in his father's orange orchard. The illustration in Dryden is by Wenceslas Hollar, stolen from Ogilby by the publisher, and really a cheat, since the bits and pieces of the plough are jumbled up on the ground, and the workmen do not look as if they know how to put it together.

It is possible to spend many happy hours over Virgil's plough, but all it tells us about Virgil is that he was not an expert on plough-building.

Young Elms with early force in Copses bow,
Fit for the figure of the crooked Plough
Of eight foot long a fastned Beam prepare,
On either side the Head produce an Ear,
And sink a Socket for the shining Share ...

He moves on from this difficult subject to 'threshing floors of puddled and rolled clay' – an advance I must grudgingly admit on the paved 'marble threshing-floors' of the Greeks. Still, he has to issue warnings against mice, moles, snakes, toads, weevils and ants, which Milton calls the parsimonious Emmet, if that is any improvement.

The question of the size of yield follows at once, and so the question of the signs of a good harvest, when the nut-blossom is thick and scented in the forest. This introduces the central message of the whole poem, the natural degeneration of seed, which seemed easy to observe to the Romans, so that man has to pull hard on his small boat, rowing against the stream of nature (197-203).

We return to the hard glitter and variety of the stars, and the Sun's backward slide through the twelve constellations of the Zodiac, which defines the year. Yet calculations were not perfectly accurate, and Virgil wisely relies like other agricultural writers on the most obvious signs, Arcturus, the Pleiades and the Dog-star. He mentions the Hyades, the Kids, the Crown, and the Snake or Dragon, which since it never sets is no use for telling the season, but it is a glittering and decorative constellation and Virgil likes it.

He has great fun matching the Kids and luminous Snake to sailors off to Istanbul for oysters, the Scales to muscular barley-sowing, with flax and poppies, and to ploughing. This Georgic constantly exudes an atmosphere of health, not just healthy exercise, like a travel poster for the railways of the nineteen twenties.

The climax is Virgil's explanation of the five zones of the earthly globe, which scholars cunningly derive from Crates of Mallos (c. 150 BC) from whom the truth was trumpeted to Macrobius: but Virgil had already got it from Eratosthenes. The Bodleian Library has a fine green and white illustration of the scheme in a tenth or eleventh century German manuscript of Macrobius's commentary on 'Scipio's dream', with the polar ice at top and bottom with a forbidding Ocean fringed north and south with desert splitting the northern from the southern hemisphere.[4] If anyone should ask why in that case did people in the Middle Ages not know the earth was round, the answer must be their thick wits and laziness and their lack of science.

Two Poles turn round the Globe: one seen to rise
O'er Scythian Hills, and one in Lybian Skies:

The first sublime in Heav'n, the last is whirl'd
Below the Regions of the nether World.
Around our Pole the spiny Dragon glides,
And like a winding Stream the Bear divides:

So far so good, but below the southern sea 'perpetual Night is found, / In silence brooding on the unhappy Ground', because the turning of the earth had not fully occurred to Virgil or Lucretius (3, 26) – though Eratosthenes had insisted that corn grew in both temperate zones and men dwelt in both, *antipodes* (feet facing feet). The conundrum of antipodean gravity had not been solved, and the entire arrangement of the world was treated by poets, even by Manilius, as a mystery. Mynors thought the south pole must once have seemed to be the underworld: did the dead cling to it like bats to a roof? Having stated his more rational view, Virgil cannot resist elaboration:

Or when Aurora leaves our Northern Sphere,
She lights the downward Heav'n, and rises there,
And when on us she breathes the living Light,
Red Vesper kindles there the Tapers of the Night.

This thrilling digression over, and intellectual curiosity satisfied, Virgil takes us again through the labours of the seasons (252-75), ending with the loading of the donkey with oil or cheap apples for the town, and coming home with pitch or a stone quern. We are informed of lucky and unlucky days by the moon (276-86): this superstition, by which things wax and wane as the moon does (oysters in Pliny's Natural History for example), is ancient, but Virgil does not seriously believe in it, and follows some source of his own. Then come another ten verses on the work of darkness and of night. He has filled up his Georgic almost too densely with tasks and labours:

For Moisture then abounds, and pearly Rains
Descend in Silence to refresh the Plains.
The Wife and Husband equally conspire
To work by Night, and rake the winter Fire.
He sharpens Torches in the glim'ring Room,
She shoots the flying Shuttle through the Loom:
Or boils in Kettles Must of Wine, and skims
With Leaves the Dregs that overflow the Brims.
And till the watchful Cock awakes the Day,
She sings, to drive the tedious hours away.

Season by season, Virgil makes the year homely and rather English, with tasks as many and varied as there used to be in any village until modern times: acorns, myrtle-berries, crane-stalking and deer-trapping and hare-hunting all had their special times: only fox-hunting being an impractical pursuit did not exist,

> Then when the fleecy Skies new cloath the Wood,
> And cakes of rustling Ice come rolling down the Flood.

Virgil moves from this to autumn and the signs of autumn storms. His storm-scene, which swiftly follows, is as memorable as the one in Beethoven's symphony: in fact it is apocalyptic (and surely Alpine). 'though Jove flings down Athos or Rhodope or Acroceraunia' (332).

We should watch the strange gyrations of the planet Mercurius and the cold lurking place of Saturn, and say our prayers. We should pray to Ceres in early spring, when lambs are fat and the wine soft (341), when sleep is sweet and the mountain shadows are dark; let all the rustic youth adore Ceres, with milk, honey and wine, let the victim go three times round the crop with everyone cheering, and let no one set a sickle to new corn before dancing the antic dance and speaking the chants for Ceres, with oak leaves twisted round their heads (350).

The signs of weather follow Aratus, 'the Mountains whistle to the murm'ring Floods', cormorants fly inland, herons upwards, coots skim the shore, stars fall 'And shooting through the Darkness, gild the Night.' The poetry is in the procedures of nature and the seasons, but mostly it is to be found in the details, as it was in the Eclogues. These signs of rain are as wonderful and as refreshing as anything in Latin poetry (360-93).

> Huge flocks of rising Rooks forsake their Food,
> And crying seek the Shelter of the Wood.
> Besides, the sev'ral sorts of wat'ry Fowls
> That swim the Seas, or haunt the standing Pools:
> The Swans that sail along the Silver Flood,
> And dive with stretching Necks to search their Food.
> Then lave their Backs with sprinkling Dews in vain,
> And stem the Stream to meet the promis'd Rain.
> The Crow with clamorous Cries the Show'r demands
> And single stalks along the Desert Sands.

Fine weather is easier to foresee, and the evening owl-call is said to predict it. Somehow this gives Virgil a chance to discuss Nisus and Scylla transformed into birds. He has mentioned them in an Eclogue and they are fully treated in the Ciris in the *Appendix*, though not by him. The small bird called a Ciris said to be hunted by the 'sea-eagle' appears to be mythical, and no one knows where Virgil got the story, if not Callimachus: but Aemilius Macer (Courtney, 1993, 292f.) is I suppose a possibility.

This vein of signs and wonders is a fertile one, and Virgil follows it, returning to Aratus, the moon (424) and the sun, to lead us into the climax of his book, nor is there any shortage of lovely lines on the way, like one with the sea-saviours Glaucus and Panopea and Melicertus's son Ino (437), or another where pale Aurora 'Rises from Tithonus his crocus bed' (447), as Ogilby puts it.

Suddenly at line 463 the Sun gives signs, who dares say the Sun lies? He warns of riots, frauds and open wars: when Caesar's light went out, he pitied Rome:

> In Clouds conceal'd the Publick Light:
> And Impious Mortals fear'd Eternal Night.
> Nor was the Fact foretold by him alone:
> Nature herself stood forth, and seconded the Sun.

The lines that follow are remarkable in themselves, but more so in their influence, because it was by imitating and exaggerating these lines of Virgil that Lucan composed his first book on the Civil War, and it was by translating those lines that Christopher Marlowe learnt his job as a tragic poet, and from Marlowe Shakespeare learnt the dire brilliance of his early style. Compared to that powerful transmission of energy, Dryden is feeble of course, but let him stand here.

> What Rocks did Aetna's bellowing mouth expire
> From her torn Entrails! And what Floods of Fire!
> What Clanks were heard in German Skies afar
> Of Arms and Armies rushing to the War!
> Dire Earth-quakes rent the solid Alps below,
> And from their Summets shook th' Eternal Snow.
> Pale Specters in the close of Night were seen;
> And Voices heard of more than Mortal Men.
> In silent Groves, dumb Sheep and Oxen spoke ...

His terrible vein continues for another 20 lines, to end with the peasants of another age, digging up rusted arms at Philippi. In the course of his sacred rage, after the bronzes sweating and the ivory faces weeping, comes 'rising in his Might, the king of Floods', the Po, tearing away flocks and farms in his course.

It is scarcely surprising that Virgil ends his outpour with a prayer to the gods of the soil, to Romulus and Vesta, the hearth-goddess of Rome, to join with Augustus, 'Nor hinder him to save the sinking Age'. There are so many wars in the world, so many faces of crime, no proper honour to the plough, ruined fields and farmers driven away, and sickles turned to swords, war on Euphrates, war in Germany, neighbouring cities taking up arms and tearing up alliances, and wicked Mars raving across all the world. It is like the start of a race when the chariots rush on, the teams are crazy and out of control, the charioteer can do nothing, and the reins are useless.

That is the surprising end of the first Georgic. The second (537-40) ends with only a hint of these horrors, but the third also ends in tragedy. Virgil's formidable voice of doom turns in his prayer to the *genii loci*, one of whom Aeneas himself had become, so Ovid tells us, a powerful expression of rage and grief, such as he never again uttered. There is a sense in which this first and by a short head briefest of the Georgics is the only one: Virgil has shown what can be done (for that reason we shall not follow him in quite so much detail through the other three).

Second Georgic

Why are there four Georgics? Maybe because of the four seasons, but scarcely because the logical division of material demanded them. Within the first Georgic the divisions make Virgil cover the same ground again and again. The effect of bewildering variety depends on phenomena like the storm to end all storms coming just before, not after, the signs of approaching storm. Animals appear who should be reserved for the third Georgic, and Virgil scatters his stars with profligacy to cover all the seasons and the entire year. But there are differences.

Virgil has done with Ceres and the wooden plough, and we turn now to Bacchus, whose gift in the prologue was the trick of mixing water with the wine, which was otherwise barbarous or undrinkable. Here he will play a heartier role, exaggerated by Dryden.

> Come strip with me, my God, come drench all o'er
> Thy Limbs in Must of Wine, and drink at ev'ry Pore.

The despised Ogilby is more accurate: 'O Father come, and lay thy Buskins by, / With me in must then stain thy naked thigh.'

In this Georgic we are to deal with vines, the groves and woods, and the olive. After the invocation of the wine-god to the pressing, we begin from natural trees and plants such as river reeds, 'sprung from the watery Genius of the Ground', and as common in undrained Campania as they were in the Po valley I suppose. Willow, poplar and broom arise as easily as reeds, and chestnut, oak, elm and wild cherry arise from seeds that are self-sown. He includes the bay. It is of course easy enough now to improve on his information, but there is no denying that the natural woodland of Italy – through which the first roads were still being cut – criscrossed only by herdsmen, sounds a delightful place. His planting and grafting have a busy air, but there is still a spacious innocence about them.

> Thus Pears and Quinces from the Crabtree come
> And thus the ruddy Cornel bears the Plum.

This brings him to the virtues of different soils, so he invokes the help of Maecenas (41) and promises not to offer versified fiction (45) or long prefaces, but the truth. He has told us southern Thrace is the place for vines, and they have flourished there from the time of Homer to that of the late Iannis Carras, and that Taburnum, a stony hill twenty-five miles north-east of Naples, is the place for olives, which we must take on trust.

Now with a flourish from Lucretius (47) Virgil makes a renewed and determined attack on natural vegetation, grafting, and the imposition of Roman discipline on trees. Grafting excites him in its more extreme examples, the shaggy arbutus bears the true nut, the plane strong apples and the chestnut beech-mast: the ash has whitened with pear-blossom and the pigs have eaten acorns under elms (72). On how to graft, a subject on which his view is so simplified as to be unsound, and may well therefore derive directly from some ancient gardener, he is at least clear.

Virgil gives 10 lines (73-82) to the subject, and then plunges into the varieties of fruit and of vines. The vines are riotous, they are persons and have their vanity, and in the end the varieties are innumerable. This of course is true, so that the game in viniculture is to preserve a pure species: in wild vines such as are to be found in Afghanistan, every vine is a species of its own, and the abundance is infinite.

In this baroque evocation of vineyards we begin to sense the variety which is the nub of the second Georgic, which will contain the varied praises of all Italy. The catalogue of what grows where (109-35) is only the introduction to Virgil's Italy (136-76). The praises of a place were a common set piece in the schools of oratory, and we have praises of Athens from the fourth century BC, but this is something new, since he dares to name Italy and to treat it from the Alps to the south.

Virgil knew a good deal about Italy – one must assume that his Italian journeys depended on the help of Maecenas since Horace's journey to Brindisi hardly opens the subject. Virgil knew Silarus and the toe of Italy, and he knew the old gardener in the fourth Georgic near Tarentum, as well as the mighty lakes of the north. There is no mythology in the praise of Italy either. It is possible of course that poetry followed prose, and that Virgil had in mind a lost work of the antiquarian Varro (Macrob. 3, 16, 12) but we do not know if so how he moulded it. He passes from nature to man, and includes civil with military power. The entire passage is a remarkable tour de force.

> But neither Median Woods (a plenteous Land)
> Fair Ganges, Hermus rolling Golden Sand,
> Nor Bactria, nor the richer Indian Fields,
> Nor all the Gummy Stores Arabia yields,
> Nor any foreign Earth of greater Name
> Can with sweet Italy contend in Fame.

No fire-breathing bulls turned the Italian turf and no dragon-teeth were sown there, but vines and olives and 'harvests heavy with their fruitful weight'. The olive was really a Greek import, but never mind that:

> The Warrior Horse, here bred, is taught to train,
> There flows Clitumnus thro' the flow'ry plain;
> Whose Waves, for Triumphs after prosp'rous War
> The Victim Ox and snowy Sheep prepare.

From Monte Massico (142) at the north of Campania, which he mentions casually for its wine, Virgil is in his own territory: Clitumnus is a lovely spring in Umbria that Highet describes in *Poets in a Landscape* (1957). It rises near Spoleto, where the white cattle, becoming rare as he grew older, made Mynors quote Carducci, 'sweet-eyed and snow-white, that mild Virgil loved'.

The poet blesses the region with perpetual spring, and two generations of cattle a year and two apple-crops: Italy is a survival of the golden age. There are no lions or tigers or poisonous aconites,

> Nor in so vast a length our Serpents glide,
> Or rais'd on such a spiry Volume ride.

Virgil praises the cities, the forts, the overseas trade, and the great Lakes, 'thee Larius first', then stormy Benacus, which is Lake Garda and home territory.

From these he turns to the great harbours created by Agrippa in 37 and 36 BC, out of lakes that lay near the sea on the gulf of Pozzuoli, Avernus and

Lucrinus. Agrippa had strengthened the dykes and opened a canal into and through the shallow lagoon of the Lucrine, to a shelter in the deep water of a volcanic crater, Avernus. Italy ran with rivers of silver, bronze and gold, the last in the alluvial gold of the Po's northern tributaries. Lucretius (5, 1255) had streams of gold and silver running down molten from a burning forest.

Virgil goes on at once (165-6) to praise the tough human beings Italy used to breed, Marsians and Sabines who are mountain people, Ligurians (mutton-eaters and drinkers of a barley brew) and Volscians (hill men), the great families of the Decii Marii and Camilli, and Caesar,

> ... whose victorious Arms
> To farthest Asia carry fierce Alarms
> Avert unwarlike Indians from his Rome,
> Triumph abroad, secure our Peace at home!

We have heard policies of the same kind enunciated in our own times, and it is to be hoped that we have less confidence in them. It must be said in Virgil's favour that he puts the matter with an awful clarity: conquering the Indians was self-defence, he thought.

> Hail, sweet Saturnian soil! of fruitful Grain
> Great Parent, greater of Illustrious Men.
> For thee my tuneful accents will I raise,
> And treat of Arts disclos'd in Ancient Days:
> Once more unlock for thee the sacred Spring
> And old Ascraean Verse in Roman Cities sing.

(Saturn was both a god and king of Latium in the golden age. Ascra was the village on Helicon where Hesiod lived, whose Works and Days are the great-grandfather of the Georgics. Cities is a mistranslation, the Latin word is *oppida*, the towns of the native Italians, places like Sulmo and Venusia.) These splendid lines are not an introduction however but an epilogue: Virgil now turns back to the types of soil. As Mynors puts it, 'as at 1,252 and 325, we return quietly to our business', which is the soil.

Virgil distinguishes half a dozen landscapes, which he intersperses with amazing lines given for their picturesqueness or entertainment value perhaps, and yet lightly echoing the triumphant tones of this Georgic: a sacrifice for example where 'the puff-cheeked Etruscan blasting on his ivory' is an essential attendant. Any reader who knows the painted Roman triumph from the Renaissance at Hampton Court will see how this single line encapsulates the idea (193).

III. VIRGIL'S ITALY

Compacted into its single verse it would have to read 'The Etruscan's puff-cheeked ivory altar-blast'.)

The landscape is varied between the distant glens of rich Tarentum, and 'the fields unhappy Mantua lost / On grassy rivers grazing swans of snow' (197-9) 'slow bullocks trailing homeward with their carts', and 'the antique houses of the birds, 'With their last roots uprooted', and they seek 'High air, the nest deserted.' The same phrases come to his mind at the fall of Troy. We have hill-tops with hardly the dewy rosemary to feed a bee, and the riches of Capua, the old regional capital of Campania, with Vesuvius, and small deserted Acerrae that the river Clanius flooded.

The land for wheat and for grapes entails pleasant excursions and includes a line or two about the oak roots reaching as far down to hell as the branches do up to heaven – the origin it seems of a truth I have known all my life – and of the regimental order of planting a vineyard, which is fanciful but convincing at a first reading.

Fire in a vineyard started by incautious shepherds must have been a serious hazard and it provides Virgil with a few spectacular lines, where the vines set alight the trees that supported them:

> For first the smould'ring Flame the Trunk receives,
> Ascending thence it crackles in the Leaves:
> At length victorious to the Top aspires,
> Involving all the Wood in smoky Fires ...

What attracts Virgil by contrast is the spring. He has already treated that season here and there in the Eclogues, always with a sort of Shakespearean lightness, which in this part of the Georgic he repeats.

The key to it is his inner freedom from the spooky and often malignant gods of the country, and his real sense of what nature is and does. It must be called Epicurean, whether it is orthodox or not.

> For when the Golden Spring reveals the Year,
> And the white Bird returns whom Serpents fear ...
> The Spring adorns the Woods, renews the Leaves;
> The Womb of Earth the genial Seed receives.
> For then Almighty Jove descends, and pours
> Into his buxom Bride his fruitful Show'rs,
> And mixing his large Limbs with hers, he feeds
> Her Births with kindly Juice, and fosters teeming Seeds.
> Then joyous Birds frequent the lonely Grove ...

87

In this sunny mood Virgil could go on indefinitely, but we must notice that it is not exactly Jove who performs the miracle in the Georgic, it is Aether (325). The 'white Bird' is the stork and Aether is the sky, and the Grove is not lonely but trackless. It promotes a deliberate wordplay between *avia* (trackless) and *avibus* (birds). 'The trackless coppice echoes with songbirds' would be more accurate.*

> In this soft Season (let me dare to sing)
> The World was hatch'd by Heav'n's Imperial King:
> In Prime of all the Year, and Holydays of Spring ...
> When laughing Heav'n did the great Birth attend ...
> For what remains, in Depth of Earth secure
> Thy cover'd Plants, and dung with Hot Manure.

So with the usual cyclical movement we return to agriculture, though in this Georgic in particular cheerfulness keeps breaking in. The animals to keep out of a vineyard include the mysterious *urus*, who comes into a German forest in Ceasar's Gallic Wars and may be the auroch, a wild ox built like a tank, whose alarming skeleton is to be seen in the Prehistoric Museum at Copenhagen. It is to me inconceivable that Virgil intended such a monster, though he was domesticated many thousands of years ago, and so I take the *urus* to be that useful animal the water buffalo.

The passage ends with a rustic festival which has an antiquarian sound, and much of it, including the masks hung on pine trees, seems to be attached to Athens and its first strolling players. But Virgil seems to refer to something that happened in rustic Italy. If so, then he has got it from a book or seen it in the remains of Greek Italy, where I think that he knew the river Acheron in the hills behind Sybaris. The best guidebook to that area is still *Old Calabria* by Norman Douglas (1915), which is still in print. This Bacchic festival ends (395-6) with the sacred goat, 'led by the horn now at the altar stands, / And we on hazel sticks roast his fat guts'. There is fruit to follow, and as in the fourth Eclogue 'among the untamed bushes gleams the grape' (29) so here:

> Apples when they feel the strong tree-trunk,
> Their sappy power, climb up among the stars;
> Then all the woods are heavy with increase,
> And wild-birds' houses, gleams of bloody fruit. (426-9)

---

* *Avia tum resonant avibus virgulta.*

At 456-7 the poem stutters to a climax in a buzzing of bees and a string of Greek names for the fabulous centaurs, who got drunk and misbehaved at a marriage feast. Then Virgil breaks out into more than 70 lines of strong feeling, first about farmers and their happy life (if they but knew it) unplagued by war and relying on the earth for justice. They have no worry about patrons or luxuries,

> But easie Quiet, a secure Retreat,
> A harmless Life that knows not how to cheat,
> With homebred Plenty the rich Owner bless,
> And rural Pleasures crown his Happiness ...
> Cool Grots, and living Lakes, the Flow'ry Pride
> Of Meads, and Streams that thro' the Valley glide,
> And shady Groves that easy Sleep invite,
> And after toilsome Days, a soft Repose at Night.

The pleasures of the country are more abundant than those of Horace's Sabine Farm, but they do not differ in principle. Horace knows as well as Virgil where to get oysters or the best apples, but in this passage Virgil has concentrated his philosophy as well as his sense of the countryside. The longer I study them both the more I have the impression that they were intimate friends and companions.

'From hence *Astraea* took her Flight, and here / The Prints of her departing Steps appear.' Astraea was divine justice, who was frightened off or disgusted by the onset of the Bronze Age, and found refuge in the constellation Virgo. Aratus thought she was angry because men were eating working oxen, and that she vanished 'among the echoing hills', but Virgil not unreasonably remarks that her last earthly dwelling-place was among country people. With her departure the golden age ended.

But Virgil has not finished, since it is not just country pleasure and country honesty he has in view. He means to enter into his own vocation and philosophic position.

To me the Muses are before all things sweet, I bear their signs, am battered by their mighty love: may they accept me and show me the roads of heaven and the stars, the fainting of the sun and the multiple labours of the moon, where earthquake comes from, what makes the deep sea swell. His work on the poem has raised serious scientific questions, and he would like to devote the rest of his life to solving them.

As for earthquakes, if one follows Virgil's use of the word 'vein' in the first Georgic, it is possible to detect traces of the view that earth like men has veins

89

and that air circulates in them. There was a theory of earthquakes that said the earth panted and air caused earthquakes. Not only Ovid but Pausanias (who was at least no poet) believed that.

Why does the sun set faster in winter and rises slowly, Virgil asks. One feels, as so often with poets, that he is on the verge of a breakthrough, yet he swiftly changes the subject: But if I cannot get at this area of nature, and the cold blood around my heart prevents me, let me love the country and forests and river, ingloriously (483-6). I cannot explain the iceblock round the heart and how it prevents him, but what is worse I am puzzled by *obstet* at line 482, where delay prevents the tardy dawn, and *obstiterit* at line 484 where the cold or frozen blood prevents his breakthrough. Mynors scorns or neglects this worry.

Virgil rushes on to the meadows and Spercheos and Taygetos where the Spartan virgins run riot, the icy valleys of Haemus and the mighty shadows of its branches. The river Spercheos is in southern Thessaly, Taygetos is the mountain of Sparta, which Virgil makes a female mountain, perhaps following some old poet like Alkman, who mentions the riotous virgins; the freezing Haemus was a fine forested mountain in north Greece. All this must have some lost source in poetry. It is rare in the Georgics to find so ecstatic and irrelevant an outburst about foreign places.

Happy is the man who has been able to know the causes of things and has put all fears and the inexorable fate of man, and the strumble of hungry Acheron under his feet (490-2). Virgil must mean the south Italian Acheron, which is a thousand feet of cliff below one's feet at the iron-working village explored by Norman Douglas (where I have supposed that Horace also went). The doctrine of these lines is purely Epicurean: no doubt the circle at Siro's villa did spend much of their time on scientific enquiry, as Lucretius advises. But after hungry Acheron there is only a colon: and happy is he too, who knows the country gods, Pan, old Silvanus and the sister Nymphs. He will not worry about politics, 'Roman issues, and kingdoms that will fall'. He does not grieve over the poor or envy the rich, he plucks the fruit the bough offers, what the willing country gives, he does not notice iron law, crazy courts, or the public records. So much for Horace who worked in the record office: yet Horace might agree. Michelangelo pulled it down to build his dazzling palace of the Capitol, which rests on its foundations. Even Dryden's plate illustrating these lines, the last for the second Georgic, is Hollar's engraving of the forum with more ruins than one sees now.

Virgil goes on to decry luxury and civil war, and to praise by contrast the virtuous farmer. No rest for him even in winter, the pigs get their acorns, the olives need pressing, the mild vintage cooks on the sunny rocks (522). Sweet infants hang on his kiss, the house is chaste, the cows give milk, the goats fight. All this is echoed in Horace. It is the life of the old Sabines (532) which made

Tuscany and made Rome the most beautiful of all earthly things (534). This was the life of the golden age that Saturn led on earth, no trumpet blasted, no swords were hammered.

The poem ends here, and there has never been so full and clear a statement, to my knowledge, of Virgil's pacifist personal sympathies. He may not be a 'soul naturally Christian', as he used to be called, but given Christianity he is surely close to being a natural Quaker.

Third Georgic

The third Georgic begins with an invocation of Pales, an old Italian shepherds' goddess with a feast on April the twenty-first, and Apollo in disguise as a shepherd on a river in Thessaly. The curious couple is linked with the mountain Lycaeus in central Arcadia; everything else has already been tried, this is my way to fame, says Virgil (18-19). He is going to bring down the Muses and plant Palestinian palm trees at Mantua, and in the green meadows plant a marble temple. Marble is a Roman word from the glitter of white marble – the Greeks just called it 'white stone' -so his temple will sparkle like a swan, 'beside the water,'

> Where Mincius wanders slow turn by slow turn,
> And covers all his banks with slender reeds. (14-15)

In the middle will stand Caesar, and Virgil, victorious in purple robes, will marshal a hundred four horse chariots: the Olympic and Nemean games will be deserted for these. He will bring gifts, there will be cattle-slaughters and processions and embroidered Britons shall bear curtains up. We shall have Caesar's Indian war, mourning Armenia, and Parthians withdrawing (16-29). This absurdly over-rich scene would I suppose be worse if it were any better. It is the first sketch of the Shield of Aeneas: like Dante we should gape for a moment and pass on.

Virgil must treat forest and mountain which, he says, Maecenas has suggested (41). For a moment we hear the cry of hounds, otherwise notoriously missing from the Georgics (43-4). Soon Virgil will tell of Caesar's battles (46-8). Now he turns to the breeding of horses and cattle. Whether because of the subject or Virgil's vague eyes for it, or because the detail of the verse is less sharp, I do not find myself gripped by the opening of the third Georgic, perhaps after his mighty spurt in the last hundred lines of the second, the poet was tired. But Virgil loves horses, his stallion is splendid at least.

Upright he walks, on Pasterns firm and straight,
His motions easy, prancing in his Gait:
The first to lead the Way, to tempt the Flood,
To pass the Bridge unknown, nor fear the trembling Wood:
Dauntless at empty Noises, lofty neck'd,
Sharp-headed, Barrel belly'd, broadly back'd ...

He likes them dappled or bright chestnut, but faint white and dun are hardly worth rearing. Behind these views I seem to detect the chestnut ponies (we would call them) of Thessaly, inspected once a year at Athens and owned by the Knights or Riders. It is possible that the strain has survived in the wild ponies of Skyros, which Joy Koulentianou has written about.

In such a shape, old Saturn did restrain
His heav'nly Limbs, and flow'd with such a Mane ...

The mating of horses is as thrilling in this suddenly swift verse as their description. Morality and science drop away as we turn our serious attention to the breeding of these extremely beautiful animals, and their treatment from youth to pensioned age.

When we move on to cattle, they are almost at once running wild in the mountains (213, cf. 146f.). There at the southern end of the long lanes of transhumance, the bulls fight. The nearest to a modern treatment of this is Ralph Hodgson's *The Bull* published between the wars. Virgil was greatly excited by the idea, and it recurs or is reworked at the climax of the Aeneid (12, 715). The river Silarus marks the border of Lucania from Campania north of Paestum, but after Virgil's day it became swanky. The ancient Greek temple of Hera was there, first explored by the anti-fascist archaeologist Zancani-Montuori in exile in the swamps during the 1939 war, in order to give her guards some disagreeable exercise. The exciting remains are in the Paestum museum. The fact that the battles of bulls are like those of men, or surpass them, was spotted by Apollonius of Rhodes, and long before that of course in the Irish epic called *The Tain*. The scene was commonly illustrated by the Greeks, as Weitzmann (1959) pointed out.[5] The forest called Sila where Virgil puts his bulls is further south, to the east of Cosenza, on a mountain of nearly two thousand metres, unless the ancient forest was Aspromonte, still further south, as following my betters I suspect .[6] Mynors reproduces a naive version in colour of the bulls from a Venetian manuscript[7] on the paper cover of his Georgics.

We rise to romantic lovers (260f.), the Sabine pig (255) and the lynxes of Bacchus, but the mares are champions. The point to notice about this natural history of sex is that Virgil is homosexual. Though it may give one no special delight to stress the fact, it surely does throw light on the vigorous male animals who abound in this Georgic, and when we think the mare's moment has come (266f.) she becomes pregnant by standing in the wind: love drives them crazy (Hor. ode 1, 25, 14). Homer had said something of the kind, Aristotle said with an air of wisdom that it happened in Crete, and Varro said it happened in Portugal. However you take this opinion it was bookish and Virgil must have got it from a book, as he may have got the battle of the bulls as well. But it is Acheron below one's feet that convinces me that he knew the forests of Bruttium.

Now at last (294) he comes to speak of sheep and goats, committing himself to Pales. The sheep are bedded on fern and goats get 'Winter brouze', and a steading or sheepcote open to the south for basking.

> On Shrubs they brouze, and on the bleaky Top
> Of rugged Hills the thorny Bramble crop.
> Attended with their bleating Kids they come
> At Night unask'd, and mindful of their home,
> And scarce their swelling Bags the threshold overcome.

In spring sheep and goats must be out early for dewy herbs and young grass.

> When creaking Grasshoppers on Shrubs complain,
> Then lead 'em to their wat'ring Troughs again.

They must feed again at sunset and moonrise, when the sea-shores are loud with alcyone and the thickets with acalanthis, both humans transformed into birds. Readers without Latin must take my word for it that the line is mysterious and delicate.

Immediately Virgil turns for ten lines to the shepherds of Libya: nomads who wander in the vast desert (339-48), and the Scythians (349-83) who use axes on their frozen wine. Without turning a hair as it were over these lengthy digressions, Virgil returns to wool, milk and dogs (384-413), and how Pan betrayed the moon in Arcadia with a snow-white fleece: a story filched from the poet Nicander, or so we are told – Nicander was a second century BC poet who was an expert on snake poisons, and his long poem on the subject existed in an illustrated form.

> 'Twas this with Fleeces milky white (if we
> May trust report), Pan, God of Arcady,

Did bribe thee Cynthia; nor didst thou disdain
When call'd in woody shades, to cure a Lover's pain.

The peasants press their cheese in the morning for evening eating or else they
keep it overnight and carry it to market before daybreak. Their dogs are animal
guard dogs, or else they guard you against Spaniards creeping up behind your
back. You can even hunt wild donkeys, hares or deer, or perhaps rouse the wild
boar. It is clear from the brevity of this passage that Virgil is not a hunting man.
He warns us of the dreadful Calabrian serpent in far more words.

Virgil is careful about sheep-medicine too, and this brings him to the cattle-
plague, the Lucretian climax of the third Georgic.

We see the naked Alps and thin Remains
Of scatter'd Cotts and yet unpeopl'd Plains
Once fill'd with grazing flocks, the Shepherds happy Reigns.

His account of the cattle-plague really is appalling and I have seldom brought
myself to read it through. The climax is the Fury.

Tisiphone, let loose from underground,
Majestically pale, now treads the ground.

It happened in Noricum, a kingdom in the Austrian Alps taken over by Rome
only in 15 BC. The deserted castles on the mountains that were to be seen there
were probably the remains of iron age forts. Perhaps this 'kingdom' went north
from Aquileia to the Julian Alps, perhaps it included northern Croatia: we
cannot know.

The plague was 'long ago' and not in Virgil's memory. He models himself on
the great plague in Lucretius, which in turn is a version of the great plague of
Athens in Thucydides. That is one of the oddest things I know about Virgil and
his poetry. It was much imitated as you might expect, but not rivalled within my
range of reading at least. Tisiphone was a sister of Allecto whom Virgil would
use to stir up the civil war in the Aeneid.

The fourth Georgic is the most remarkable, and in it Virgil emerges as a new
kind of poet altogether. It certainly requires a chapter of its own.

IV

TRANSFORMATION SCENE

The fourth Georgic marks an unexpected transformation. It is evident that the story of the hero and the goddess is so integrated into the rest of the poem that it must have been planned when this Georgic was first written. It might have been planned even earlier, when the four poems were plotted perhaps in prose, except that (as it appears to me) the third shows a falling off and a lack of the abundant material of the patchwork first and second. If that is so, one could easily imagine Virgil wanting the climax of a long and brilliant story in the fourth. The climax of the first Georgic returns the story to Augustus; the second ends with the inspired energy of his personal credo in which only the Greek place-names, Taygeta and Spercheos (cf. p. 118) fail to make much sense; and the third has ended for better and worse with the Austrian (Norican) cattle plague and the fascinating ruined fortifications in the Alps; but the fourth contains a narrative like an unclouded diamond, which it is a pleasure to write about.

The bees of the fourth Georgic have buzzed several times in the earlier Georgics, and the honey dripping down the oak in the forest is a sort of obsession of Virgil's, and his chiefest symbol of the golden age. Honey and the sun and gold and amber if you keep it covered up are the only things that time does not alter or tarnish. The American excavators of Corinth before the war found an amphora of honey, still perfectly golden after two or three thousand years, so they ate it day by day for breakfast, coming to an alarmed halt only when they found a baby buried in the bottom of it. (They should have known from ancient mythology what to expect, but archaeology and mythography are far apart.)

Virgil's transformation-myth is Hellenistic and quite innocent. It has the merit sought for by poets since Callimachus and Theocritus: it is obscure. It is a story you do not expect, that has amazing twists. Ever since the sixth Eclogue Virgil has been threatening us with a myth or a transformation, and it will be the resurrection of the bees: their eruption from a corrupt carcase. It is the myth of 'airy honey', which it is fair to say emerges from all his contemplation of the seasons of the earth and the processes of nature.

Now shall the heavenly gift of airy honey
Be my theme: Maecenas this is yours. (1-2)

There is no invocation of any god, because divine intervention will come as
a surprise. Who really was the god of bees? If the hives were in a garden or an
orchard I suppose it would be Priapus. But that stock of painted wood would
not fit Virgil's story. Bee-keeping had been legislated for and officially noticed
since the time of Solon, but Apollo (7) is called in only as the god of poets.
Perhaps the bees are Epicureans and take no notice of gods? We shall see. It is
worth recording at once that both Noricum of the cattle-pest on one side of
Mantua and Liguria on the other were exporters of honey in Virgil's time.

I will speak of the wonderful sight of affairs without weight, high-spirited
chiefs and the manners of the whole people: my labour is on a tiny scale, but the
glory is not so tiny if Apollo hears my call (2-7). In fact Virgil proposes a theme
like that of the wars of the frogs and the birds, conventionally supposed in his
day to be Homeric: a kind of mock heroic epic. This may be an excuse for his
bee poem, but it is certainly not as wonderful as what he delivers.

Bees have to live in a place out of the wind, where no sheep or butting goats
crop the flowers and no wandering cattle shake the dew from the meadows or
eat the young grass (10-13). It sounds like those secret enclosures of the gods,
an *abaton* where no one may tread, such as Euripides celebrates in the *Hippolytus*.

Mynors maintains the surprising opinion that the ancient world assumed
honey was the nectar in flowers, and was also distilled out of the air onto the
leaves of oak trees, and the same as 'the honey-dew secreted on foliage by
insects'. No doubt he is right. We used to suck the honey out of clover and certain
other flowers like honeysuckle when we were children, though to suppose that
honey was a distillation of the air on leaves was beyond our imaginations.

The enemies of bees are as strange:

> The painted Lizard, and the Birds of Prey,
> Foes of the frugal Kind, be far away.
> The Titmouse, and the Peckers hungry Brood
> And Progne, with her Bosom stain'd in Blood ...

Bees are the 'frugal Kind' of course, and the birds are Merope, the bee-eater,
and Procne the swallow, mother of Itys, whom she fed to Tereus her husband.
The swallow was notorious for eating on the wing, and Chaucer calls her 'The
swalow mordrer of the flyes smale / That maken hony of floures fresshe and
newe'. The bee-eater has in Egypt a green variety (so Servius, who knows it, may

96

be an Egyptian) and Aelian rather endearingly assures us it could fly backwards, but perhaps he means a humming-bird of some kind.

Merope and Procne were coupled because they had the same twittering voices, in a late antique poem called the Song of Philomela: *zinzizulare sciunt*, they can buzz. But there is no reference there to bee-eating, and no one really knows why Virgil said swallows attack bees. He is keener on wind-breaks, wet moss and tufts of grass to let the little creatures drink water. He wants to plant the palm and olive to protect and over-shadow them, and he worries about the raw recruits in the spring swarms who will need a rest in a cool place by water.

Virgil imagines the Queen is like Aeneas leading out a new colony, though the habits of actual bees are not so bold. The swarms are in June or later, and the Queen on whom they depend and whose scent they follow does not 'lead' the swarm (21f.). A swarm is an alarming sight.[1] Once it is away, the bees go streaking across country like a pack of hounds, stopping for nothing. They will stop a cricket match in mid-action. They get so thirsty that they will settle like a long beard on the wet mouth of a sleeping man: I have seen them do so.

> Then o'er the running Stream or standing Lake
> A Passage for thy weary People make,
> With Osier Floats the standing Water strow,
> Of massy Stones make Bridges, if it flow:
> That basking in the Sun thy Bees may lye,
> And resting there, their flaggy Pinions dry.

Virgil knows that bees like the smell of Thyme and Savory and Rosemary and Violets, and he knows that hives can be made of bark or twisted osiers, and that the bees themselves

> With dawby Wax and Flow'rs the Chinks have lin'd'.

The dark gum that the bees make is very sticky, and they make it from gummy buds and the bark of trees (40); they stop up chinks with it, but they do not really live in what Milton calls their straw-built citadel. The straw is tied or plaited like a wigwam round the outside of the wooden hive, which is hidden under it, with only the entrance showing: this at least was the custom in Yorkshire in 1854, when it was drawn by Henry Moore. But plaister thou the chinky Hives with Clay, says Virgil, And leafy Branches o'er their Lodgings lay' (45-6).

Bees will not thrive in yew-shade, and Virgil warns against the smell of burning crabs. This peculiar and unlikely sounding hazard had something to do with the foul smoke of dung-fires and ox-horn fires and crab-fires which the

Romans used to employ in their vineyards; there had to be three crabs and it had to be the left horn of an ox. Virgil also warns they dislike echoing rocks, but that sounds like Epicurean dogmatism, and White of Selborne used to yell at his bees through a loud-hailer to see what happened, and they did not take the least notice of him. They leave the hive to look for food, to swarm (58-66) and to fight (67f.), which I have never seen bees do or heard of them doing, except united against a common enemy, such as an animal that has knocked over a hive, and in those cases of course they can kill. Virgil is plainly fascinated by all their operations, and we should peer closely at the 60 something lines he spends on them.

When the gold sun beats winter underground, and shows heaven by summer light, they rush about the glens and woods and reap bright flowers and lightly sip the surface of rivers. Hence gladdened by who knows what sweetness they care for their offspring and their nests. Here they strike out new wax and sticky honey (51-7). It is a pity that Virgil never saw a glass beehive, and knew little of what went on inside a hive, or even in a natural bees' nest in a hollow tree.

But when you see a swarm let out of their cells to the stars of heaven, swimming through liquid summer, and you wonder at the dark cloud drawn along the wind (58-61). Virgil emphasises the wonderfulness more than with other animals (the stars of heaven just means the sky). Aristotle, who is Virgil's best authority, uses it of drones. There is no hint intended that earthly creatures might respond to the magnetic field of the stars, though I have heard it said that migrating birds do so. You must, says Virgil, spot where they are going.

> Then Melfoil beat, and Honey-suckles pound
> With these alluring Savours strew the Ground
> And mix with tinkling Brass the Cymbals droning Sound.

This brings the swarm swiftly home to make the rough music Mynors recommends the front-door key and a warming-pan.

Virgil then describes civil war in the hive, and although it is dressed in heroics, he does not quite desert the reality of bees: Scarce can their Limbs their mighty Souls contain ... / With hoarse Allarms the hollow Camp rebounds, as if with Trumpet calls. Dryden and certainly Virgil mean the old European cavalry trumpet, an instrument with a solemnity to match its antiquity, but rather few notes, like a Danish Lur. Horsemen bees and Knight bees rush around looking important, and / On their sharp Beaks they whet their pointed Stings. / And exercise their Arms, and tremble with their Wings.

All this happens in what the Bible calls 'the Spring of the year, the time when Kings march out to war', and Virgil makes the same observation:

> And Heaps of slaughter'd Soldiers bite the Ground;
> Hard Hailstones lie not thicker on the Plain:
> Nor shaken Oaks such showers of Acorns rain.

This entire scene is imaginary. Only the warsong of the Queen does seem to have some basis. Maeterlinck knew it, and said it was like 'the note of a distant trumpet of silver ... clearly audible in the evening especially, two or three yards away from the hive'. What it appears happens is that the Queen inside the hive above the breeding cells stalks about trumpeting in case she has a rival. Usually the worker bees kill any rival Queen, but if one escapes them then one or other of the two will take off a swarm to find a new home. If there are two Queens in the swarm it will split, and the workers of the weaker swarm will kill their Queen and rejoin the rest. Bees are fierce monarchists.

What is curious is that Virgil does not mention wasps. Indeed the whole evolutionary idea of specialisation to fill a gap in nature has not dawned on him, but what makes the omission of wasps curious is *The Wasps* of Aristophanes, which he must have heard of, because Aristophanes was one of Horace's favourite writers. The wasp enters visual art earlier than the bee, because those bronze age Cretans called the Minoans made them the basis of jewellery. If Virgil had wanted an aggressive creature, the wasp might have suited him.

Yet the magic of bees is their honey, and bee-swarms are one of the most dramatic sights of summer. So this Georgic had to be about bees, and he can distinguish one kind of bee from another, though he simplifies Aristotle's four kinds of bee (including drones) to two, to suit his civil war where there must be natural victors and vanquished. But Virgil is not writing without irony, and is more influenced by folklore than by his learned sources.

> All these passions and battles which are so great
> Are put to rest by a handful of small dust. (86-7)

Lecturing on the Georgics forty-three years ago, Mynors memorably compared this line to the rattle of earth on the coffin-lid of human beings.

The types of bee follow for a few lines: they have an extraordinary beauty in their pre-scientific way.

> His Royal Body shines with specks of Gold,
> And ruddy Skales; for Empire he design'd,
> Is better born, and of a Nobler Kind.
> That other looks like Nature in disgrace,
> Gaunt are his sides and sullen is his face ...

It is perfectly possible that even here Virgil may have been looking at contemporary paintings. Certainly none of bees have survived, and yet bees carved in marble nestle among the flower garlands of the Ara Pacis Augusti, which was soon to be built, and they are easier to draw or paint than they are to carve. In Virgil's 15 lines on their appearance, they glitter like drops of honey in the sun. Dryden introduces Mead, which is honey-based, and which he calls Metheglin, to confuse this discussion, but he does give the spirit of Virgil's climax (100-102).

> Huge heavy Honey-Combs of Golden Juice,
> Not only sweet, but pure and fit for use:
> T' allay the Strength and Hardness of the Wine,
> And with old Bacchus, new Metheglin join.

You can keep the bees at home with the pleasures of 'sweet Gardens, full of Saffron flow'rs'. Priapus with his wooden sickle will be their gardener, and fetch thyme and viburnum from the mountains, though the hard work hurts his hands (112-15). Pausanias (9, 31, 2) on Mount Helicon tells us 'this god receives honours wherever goats and sheep graze, and bees swarm', and whether because of their sexual prowess or because they were as ridiculous and 'low life' as he was, donkeys were sacrificed to him. Priapus, so Virgil says, will plant and water the bee-garden and this may mean that Virgil considers it natural, not planted by human beings.

By the way, he goes on, lest I should finish this Georgic too quickly, let me tell you something about gardening (116-17). He gives us 40 or so lines on the subject, but they are so crisp and enchanting that whole books have been based on them, one of the most interesting being by Père Rapin, whose work Dryden knew, and Creech translated his essay on pastoral poetry as a preface to his Theocritus (1684). At the end of my first Oxford term in 1954 when Mynors had lectured on the Georgics, I rushed to the Bodleian Library to read Rapin, but I then found him a blind alley (perhaps it is only now that I am ripe for so dull a poet).

> My Song to Flow'ry Gardens might extend:
> To teach the vegetable Arts, to sing
> The Paestan Roses, and their double Spring:
> How Succ'ry drinks the running Streams, and how
> Green Beds of Parsley near the River grow,
> How Cucumbers along the Surface creep,
> With crooked Bodies, and with Bellies deep:

IV. Transformation Scene

The late Narcissus, and the winding Trail
Of Bears-foot, Myrtle green, and Ivy pale.

Virgil says long-sleeping or late-waking Narcissus, the stem of bending acanthus, pale ivy and shore-loving myrtle (122-4). The late narcissus emerges in autumn, after the first autumnal rains, succory means endive, and the roses of Paestum were proverbial, they came into Cicero's fifth attack on Verres. There do exist a number of roses that flower twice even in Gloucestershire, but Paestum was far to the south of Naples, and beyond the boundaries of Campania which were on the river Sele.

Virgil having got so far, two or three days from home, now brings us to the magically remote spot where Oebalus King of Sparta sent out Phalanthus and those Spartans who had slept with slavewomen to found the city of Tarentum. But the myth of Tarentum was heroic and full of lies, and the character Oebalus is suspiciously obscure: obscurity of this kind was a favoured device among Hellenistic poets. But we know Virgil means Tarentum (which is not mentioned in the Latin) because of the river Galaesus:

> For where with stately Tow'rs Tarentum stands,
> And deep Galaesus soaks the yellow Sands,
> I chanced an old Corycian Swain to know.

Tarentum was an old Mycenean trading post on a spur of land between a lagoon and a sheltered bay full of islands. Venusia where Horace was born was not far inland, and Horace liked Tarentum as much as Virgil did.

This is the only personal anecdote in the works of Virgil, but we are not told how he met the 'old Corycian Swain'. It may have been on the journey to Brindisi with Horace, or another journey with or without Maecenas. Virgil calls the Galaesus not deep, by the way, but 'black' and the cultivated ground yellow. 'Corycian' means from a mountain in Asia Minor which was a nest of pirates resettled by Pompey (67 BC) in Calabria and in Greece. Mynors felt the story, which is in Servius and elsewhere, was dangerously unconfirmed, but I am reluctant to abandon the belief that this old but active gardener was a retired pirate. Patrick Leigh Fermor has pointed out the possible connection of the formidable towers of the Mani with the towers in Asia where these pirates once had their lairs. At any rate, like Priapus the Corycian will have had 'hardy horny Fingers that ached with Pain'. He was:

> Lord of few Acres, and those barren too,
> Unfit for Sheep or Vines, and more unfit to sow.

101

Still he contrived to cultivate pot-herbs and vervain, and he lived on whatever he could grow:

> Sometimes white Lillies did their Leaves afford,
> With wholesome Poppy-flow'rs, to mend his homely board.

He was pleased with what he had and thought it more than a king's wealth. He loved it because it was his own.

The Corycian seems to have strayed out of a poem by Horace in fact. He was the first in spring to gather roses, and in autumn to pick apples, and 'when the unhappy winter cracked the rocks and reined the tracks of waters in with ice, he cropped the leaf of his soft hyacinth' (135-7). Grammarians of late date were worried by the Greek sound of the rhythm, and preferred to substitute acanthus. The line is lovely, and it is only the botany that worries me, unless his flowers grew in pots indoors in a sunny window, otherwise the defiance of frost is a bit strange. Dryden prefers acanthus.

> He stript the Bears-foot of its leafy growth,
> And calling Western Winds, accus'd the Spring of sloath.
> He therefore first among the Swains was found
> To reap the Product of his labour'd Ground
> And squeeze the Combs with Golden Liquor Crown'd.
> His Limes were first in Flow'rs, his lofty Pines
> With friendly Shade secur'd his tender Vines.
> For ev'ry Bloom his Trees in Spring afford
> An Autumn Apple was by tale restor'd.
> He knew to rank his Elms in even rows,
> For Fruit the grafted Peartree to dispose,
> And tame to Plums the sourness of the Sloes.
> With spreading Planes he made a cool retreat
> To shade good Fellows from the Summer's heat.

The story of the gardener is over (147-8) when it has hardly begun. Perhaps Virgil sat with him under his planes in the early season, though his account sounds as if this garden was high up the river and some way from the city. Did the Corycian have no sheep or goats at all? It is possible that they were away in the mountains guarded by shepherds.

But the whole point of Virgil's vignette is that the man is a subsistence farmer, who grows the minimum and lives on that. The trees are older than thirty years all the same, and if there are no slaves on this tiny farm or plot, it must have been extremely, preternaturally hard work. He is a gardener for the sake of his bees and we know there were market gardeners on a larger scale in this part of Italy: Cicero knew one outside Brindisi. We know also that the Greek instep of Italy thrilled Virgil as well as Horace. Why are we told that when Virgil lay dying at Brindisi, he was planning a visit to Metapontum? A lonely temple is still standing there, just west of Tarentum, and it may be that Virgil knew the mosquito-infested Greek ruins already.

The old Corycian is introduced in an atmosphere of gardens (109 and 118) in which bees delight and he is then presented (139-41) as a beekeeper on land where nothing much will grow. Flower gardens or pleasure gardens were urban and not rustic, so the rich illustrations of Roman gardening that the Italians have recently recovered are no use to us here. The Corycian might almost be the elaboration of an epigram. And yet he is so well done and so appetising that one is reluctant not to believe he was a friend of Virgil's, even if he was then conventionally dressed up in Horatian morality and Hellenistic luxuriance of texture.

His bees (139-41) are the key to the Corycian and to his relevance in the rational analysis of the Georgic, but in its operation as a poem he is a bold digression from the minutiae of apiculture, a step into new and wonderful country and towards the myth which will be the climax of the poem. 'What apples in fresh blossom dressed the tree / So many ripe in autumn she still held' (142-3) touches again on a deep theme of the four Georgics, as well as on the blessedness of the Corycian's sunny old age.

Virgil moves on (less briskly than it seems) to the singing sound of the Cretan dwarves, the Curetes, and their clanging cymbals, and how the bees fed the king of heaven as an infant in his mountain cave. Bees are the only animals to have their children in common and to live in cities under laws (153-5) and have a loyalty to their home and country. This degree of social organisation was their reward (it appears) for feeding little Zeus. The noise of the Curetes was to disguise his infant cries and confuse his father who intended to eat him but was luckily duped with a large stone. This somewhat surprising story comes from Callimachus, but essentially it is ancient Greek mythology. There is no use in worrying why the wasp, the hornet and the ant should be disregarded here. The bee is the citizen of a Platonic Republic, and that is that. (Why I wonder did this never occur to Plato? The first philosopher to show serious interest in bees was Aristotle.)

The bees hoard their food in common, and their jobs are specialised: some forage, some guard the store and make the comb,

> Lay deep Foundations for the labour'd Comb
> With dew, Narcissus Leaves, and clammy Gum.

103

To pitch the Waxen Flooring some contrive:
Some nurse the future Nation of the Hive:
Sweet Honey some condense, some purge the Grout,
The rest in Cells apart the liquid Nectar shut ...
With Diligence the fragrant Work proceeds ...

The bees are as strong and as hard-working as the Cyclopes (170) when *Aetna* rumbles with their anvils. Instinctive love of having urges the Athenian bees. They build the combs and roof them like the singing masons building roofs of gold in Shakespeare's Henry V, which must derive from these lines. At nightfall they come home heavily laden.

The Gleans of yellow Thime distend his Thighs:
He spoils the Saffron Flow'rs, he sips the blues
Of Vi'lets, wilding Blooms, and willow Dews.

All night they sleep and all day they work. There are no violets in their diet, only blue-green willow, sweet casia, blushing crocus, the rich lime-blossom and iron-blue hyacinth. The words for colour are so strange as to be almost unnatural: the crocus gleams rather than blushes, with its gold, but the glaucous or blue-grey willow already has you off balance: Crocus and Narcissus were both transformed from boys, and so was Hyacinth.

Virgil organises the lives of the bees as regularly as if they were monks. He notes their buzzing to get in and their night-time silence, their carefulness in bad weather, and their habit of carrying stones to help them navigate as ships carry ballast (194-6). Ancient writers from Aristotle to Plutarch had no doubts about this curious habit, which has no basis in reality. Though Mynors thinks the bees were throwing out refuse or bringing in building materials, I think it is just a lie boldly repeated by author after author.

From this Virgil goes on to discuss even more bizar behaviour of the bees. They have no sex life, they gather children by licking them from leaves. They live seven years, but their race and family live immortally. They are loyal unless or until a king dies. There is then chaos and civil anarchy until they elect another (197-202). There is no real doubt here that Virgil is giving us his version if not of the Republic then at least of a Platonic myth.

Induc'd by such Examples, some have taught
That Bees have Portions of Etherial Thought:
Endu'd with Particles of Heavenly Fires:
For God the whole created Mass inspires;

Through Heav'n and Earth and Ocean's depth he throws
His influence round, and kindles as he goes.

Flocks, herds and men and every kind of beast return to God and there is no
space for death. They fly away as numerous as the stars into high heaven.

The language of this has a Lucretian solemnity, though not quite all the
Christian overtones that Dryden gives it.[2] Aristotle suggests everyone believed
in some special divinity in bees. So Virgil's doctrine has a strong Greek resonance
and perhaps a Stoic colouring, though it is also to be found in Virgil's fellow-
Epicurean Lucretius (2, 991 and 5, 318). We shall encounter another strange
outbreak of Stoicism in the sixth book of the Aeneid, the hub of the epic, where it
would be better discussed. It is clear enough in the present context that the language
of poetic exaltation has contributed something to the philosophic idea. Here
(219-27) its context is to explain the death of loyal bees who may die in battle.

Having assured us of the happiness and heaven of bees, Virgil instructs us how
to steal their honey, with sprinkled water and with smoke, as it is still done. The
two harvests of honey are when the Pleiades rise and when they sink, that is early
summer and autumn. No doubt Italian hives had more honey than ours, so it
was the length of summer and not the rapacity of the Romans that made Varro
suggest three harvests. In England one is often as much as you should take, unless
you are supplying your bees with winter food to replace their honey.[3] The honey
tasted best if it was taken in late June when the bees had been on the lime-
blossom for weeks. Virgil has an intricate bit of astronomy (234-5) about the
setting of the Pleiades, and it is hard to make sense of what he says about the
Fish, though it is clear enough he must refer to the coming of winter. Bees do
not hibernate, they only slow down in winter, so a sunny day brings them out,
but Virgil's second harvest cannot be later than November, by which time
activity is closing down for the year (in England this would happen far earlier).

From the loss of their hard-won honey Virgil proceeds to the pests other than
man that can attack the hive, like the gecko and the aggressive beetle, the drone
and the larvae of the wax-moth:

Or secret Moths are there in Silence fed:
Or Spiders in the Vault their snary Webs have spread.

Bees like men 'fall away And languish with insensible Decay'. They are carried
away dead by their relatives and friends. Virgil has turned this habit into a
symbolic sign of their decline.

Why have we come back to death, already two or three times dealt with in
the poem? Because Virgil is preparing the complete catastrophe, like the cattle

catastrophe in the third Georgic, which will usher in the wonderful tale he has to tell.

> They change their Hue, with hagger'd Eyes they stare,
> Lean are their Looks, and shagged is their Hair ...
> ... Soft Whispers then and broken Sounds are heard,
> As when the Woods by gentle Winds are stirr'd:
> Such stifl'd noise as the close Furnace hides
> Or dying Murmurs of departing Tides.

The only cure is sweet smells, and honey infused through tubes, wine and raisins and old rose petals, thyme and centaury. Virgil claims that beekeepers boil up the roots of Amellus from the river Mella that Catullus mentions (67, 33) in the Alps north of Brescia. Mynors calls this magic flower wild starwort or michaelmas daisy, which is an American native, but I think he means *Aster caeruleus Atticus*, a Mediterranean variety. The Alpine flower 'Amellus' is quite unknown to modern science or bee-medicine.

If all the worker bees are already lost, then

> 'Tis time to touch the Precepts of an Art
> Th' Arcadian Master did of old impart:
> And how he stock'd his empty Hives again
> Renewed with putrid Gore of Oxen slain ...

Having announced he is about to tell us an ancient mystery, the first thing Virgil does is to shift the scene to Egypt, the home of antique mysteries. Herodotus produces bees from a dead man's skull (5, 114) and the Bible from a dead lion (out of the strong came forth sweetness) though classical scholars will not accept this behaviour in bees, and suggest a fly.

Virgil gives us the Nile, and its people in painted boats, with much resonant symbolism about the black men up river, the dark and rich earth and the greenness of the delta after the floods. Here he says they make four-walled and four-windowed houses. A two-year-old calf with curving horns is choked to death and left in its house, surrounded by sweet herbs, in the spring season, before flowers appear in the meadows, before the chattering swallow nests in the eaves. This account is a little reminiscent of a conjuror rolling up his sleeves (305-7), but he says that sure enough the marrow of the bones boils up until the corpse is swarming with mites that grow into bees.

Now we happen to know that Philetas before Theocritus believed bees were born from dead oxen. What is so curious is Virgil's prosaic and precise, rather

Herodotean description. Where can it have come from? I do not think Gallus is a likely source, but some Egyptian Greek may have witnessed half the process and imagined the rest? Theocritus believed in the magical or sacred powers of bees, but his account – if he wrote one – would be more romantic. Here only the end is so: the bees burst out like summer rain-cloud or like the buzzing arrows of the light Parthians (313-4).

What god revealed this clever trick? The shepherd Aristaeus fleeing away from Tempe, having lost all his bees, so they say, by disease and hunger. He stood at the sacred head-spring of the river, lamenting to his mother.

> Mother Cyrene, Mother whose abode
> Is in the depth of this immortal Flood:
> What boots it that from Phoebus loins I spring,
> The third by him and thee from Heav'n's high King?

Aristaeus had an Arcadian base as early as Pindar (fr. 251) but he was a head shepherd who wandered around with his flocks, hence here he is the 'Arcadian Master', or probably Master of the bees, the 'bee gaffer' as they were called. The river must be the Peneus. It is a magic place, the entry to a wonderland. It flows down a narrow gorge associated with Apollo, between Mount Olympus and Mount Ossa, and Pindar says Cyrene lived beside its waters.

The religious cult of the comparatively obscure hero Aristaeus apparently began in Thessaly, where he was the protector of cattle and fruit trees. His mother was carried off to Libya by Apollo, though she seems to have had a homing instinct for the Peneus. This is the ordinary introduction of a Hellenistic story in prose or in verse, as Reitzenstein pointed out long ago, and it is amazing how they all conform to a model which does not exist. But Virgil will now put out all his powers in a mythic narrative of nearly 250 lines in which his tale merges into the second and greater subject of Orpheus and Eurydice.

'Why did you bear me? Where did love of me drive you? Why did you bid me hope for heaven?' He tells her in wounded and contorted words that he deserved better; 'what good were his care for flocks and crops and his intelligence? Why if she is so tired of his praises, does she not pluck up his forests, bring fire against his steadings and his harvests, burn the sown ground and wield an axe on his vines? (321-32)

This is the speech of a furious young man which Cyrene, like a good Epicurean Nymph, scarcely hears. But she did feel a sound under her roof in the deep water. Aristaeus is standing at the source of the river – though the same word *canut* can mean its mouth (Aen. 8, 65). The deep water where the

Nymph was hiding is a mystery and was meant to be one, perhaps it is inside the rock.

Around Cyrene sit the Nymphs spinning wool like proper Roman ladies: the wool is Milesian so it is very fine, and its dyed colour is crystalline green. Virgil's list of their names is not Homeric. They are chosen for their beauty and an air of antiquity: Drymo, Xantho, Ligea, Phyllodoce with the hair glittering on their white necks, Cydippe and yellow-haired Lycorias, one a virgin, one fresh from childbirth, Clio and her sister Baroe daughters of Ocean, both wearing gold and belts of fur, Ephyre and Opis and Asian Deiopea, and swift Arethusa with arrows put by. Among them Clymene, one of the Nymphs, tells of Vulcan's useless care and Mars's trickery and his sweet theft. The story is Homeric and what Mars stole was not honey but sex with Venus.

Clymene goes through the innumerable loves of the gods from Chaos on, and they are captivated by the song as they weave their soft wool. But again the grief of Aristaeus reaches his mother's ears, and they all sit staring on their shimmering thrones. Before her sisters it is Arethusa who sticks her yellow head out of the surface of the river, and speaks from a distance.

'Sister Cyrene it is sad Aristaeus, your greatest care, who stands weeping by the waves of Peneus your father'. (The river was her grandfather, her father was the King of the Lapiths.) 'He calls you cruel by your name' (353-6). Struck with fresh fear his mother spoke to Arethusa.

'Bring him, bring him to us. It is right for him to tread upon the threshold of the gods' (358-9). She bade the deep rivers split wide apart, to let the boy step in, and like a mountain the wave stood up and curved its head round him, took him in its vast bosom and sent him down to the bottom of the river, and he wondered to see his mother's house and her wet kingdom.

This is not the only aqueous revelation in Virgil, but it is the most surprising. These underwater cave-palace scenes became popular with Homer's Odyssey: there is one of a young hero on the sea-bottom painted on a fifth-century Athenian vase in the Louvre. But I do not think Virgil has anything like it in mind. The underwater greenish shimmer, the vast height of the wave and the yellow head of Arethusa are a matter of words. Lucretius (6, 536) knows that there are watery caverns, but no one else has described them in such detail.

I fear I left Virgil in mid-sentence (363). Dryden presents an illustration of the scene stolen from Ogilby of an opera with the candles burning along the edge of the stage, but even Hollar could not represent the amazing spectacle as it confronted Aristaeus,

Of Lakes that pent in hollow Caverns roar.
He hears the crackling Sound of Coral Woods,
And sees the secret Source of subterranean Floods.

Aristaeus sees Phasis and Lycus and where deep Enipeus's head first rises. The first two are Armenian, Enipeus is in Thessaly, but the congregation of great waters proceeds headlong without regard to geography: father Tiber and the Anio, and rocky Hypanis (in Scythia) and Mysian Caicus (Mediterranean), and last the Po,

Twin-horned, bull-faced, gilded Eridanus,
Than whom no other stream more violent
Rushes through rich fields to the purple sea.

When he comes under the hanging pumice roof and Cyrene had seen her son's vain tears, they gave him streams to wash himself and woollen towels. (His reception is Homeric.) They lay a table with a banquet and full glasses.

The roots of all rivers in one great shimmering cavern is an astounding and surrealist idea. The hanging roofs of pumice do sound like the area of Naples, and I am not inclined to think that Virgil intends coral or stalactites of any kind. These roaring, gleaming waters are surprise enough. Yet within the cave life is domestic though heroic, it is automatic that the weeping boy washes his face (understood) and his hands before a meal. The highly improper song by Clymene about the affairs of the gods, which Virgil calls 'dense', has now ceased.

There are a number of small touches of comedy in the scene, but one must keep one's eyes open to spot them. The Nymphs are earthly even if they are rivers like Arethusa, but they may be daughters of Ocean, who is one of the most ancient of the gods. The altars in the cave are alight with incense-burning flames. Cyrene offers the boy wine to pour to Ocean: the wine is 'Maeonian', that is Lydian, of high quality like the Panchaean incense, and is served in a preposterously antique cup, a kind of 'flute' with two handles.

So she prays
To father Ocean and her sister Nymphs
Who keep a hundred woods, a hundred streams:
Three times pours nectar on the burning Hearth
Three times the flame leaps up to the high roof.

The scene is both palatial and baroque. As she pours liquid nectar the flame of course dies down but then at once it leaps up 'to the topmost roof'. The place where she pours is called Vesta, so this is her ritual Hearth and her home. The omen of the flames is a good one and it gives her confidence. She begins her speech in the old manner of story-telling.

Suddenly we have entered a new phase of the adventure. The same formula occurs many times in Virgil, and without any self-consciousness (About the buzz-fly of Silarus for example (Geo. 3, 146) and in Ennius. Virgil is still for all his dazzling variations and surprises a traditional story-teller.)

> In the Carpathian Bottom makes abode
> The Shepherd of the Seas, a Prophet and a God:
> High o'er the Main in wat'ry Pomp he rides
> His azure Carr and finny Coursers guides:
> Proteus his name ...

Karpathos lies between Rhodes and Crete, and Virgil has given the sea-bottom, known in his day to sponge-divers and to shell-divers, to the Old Man of the Sea. Homer had put him off-shore of Egypt. The Carpathian deeps may have come into the lost poetry of Theocritus or they may be Virgil's private fancy.

There is a prophet in the Carpathian deep, blue Proteus, Cyrene says. Everything in this part of the poem gleams or glimmers or is blue. Proteus measures the great sea with fishes and a yoked car of two-footed horses (that is, sea-horses, as we know them in art). The fish may be dolphins but whether or not they are harnessed remains a mystery. They are not the seals he has in Homer. The *hippocamps* or sea-horses pull his car, so what the fish are for is an insoluble difficulty. I think they are just the attendants of the prophet, and he may take a ride on one if he feels inclined. In the depths of the sea of course they are not clearly visible.

Cyrene sees him when he revisits the Macedonian harbours and his old country Pallene, which is the westernmost of the three great prongs of land east of Saloniki. Proteus was the shepherd of seals, from Homer onwards, and Callimachus seems to have said he used to visit Pallene, no doubt because the seals did in summer. The Greeks were conscious of where the seals bred and where they were to be found, because a type of rennet, that was vital for cheese-makers, came from the bodies of these great creatures. The smell of cheese-making occurs in Theocritus (Id. 7) on the island of Kos, and must be the explanation of what the innocent Odysseus thinks is the appalling stink of seals in a cave, which has always been a puzzle because in nature they are not at all smelly. Pallene is a useful place to observe them, because it guards the mouth of Cyrene's river the Peneus (319-20).

At Pallene the Nymphs pay their respects to Proteus (391) and so does hoarily antique Nereus, an even older old man of the sea. The prophet knows all things, what was, what is, what is to come, like other prophets Greek, Hebrew, and assorted. Neptune gave him the gift,

> Because he grazes his gigantic herds,
> And his disgusting seals below the deep. (394-5)

The seals are 'disgusting' only for the imaginary cheesy smell surely, not for their faces – which are charming – nor for their queer song. That ass Ovid calls them 'deformed' (Met. 1, 300) and he may safely be ignored.

> But first the wily Wizard must be caught,
> For unconstrain'd he nothing tells for naught,
> Nor is with Tears or Bribes or Flatt'ry bought.
> Surprise him first, and with hard Fetters bind:
> Then all his Frauds will vanish into Wind.
> I will myself conduct thee on thy Way,
> When next the Southing Sun inflames the Day:
> When the dry Herbage thirsts for Dews in vain
> And Sheep in Shades avoid the parching Plain.
> Then will I lead thee to his secret Seat ...

If this looks like some thrilling entry to the underworld, the reader is not quite deceived. It should be borne in mind when Aeneas seeks directions from the Sibyl, to visit his father in the underworld. But here it is a purely wonderful fiction, one of Reitzenstein's Hellenistic *Wundererzählungen*. And Virgil proves himself a master of narrative fiction, towards which the entire generation of Gallus and Cinna had aspired.

When the young man, transformed into a hero by a waft of nectar, undertakes the adventure she has sketched out, it is still more wonderful. But first she continues her warning:

>   ... scorch'd with Heat
> The wayward Sire frequents his cool Retreat:
> His Eyes with heavy slumber overcast.
> With Force invade his Limbs, and bind him fast ...

Proteus is to be tied up as Silenus was tied in the sixth Eclogue, but not so easily, because he will turn into a boar with foamy Tusks, roar like a lion, crackle like fire, 'Hiss like a Dragon, or a Tiger stare' or else 'In fleeting Streams attempt to slide away'. Then he will tire of his repertory of tricks and turn back into his old shape. Only when Cyrene has told him all this, she covers him in nectar,

> Infusing Vigour through his mortal Joynts:
> Down from his Head the liquid Odours ran,
> He breath'd of Heav'n and look'd above a Man.

We are moved in mid-line to a huge sea-cave (418) where ships might shelter from a storm, and here the Nymph places the boy in ambush, while she takes herself off in a cloud. Already the swift dog-star was toasting the thirsty Indians and the flaming sun devoured mid-heaven: the grass burnt and the hollow rivers cooked dry-jawed to mud in the sunrays, when Proteus from the sea sought out his cave, and the wet people of the vast sea leapt around him and sprinkled far and wide their salty dew (425-31).

> His finny Flocks about their Shepherd play
> And rowling round him, spirt the bitter Sea.
> Unwieldily they wallow first in Ooze
> Then in the shady Covert seek Repose.

I doubt whether the blazing heat of a Greek noon or the sea-wetness of the marine farmyard have ever, in any language, been more sharply conveyed. Fire and water and gods and animals are commingled. The god is like a shepherd counting his flocks, like the headman of a yard when the evening star brings home the calves, and the bleating of the lambs excites the wolves.

But Aristaeus hardly lets the old fellow compose his limbs when he has him chained. Proteus tries to escape in fire, in animals and in running water, but he cannot, 'And wearies all his Miracles of Lies'. How dare a man attack a god? 'You know my name and business', Aristaeus rather pertly replies.

> The Seer could not yet his Wrath asswage,
> Rowl'd his green Eyes, and sparkled with his Rage:
> And gnash'd his Teeth, and cry'd, No vulgar God
> Pursues thy Crimes, nor with a common Rod.

'Thy great Misdeeds have met a due Reward / And Orpheus dying Pray'rs at length are heard.' The love of Orpheus and Eurydice was well-known: it was one of the scenes carved in relief in Athens in the fifth century BC to fit round the Altar of the Twelve gods which was known as the Altar of Mercy, or of Pity.

Eurydice was known also from Plato (Symp. 179d), from Euripides and from Greco-Italian painting.

The introduction of the story here however is a lightning-flash of revelation: one wonders at once, what is the young Aristaeus's sin, and what Orpheus has to do with the death of his bees. Orpheus was not unnaturally furious at the death of his wife (456). We are told by Proteus,

> She as she fled from you headlong by streams
> In tall grass failed to see a mighty snake
> Guarding the river-bank where she must die.
> Her sister dryads cried out to the hills.

The narrative is swift and clear enough, but why was Aristaeus chasing her, and where was her husband? If Virgil knows he is not telling us. Although it is easy enough to assume an attempt at rape, it is odd that we are not told that. The dryad being by a river may have undressed, and Aristaeus may not have pursued her, he may just have disturbed her in this wild place. We only know (455-6) that he deserved worse.

I am inclined to put the fault in the story down to the source poem that Virgil followed: we do not even know of its existence, though Maurice Bowra thought it did, and more or less wrote it, as his manner was (C.Q.,1952). It is suggestive that Eurydice the wife of Orpheus first becomes Eurydiceia in the lament for Bion written perhaps as late as the time of Sulla (124 BC); the subject was not forgotten.

Still, the sin of Aristaeus does not interest Virgil, it is a mere transition to introduce Orpheus and Eurydice, which is a tale told by Proteus. An amazing list of exotic Greek geographic names weep for Eurydice, and Orpheus in full neoclassic eloquence bewails his dying love on his tortoise-shell. You dear wife, you on the lonely shore, he sang you as the sun rose, and as it fell (466). He went to the jaws of Taenarus, the high porch of Dis and the grove darkened with black fear; he came to the ghosts and their tremendous king, to a heart that does not know how to melt at human prayers.'

Orpheus has entered the underworld by one of its classic openings, a frightening sea-cave on the formidable Cape Matapan, still one of the stormiest places in the world.

From the bottom of Erebus came the thin ghosts of the dead disturbed by his song, like those thousands of birds that take shelter in the leaves when the evening star or the winter rain drives them from the mountains, mothers and men and lifeless bodies of great heroes, boys and unwedded girls, and young men put on pyres before their parents' eyes. Around them the black mud and

113

formless reeds, the marsh of Cocytus with its slow stream unloved binds them in and Styx nine times self-intermingling fetters them. The very house and lair of Death stared in amazement and inmost Tartarus and the Furies twined with blue snakes; Cerberus gasped and held silent his three mouths, Ixion's wheel stayed hanging in the wind. Then treading back, avoiding all hazards (485) he with Eurydice given back was coming to the upper air, she behind him by Proserpina's condition, when sudden madness took the imprudent lover, forgivably if the ghosts could forgive. He stood, was overcome, and looked, alas, at his Eurydice on the very edge of light, triple thunder sounded on the lake of Avernus.

This remarkable passage offers a foretaste of Dante and of course the Aeneid, but it is as notable for what it leaves out as for what it puts in. The old man of the sea is an accomplished teller of tales. Were they returning to the light by Lake Avernus not far from Naples, rather than the dark jaws of Taenarus?

Virgil owes a great deal to Homer, even the metaphor of the leaves which in Homer means the successive generations of men, but here the birds that shelter in the leaves are Virgilian and I suspect Alpine. There is no doubt that the underworld is a terrible muddy dark place, like the delta of the Po, nine times self-intermingling. Ixion's wheel gives a touch of solemn antiquity, that is all.

'An Iron Slumber shuts my swimming Eyes', and Eurydice dies again, 'like subtile Smoke dissolv'd in Air'. Vast night surrounds her, and she stretches out her hands in vain. Hell's ferryman will not let her cross the marsh. She was already cold as she disappeared in the Stygian punt.

They say for seven whole months under an airy rock he wept by the waters of Strymon (back in the north) and in those frozen caves composed a song

> That melted tigers and drew oaks to him:
> As Philomel in the black poplar shade
> Mourns her lost young that the hard ploughman drew
> Featherless from the nest where he found them:
> She weeps away the night sat on the bough
> With her unhappy song and fills the place
> With her unhappy lamentations.
> No love, no thought of marriage bended him,
> Wandering alone across the Polar ice
> And snowy Tanais and all those grounds
> Where the Riphaean frost never withdraws.

The formula is still the same as it was in the Eclogues: this Georgic is as much a patchwork as any. But Virgil's transitions are as smooth as they are swift. We moved from the sudden jaws of the underworld at once to the ghosts of the dead, and the underworld marsh. The Queen of hell and the Ferryman were noticed only in retrospect or on the return journey.

The second death of Eurydice is moving in another way altogether: we are moved because we know the underworld is not. Orpheus composes his song in tears when it is all over, and his grief is all in the metaphor about the nightingale, not a mythical bird but a real one. Why a poplar shade if not by the Po? An alder would be likelier but the Latin word *populea* is musical. The black poplar is really a kind of aspen, but it is an impressive and lugubrious tree and it will do; it has low branches that could attract the bramble-haunting nightingale.

Orpheus sought for his kidnapped Eurydice and the vain gifts of Dis; and the Thracian mothers in the mysteries of the gods and night orgies of Bacchus tore the young man to pieces and scattered him far over their fields. They appear to have been incensed because he would not marry any of them.

> And his head from his gleaming shoulders torn
> Hebrus in mid-flood carried far away:
> Eurydice, his voice and his cold tongue
> Called as his soul fled. Poor Eurydice!
> And the river sang back, Eurydice. (523-7)

This is the end of the story that Proteus has to tell. It will be observed that he has not given a word of advice to Aristaeus who, under the influence of his wonderful story, has lost all interest in the bees. It may well be that Virgil had to chop his story short at the beginning or at the end. It has clearly outgrown its setting in the Georgic as the part of Shylock outgrew his place in the Merchant of Venice, and as certain characters tower above their proper height in Tolstoy's *War and Peace*.

However that may be, one whisk of his tail and Proteus is free:

> With one leap Proteus went into deep sea,
> Twisting the foaming wave behind his head.
> But Cyrene spoke to her frightened son:
> My son, put by your sadness and trouble.
> Here is what caused the pest, it was the Nymphs,
> With whom in the deep groves of trees she danced,
> Sent this unhappy plague to kill the bees.

So offer gifts, seek peace, pray the Napaeans. This unusual title for the Nymphs means the glen-women (*Napai* is a Greek word), and knowledge of their proper name is an essential part of the remedy. Aelian speaks in Greek somewhere of 'gods of the forest and the glen', and the later Latin agricultural writer Columella pretends to know who they are, but the wooded glens (*napai*) that they inhabit are too vague to distinguish them from dryads or oreads, though the Greek word *nape* has an association with Delphi, and *napos* with Olympia, so it is no mere landscape word. These Nymphs are 'the easy Napaeans', because they do not harbour long grudges. If they are not invented by Virgil, they must come from Maurice Bowra's Orpheus poem: they do not seem earlier than Hellenistic.

Cyrene knows how to deal with these nymphs. Aristaeus must take four fine bulls of the herd that grazes for him on top of Mount Lycaeus (Lykaios), the central mountain of Arcadia, opposite Bassae and above Lycosoura. He must build four altars for them and for four heifers at the shrines of the goddesses, cut their throats, and leave their bodies in a leafy grove. It has some meaning that Aristaeus is an Arcadian. Mount Lycaeus is the central and holiest of all those wild grazing grounds, and it is associated with the bees both here and in the earlier reference to the 'Arcadian Master' (283).

Aristaeus's cattle may be anywhere: in the first Georgic (14) they were in Ceos, and now Aristaeus has been in Thessaly, somewhere around Tempe. The 'shrines of the goddesses' are nowhere in particular, so they too could be anywhere.

> Then later, when Dawn breaks for the ninth time
> Send down Lethaean poppies to Orpheus
> Kill a black ewe and tread the grove again:
> Worship Eurydice with a dead heifer.

At once Aristaeus does as he is told; he finds and repairs the four altars, and takes the four prime bulls, takes the four heifers and then when Dawn breaks for the ninth time, sends Orpheus offerings and retreads the grove. Here 'they' see a sudden miracle, a wonder to relate (*dictu mirabile monstrum*, 554);

> ... in the liquefied guts of the oxen,
> Bees buzz in wombs and boil from broken sides.
> Trail giant clouds and from the tops of trees
> Hang in ripe clusters down the bending boughs.

The ending of this Georgic has been archaic in rhythm, but it is very swift. When Virgil repeats Cyrene's orders and leads on to the result we already foresaw from his Egyptian story, he leaves out a mass of information. He treads lightly and swiftly on the ground, as it were.

Wild bees live in hollow trees after all, and the shepherds who were the first bee-masters were wandering men, so he can put the 'invention' of beekeeping and of how to generate bees wherever he likes. He hints that it happened in Lycaeum. He hints at honey dripping from the oak trees as the bee-swarm dangles like a bunch of grapes: he hints at the Golden Age. But he feels he has said enough.

All that remains is his epilogue to this poem and the poems he has written so far (559-66):

> I made this song of herds, of farms and trees
> While Caesar's lightning flashed on deep Euphrates,
> While he spoke laws to peoples, and they bowed,
> And his road opened to the Olympian gods:
> Days when the Siren nourished me to flower
> In studies of unhonoured idleness:
> I played the shepherd's songs, and brave being young
> Sang Tityrus under the broad oak shade.

This curiously independent and apparently uncalled for bit of autobiographic verse is what ancient writers called a seal, to make their name inseparable from their authentic work, or in Greek a *sphragis*.

Horace signs the end of his Letters (bk 1) in the same sort of way, and the end of his lyrics (bk 3) with a boast of amazing grandeur. The relationship of the poet with Caesar in Horace's *Odes* is variable, but several times oddly similar to the end of the Georgics. 'I am the poet of the Georgics, and I made them while Caesar was flinging his thunderbolts above the deep Euphrates, and earning his entry into heaven'. Olympus had come to mean heaven, the sky, and the Latin word *adfectat* was used for an attempt, a struggle begun, a striving, or (as here) the beginning of a journey. 'They set out towards me as bravely as gladiators', says Terence.

Meanwhile Virgil sat in the shade, being nourished by Parthenope, the local Siren, who stands for Naples. There, 'brave, being young' he wrote his Eclogues on which he looks back with affection and no shame. The Tityrus Eclogue is the closest to Augustus and these are a wonderful, in a sense lyrical few lines. Virgil does not lose a jot of his coolness.

There is almost a challenge in their different ways to life and to immortal fame, since Virgil knew how little Caesar's hairy star was really worth; indeed he knew that the heavens were remote and might be empty. The defence of idleness or the resting on it is the acme of the Epicurean creed. Virgil sounds like a man who is preparing now after his elaborate poems to retire at forty.

There is undoubtedly a mysterious inner structure to the Georgics, which has puzzled critics for at least fifty years. The puzzles have never been much help to those scholars who delved into them, because they do not add to the sense of the poems. In the first and the fourth Georgic Maecenas is named in the second line, but in the second and third in the forty-first; there is a certain mathematical regularity about Caesar's name too: he is addressed personally at carefully contrived positions in all four poems. In the Eclogues there was elaborate correspondence between poems, but where Virgil acquired this obsessive trick we do not know. As the Merchant remarked, 'It wearies me, you say it wearies you, Yet how I found it, bought it, or came by it, I am yet to learn ...' What is more obvious and more helpful about his poetry is a kind of *tachisme*, a patchwork variation that speeds the verse and amazes or amuses the reader as he plunges through every kind of weather, so that Virgil is never faithful to the scheme of four seasons, and through every landscape, so that often you do not know Mantua from Campania or Rome from the Greek ruins to the south.

What one can say of the four Georgics as one looks back over them is that somehow they work, and finally they end with an amazing brilliance, in a narrative which is deeply contrived yet wonderfully naturally expressed, and a climax which was and was not foreseen from the beginning of the poem. The end of it all is densely written and complex even beneath the surface, so that every word must be weighed against a word: there are even overtones of honey in the Siren's milk: or in her song. At that time the sweet Siren nourished me to flower in studies of unhonoured idleness. Does that certainly mean poetry, or does it mean philosophy or scientific speculation? Virgil is a wonderfully tantalising poet, is he not?

Even the date is tantalising. After Actium in 31 BC Augustus turned his attention to the east, which had been Antony's power base. About 37 BC, Antony had appointed Polemo of Pontus to rule over Armenia, which had a boundary on the Euphrates: indeed that great river was also the boundary of the civilised or let us say civilisable world against Parthia, and it was probably Parthia that Virgil had in mind when he spoke of lightning on the Euphrates: but after Actium Augustus appointed Artavasdes of Media to rule over Armenia in Polemo's place. One Hellenistic king had replaced another, because he was a "client" of Augustus and owed him a kind of feudal loyalty. The activity on the Euphrates was diplomatic. Augustus himself returned to Italy in 29 BC, and on the way to Rome Virgil read him the Georgics in his villa at Atella. By 27 BC Augustus was ready to receive his title Augustus, and we have been calling the Roman sixth month (since their year started in March) August ever since.

The fourth Georgic in particular has great generative power for the Aeneid. The bees have made Virgil think seriously about man and the state, and about monarchy, about Augustus. The submarine miracles foreshadow several episodes in the Aeneid, and the underworlds more closely suggests book six: when Eurydice vanishes, Virgil has invented and matured and image will be useful to him among the dead.

THE MARCH OF TIME

It is when one has finished reading the Georgics that one has a retrospective sense of claustrophobia. There was no cress in the brooks, there were no woodpeckers or cuckoos in the woods, and although there were vast wandering flocks and herds, one never knew where they wandered to. Out of sight was far away. I remember once meeting a migrating flock on the island of Crete, where by chance I had met them first a few days before at a shepherds' feast when they were setting out for their summer grazing higher in the mountains. The distances if you measured them in miles were not far, but at the speed of a grazing flock they were far enough, and it was thrilling to see them again. In Virgil the pace is like that. You hear a man singing as he prunes the last vine in a long rank, and that is all. He is as impersonal as a figure in a landscape, though there is seldom any landscape, we seldom enter a house, we never wander into a town.

Can Virgil really have lived such a life? Of course not, he was an intense student of poetry and of history, a bookish man whose ideal was to love the rivers and the woods, unhonoured in his way of life. There was to his mind a certain resignation, a melancholy smile, about the very idea of being a poet.

Virgil knew more about the fine details of metrical technique in Catullus (64) on Peleus and Thetis, for example, than I can ever remember. That poem as Kroll points out was like the *Diana* of Cato the poet, the *Zmyrna* of Cinna, the *Io* of Calvus, and the *Glaucus* of Cornificius, a showpiece of the new poetry which had only these showpieces to its name. Virgil in his fourth Georgic appears to have surpassed all of them. (His work survived where theirs did not and we are lucky that Catullus also survived, although he lived so brief a life. I do not like the rhetoric in either poet, though it has a place in their style, but Virgil and Catullus write with a beauty that is moving, it is not merely dandified or aesthetic.

But, as the poet writes, times alter, and if the Georgics took seven or eight years to complete, as the lives tell us, then the world had greatly altered in that time. Between Philippi and the years after Actium, Rome had been virtually refounded: Augustus had passed from boyhood to Empire.

Colin Hardie, in a published lecture on the Georgics (1970) expressed some doubts about the last books of the Aeneid, which we must take seriously. (What he liked best were the pastoral books, seven and eight, and the first half the fourth and sixth books where Virgil treats the great themes of the Georgics, love and the underworld 'more fully but not more powerfully'.) He believes that in the sixth Eclogue – from which the Georgics spring – Virgil already saw the Georgics as a step towards epic poetry. That may be right; we have an English example in Milton of such vast early ambitions so late fulfilled.

However, I do not think anyone but me thinks of Milton's development as really continuous – and if it was so it can only have been through his sonnets because Milton was engaged in politics and wrote no Georgics. The idea of Virgil as a poet whose talent and development were entirely self-disciplined and self-contained is astonishing and in a way very attractive, but I cannot help but think his poetry shows an increasing influence of the Augustan establishment. Later in the Emperor's long life, when Virgil was dead, Augustus put overwhelming pressure on Horace, and it can be argued that he interfered too much with his delicately abundant Muse. Can the same not be said of the Aeneid?

If Virgil had been free to choose, would he have chosen Aeneas for his subject? Only if he already intended a direct confrontation with Homer. The Georgics go beyond the world of love, which does seem to pervade the eclogues and their music and their idleness; the Georgics are about work and stern nature. But when Aristaeus appeals to his mother, his model is Achilles in the Iliad appealing to Thetis with tears, and when he captures Proteus he recalls Menelaus in the Odyssey who does the same. So Virgil's battle with Homer might seem to have begun. That is how Hardie looks at the fourth Georgic, though I remain dubious about what degree of foresight the little Homeric touches imply in Virgil's career as a poet. Hardie sees that career as all but inevitable towards the heights of epic poetry, and there is certainly something true in his reading of the Georgics, which is wrong in other modern interpretations. He writes with an elaborate genius of understanding, and at times reminds one of his naive predecessor John Martyn, who was Professor of Botany at Cambridge in 1740, and whose commentary on the Georgicks of Virgil is written in so inviting a style.

Augustus on the Monument* begins with the proud boasts of his youth:

When I was nineteen I raised an army by my own intelligence and at my own expense, and through it restored the republic to its freedom from the government of an oppressive minority. So when Pansa and Hirtius were consuls I was appointed to the Senate. The same year as both consuls were

---

* The Monumentum or *Marmor Ancyranum*, called after one of its copies found in Ancyra which was read aloud in the Senate after his death.

killed in battle I was made consul. The assassins of my father I sent into exile by sentence of law, and when later they made war on the republic, I beat them twice in open battle ...[1]

He often made war and won, three times he shut the Gates of War, he was thirteen times consul, and so on. He consecrated the Altar of Fortune by the Capua Gate, for his homecoming to Rome in 19 BC, the year Virgil died, and later the Altar of Peace which the poet never saw. One cannot fail to observe that Augustus's enemies in civil war are blotted out as if they had never lived, and small attention is usually paid to his allies, and Actium is carefully avoided

On the long inscription of this monument, neither Virgil nor Horace is mentioned. They were for private pleasure, not for state monuments or national propaganda, though they reflect the policies of Augustus clearly enough in their works. At one point Augustus tried to get Horace's service as a private secretary, but Horace politely side-stepped. Virgil read Augustus the Georgics in a country house on his return from the Actium campaign, in 29 BC, and speaks in the signature of Augustus active in the east; though like the Monument he casts a veil over Actium (until the baroque sun-burst of the Shield of Aeneas).[2] It was almost certainly for the Georgics that Augustus made him very rich.

In 27 BC Augustus set off for Britain, but was distracted from that campaign by news of trouble in Spain and went there instead. In Spain there began to be news that Virgil had got down to work on the Aeneid, so he sent for any fragment, any crumb or contents page, that could be copied for him, which Virgil refused. We have a few phrases of Augustus's correspondence, a sentence from Macrobius and a bit from Probus's biography, and it must all come from Suetonius, who, though he may be unreliable in other ways, did have access to the letters in the private archives of the Emperors. Much later, we are told Virgil read Augustus three books of the first half of the Aeneid: the second with the fall of Troy, the fourth with the death of Dido, and the sixth, the underworld.

It is not by any means surprising that there should have been a gap between the Georgics and the Aeneid, which shows signs of elaborate planning. At the time of the Georgics, Virgil's habit as a writer was facile in invention, so that Eros his secretary records he might make up a half-line impromptu while he was reading in public, but careful and slow in procedure, so that he put in lines he called scaffolding to stand until the solid columns took their place. He wrote a page in the morning carefully, but then corrected it all day until very little might remain. In this he compared himself to a bear who gives birth to cubs and then has to lick them into shape. His voice was excellent and his powers of expression amazing.

Virgil gave few public readings, and those he did give were mostly of passages where he was uncertain what reaction they would face. His health was variable: his stomach was delicate, and he had headaches and sore throats, also there were times when he spat blood. His house on the Esquiline near Maecenas's house sounds grand and comfortable, but he lived more in the country, at Siro's house in Campania. He had many critics all his life, but today they are like cobwebs that one blows from an old book. They contribute nothing substantial but a few feeble jokes like 'Plough naked and sow naked': 'You'll get a cold'.

There is, nonetheless, pitifully little to be found in the ancient biographies about the few years between the Georgics and the Aeneid, between Actium and the Spanish campaign, which are so important in Virgil's development as a poet. The reason for this, although we have crumbs of information from the old secretary Melissus and from Virgil's friend Varus, is probably that the more famous he became, the shyer he became. When he was recognised in the streets of Rome and a crowd began to gather, he would take refuge in the nearest house.

All the same there is no doubt that Virgil's expressed attitude to Augustus and to Rome in his poems altered, and so did his philosophy. We have already observed a strange outbreak of Stoicism, or of a general world-view which had originally been Stoic, in the fourth Georgic (though all four of them are strongly coloured by Epicureanism). Even in the Aeneid there is a kind of Platonism in the sixth book, the heart of the entire epic.

In politics Virgil's earliest poems, the Eclogues are hard to interpret and to date, and the evidence of revision does not help either. I have never, for example, been able to take seriously the idea that Daphnis stands for Julius Caesar. Only accept that, and you have Virgil fixed in a party from the beginning of his life. The arguments for this belief, which is late antique, were advanced in the nineteenth century by Nettleship (1879). He pointed to two fancies in Suetonius's Life of Julius (Caesar), one that the night before his death he dreamed he soared to heaven and touched the hand of Jupiter, the other that his horses on the Rubicon wept and would not graze before his death. Both recur in the fifth Eclogue. Also, in the fifth Eclogue (29 and 56) Daphnis introduces rites of Bacchus, just as Servius (a highly unreliable guide) says Caesar did. There is some faint shadow of colour in common in all this, but surely no more.

But in the writing time of the four Georgics, which ends by 29 BC, Virgil has become a sturdy supporter of the establishment, he identifies Augustus with Rome, he is silent about civil war. Poets were found to write about contemporary battles with whomsoever. Courtney has reprinted bits of an appalling poem about Actium, which is anonymous, and Horace wrote his wonderful lyric Nunc est Bibendum (Od. 1, 37) about the tragedy of Cleopatra (but a careful critic might maintain that the war was against the Queen of Egypt and that Antony was not mentioned in the poem). Yet, Virgil does not mention Actium until the Aeneid.

Eighty years is rather longer than a generation, but eighty years after his death Virgil was adored like a god, the Aeneid opened at random was an oracle to Hadrian, though that dandy emperor was snobbish enough to pretend that he preferred Ennius. Copies of Virgil for oracular consultation were also kept in Apollo's temple at Cumae and Fortune's at Praeneste.[3] He had out-soared orthodoxy by his powerful magic as a poet. But now so late in the day we are interested in knowing how he stood in his own times, and after the debauch of Virgil-worship from about 60 AD to 600 AD, all there is left is the poetry, which we have traced to about his fortieth birthday, and must now trace through the labyrinth of the Aeneid.

We know that Virgil saw the Aeneid as more than an academic exercise, and we can see that what he produced was far more than a state poem, which is in turn more than academic poetry, if that phrase still has a meaning.

Virgil divided his work into two parts, the first an Odyssey and the second an Iliad. The second has often disappointed, because he was not deeply enough in sympathy with the Iliad of Homer, and did not understand the fundamental principle in Homer's world, that poetry belongs to the defeated and to the dead. Virgil's hero had to be a winner and the founder of a great dynasty and future race, and a great city he never saw built: he could not like great Hector lie down in his greatness forgetting his mastery of horses. This one fact came as close as anything could do to ruining the Aeneid before ever it was written.

Virgil's study of Homer was almost too intense, too bespectacled and book-ish. Modern scholarship has shown that he read not only Homer but the numerous conflicting commentaries on Homer the Alexandrians had brought together. If they criticised Homer, he might avoid the trap and accept a solution, or he might reject the criticism and exaggerate the Homeric 'fault', but he was always conscious of the scholars, as well as of Homer as a poet. I have held this alarming opinion strongly since I came across it some twenty-five years ago. It has never as far as I know been fully worked out, nor is this the right place to give rein to those horses, but it must be borne in mind by any student of the Aeneid that between Virgil and Homer there is a gulf full of arguments and counter-arguments.

It was inevitable that Virgil in writing a kind of 'epic' poetry would try to fit it into the same mythology of gods and goddesses as Homer had done, and more or less inevitable that he would tie the foundation of Rome to the fall of Troy. Other Italian towns had legends of Greek founders, some of them Homeric, some like Horace's Daunus obscure, but the story of the wanderings of Aeneas westward with his father and his son after the fall of Troy existed in quite an elaborate form before the fifth century BC. Aeneas is to be seen escaping from Troy with old Anchises on his shoulder and young Ascanius trotting along beside him on black-figure Athenian pots, and in Etruria in sixth century terracottas. There is even one small terracotta altar from a small town in central Italy to Aeneas the Lar. The legend has Homeric roots, since in the Iliad Aeneas was honoured like a god (11, 58) and Hector's equal (5, 467), a fit match for Diomedes and Achilles, the leading Greek warriors. He loved the gods and they protected him (20, 298 and 347) and Poseidon (20, 307) prophesied that his hopeful claim to succeed Priam would somehow be successful (20, 307).

The fact that Aeneas was religious, *pius*, and that he had a mysterious future after the fall of Troy, had already been implicit in Homer's epic, and a number of coastal towns had myths about him: Ainos in Thrace and Aineia in Chalcidice because of the coincidence of his name, and the sanctuaries of Aphrodite at Leucas, at Actium, and in Sicily. N.G. Hammond in his *Epirus* discusses the phenomenon. Writers elaborated the myth: the archaic poet Stesichorus seems to settle Aeneas in Italy, but Hellanicus of Lesbos in the fifth century BC certainly did so, and his more elaborate account of the wanderings had an influence on Dionysius of Halicarnassus, who was Virgil's contemporary, and a writer on Roman antiquities who throws much light on Virgil. Xenophon (Cyn. 1, 15) knew of the piety of Aeneas to his ancestral gods. Livius Andronicus and Naevius, the earliest stars of Roman poetry, had already adopted his lordship of the Latins, to which Hellanicus was witness, and his paternity of the Roman state.

Caesar's father had never even been a consul, but even as a boy he claimed descent on the one side from the immortal gods and on the other from many kings. By the gods he meant Venus, and the association of the Julian family as long as it lasted with Homeric antiquity was one of his grandest claims. When Aeneas died he too had become a god: the Native god of the Place, as Ovid tells us at length in the *Metamorphoses*. Virgil gives various hints about that, but he will not allow any divine halo to detract from his hero's humanity. It was common enough to raise no eyebrows though, should some family with long roots in the sleepy provinces of Italy to claim descent from figures in Homeric mythology. The king of those man-eating giants in the Odyssey, the unlikely and comic Laestrygonians, was called Lamos and he lived at 'Fargates', so the Larniae, a noble family Horace and Virgil knew, claimed that Lamos was their ancestor and the founder of Formiae. The claim of the Caesars to descent from Aeneas was no stronger and perhaps not as old.

Long before Virgil's time, Aeneas was being hailed as the forefather of the whole Roman race. Lucretius began his great philosophic poem by invoking

Venus as Mother of the children of Aeneas, *Aeneadum genetrix,* and Caesar had founded a temple of Venus Genetrix. Varro, Cicero and an inscribed stone of the republic confirm that it was respectable in Caesar's time to think of Aeneas as the great Roman ancestor. Ennius in his annals spoke of Venus as *genetrix patris nostri,* our father's mother (53). The title *Aeneadum genetrix* has even been found among the scribbles on the walls of a public building at Pompeii.[4]

Nonetheless, Virgil still had a wide variety of plot from which he had to select, the travels being easy enough but the second part of his epic, the foundation of the new city and the wars that must imitate older poetic wars, being beset with difficulties.

Underlying all his choices is his constant theme in the Georgics of the need to struggle as a farmer does, to fight the degeneration of the fruit tree and the river in flood that will carry you back, and yet at the same time he does not lose his Homeric sense that for those who saw Troy fall,

No hope remains for them but to despair (Aen. 2, 354)

It is a matter of serious thought for him to believe and to try to show that the Roman race is somehow regenerated by divine guidance, rather like the bees. His choice in the matter of Dido, which I believe he developed from Naevius, betrays deeply divided sympathies, which seem to me the important basis of feeling for any epic poet who is not merely writing a victorious chronicle.

In the later parts of the Aeneid though, we shall see that Virgil's touch is less certain, and that must have something to do with victorious nationalism. Antenor (1, 242-9), the Trojan who took the same route as Aeneas was once said to have taken, is mentioned only once, and that in a prayer, in the Aeneid. He was famous in the renaissance as founder of Padua, and no doubt he was rejected as friend or enemy to Aeneas because Padua was far from Rome.

As it is, Virgil has some trouble juggling between Rome and Alba Longa and Lavinium, to fit Aeneas into legendary Roman history. Alba was a real early fortified town in the Alban Hills, founded about 1100 BC and destroyed (by the Romans?) in the seventh century. A number of great Roman families were or believed they were Alban refugees. Virgil therefore has it founded by Ascanius, but Lavinium, the central town and holy place of the Latin federation from the sixth century, was near the spot Aeneas must have landed at, Pratica di Mare. As a sanctuary of Venus and a 'Trojan' link, Lavinium was respected by the Romans, and never destroyed. It withered slowly away into a village. Virgil was therefore probably forced by contemporary belief to put his antique king Latinus in Laurentum at the mouth of the Tiber and make Aeneas the founder of Lavinium. Rome itself was known to be a later foundation, and had legends of its own

127

which Virgil carefully skirted in a long archaeological prophecy as we shall see: the Roman foundation legend of Romulus and Remus and the Wolf could not accommodate Aeneas, and I suspect Virgil hated wolves anyway.

Bertha Tilly gave an archaeological account of these places as Virgilian Cities of the Roman Campagna (1945), from which one can still learn or relearn a great deal. The mouth of the Tiber is now three miles distant from the flourishing port of Ostia that stood on the shore under the Roman empire, though to the south near the Canale dello Stagno the shore has advanced only six-hundred feet. The north stream of the Tiber is a canal cut under Claudius when Ostia was built, the southern one, Fiumara, is the old mouth of the river.

In Ostia there was a sacred area of four temples (one to Venus and the others to unknown deities), which had been carefully preserved from the third century BC, and which Virgil knew as the spot where Aeneas first set foot on Italian earth. The three doubtful temples are probably to Fortune, Ceres and Hope, and a fifth enclosure to Jupiter marks the fall of a lightning flash. The cults are referred to in the Aeneid (7 and elsewhere) and it is likely that the strange things Virgil says about the first meal the Trojans ate in Latium refer to the ritual of this place. The small fortified camp which is the nucleus of Ostia is what Virgil (7, 157, 233, etc.) calls Troy, or New Troy. Of the sanctuary between the desolate ruins of withered Ardea (home of Turnus) and crumbled Lavinium in Virgil's time, we know from Strabo that the legend of Aeneas sanctified the place. Excavation supplies little more: temples were in use from the sixth century BC to the first, though we do not learn what gods were worshipped. Servius speaks of a temple of Castor and Pollux at Ardea that showed a painting (he does not hazard its date) in which Pallas Athene (?) transfixes Capaneus with a thunderbolt. Servius is reminded of this image by the Aeneid (1, 44) which has nothing to do with it. The dramatic death of a man with a flaming thunderbolt through both temples is reminiscent of the downfall of the hero knocked off his scaling ladder in the same way in a late interpolation in Euripides.

The Lavinium of Aeneas, Pratica di Mare, is about thirteen miles from Rome and now three from the sea-coast. It is an acropolis, but it has never been excavated. It is part village and part Renaissance palace of the Borghese family. Dionysius of Halicarnassus says 'all historians agree' that it was founded by Aeneas and his band of Trojans. The straw hut where he sacrificed the white sow was preserved there, and no one was permitted to enter it. This amazing relic could not be sidestepped, but Virgil permitted himself to transfer the miracle of the sow with the thirty piglets to the banks of the river Tiber (8, 815), because I suppose Lavinium had not been founded at the time. This is little enough latitude, and all the most ancient, legendary sites were equally demanding. Even the forest through which the Tiber once flowed must have been familiar to Virgil here and there. Bertha Tilly in 1945 still found at Castel Fusano 'a belt of the maritime forest indigenous to the west coast of Italy ... in all its primeval luxuriance'.

As for the hut, holy antiques of the kind were comparatively numerous, there was one left on the Capitol and one belonging to Romulus on the Palatine. Varro had seen the sow and thirty piglets in bronze, though we do not know where, but probably at Rome, and the priests proudly showed off an extremely ancient salted sow's carcase, which they said was the very one. Over this relic, Virgil casts a veil. He is also able to dodge the question of Aeneas's *penates* or household gods, which Lavinium as the metropolis of the Latins claimed to have kept even when government moved to Alba Longa (at Castel Gandolfo), and the kings of Rome and later the magistrates had to come to Lavinium to worship them. Lavinium and Laurentum, which was close by, became later the single city of Laurolavinium, with the same aristocracy, but of the temples at Lavinium we have only scattered and intriguing bits of terracotta and votive offerings from Virgil's century, catalogued by Lanciani in 1903. The countryside was already ruined and deserted in the age of Augustus: Horace (Odes 3, 27, 3) speaks of a lonely wolf 'running down out of the country round Lanuvium'.

In other matters Virgil was freer, and one is tempted to suggest that the further from Rome some myth or place was, the freer he felt, even in Italy. The hero of Temesa for example had a legend stretching from Homer's Odyssey to Pausanias, who notices him at Olympia (6, 6, 7), and it had an Italian ritual basis, but Virgil does not feel himself bound by it. He is not over-impressed by the sailors of Diomedes either, though they lived on as the giant shearwaters of the Isole Tremole, near Horace's home town of Venusia. Although he allows Daunus (king of Apulia down south) a genealogical role as an ancestor he is careful to skirt the stories about him, because they are too bizarre, too Illyrian to be useful for the Aeneid.

Virgil does plant Turnus in Ardea, as close as he could be to Lavinium and the heart of Latinity, and next-door neighbour to Lavinium, even though Turnus was the son of Daunus and the nymph Venilia, and the nymph Iuturna was his sister. Virgil made him 'king of the Rutuli', the tribe that lived round Ardea, who really existed, being guaranteed by a fragment of Cato. One late source even makes Daunus 'king of Ardea', and it is all too possible that the name Turnus of Ardea arose from some confusion before Virgil's time with *Tyrsenios*, Tyrrhenian (or Etruscan), spelt in Greek. Turnus was Virgil's most daring invention among the earthly characters of the Aeneid, and how a son of Daunus could be a king of Ardea is left unexplained. The Rutuli were an obscure, unimportant people, and that is why Virgil could mess their history about as he chose. Cicero in his

129

Republic (2, 5) says Romulus could have put Rome where he wished: if he wanted a coastal site 'the lands of the Rutuli or Aborigines lay ready to his hand'.

The Trojans are supposed to have set sail for Italy in spring following the fall of Troy which was in autumn. They built themselves twenty boats (1, 381), though the size of the fleet seems to vary. With this fleet they went first to Thrace (Aineia? Aeneas calls it Aeneadae: 3, 18). then to Delos where Anius was the prophet, and they were told to 'seek their old mother', so they tried Crete, which was a failure. Anchises, agreeing with a dream of the Lares, then suggested Italy, so off they sailed, touching land at Actium, and celebrating the Actian Games: Virgil obviously felt this anachronism irresistible. They touched land at Buthrotum where they met a Trojan refugee colony under Helenus and Andromache the widow of Hector. Helenus being a prophet as well as a prince issued some warnings, Aeneas dedicated a shield, 'spoils from the Greeks', almost certainly still to be seen in Virgil's time at Samothrace and dating perhaps from the Persian wars(?), and off they went to Italy, where they sacrificed to Juno and buried Anchises and spotted some Greek temples. So they dodged round the outside of Sicily before the storm wind swept them away to Carthage, and to Dido. Later they returned to this north-western spot of Sicily which Thucydides knew, and left a colony there. It is not much of an Odyssey, and it clings as far as it can to reality or accepted legend. It owes more than one might expect to tiny touches from Apollonius of Rhodes.

The texture of each individual book is carefully and consciously woven together, with devices like past events recalled in Homer's Odyssey by the hero as first person. Homer is more casual of course, and Odysseus is a cheerful liar where Aeneas always seems at least psychologically to be carrying a huge bag of household gods and an aged father. But the first person narrative offers us the entire fall of Troy, which the Iliad had not treated. The Iliad was about the events of three days in a war that felt as if it lasted for ever, as the journeys of Odysseus did, with various periods of magical or sacred time before and after.

The Odyssey showed the way for an epic cut-in-two, with twelve books (Virgil cut them to six) about the hero's journeys, and twelve (cut to six again) on his home territory. The divisions between book and book are late and dubious in Homeric poetry, which cuts all too easily because it is episodic. Virgil is interested in this, and varies the connection of book and book, but the book is his unit, the book is to him a poem. I have noticed that book by book there are in some cases underlying themes that secretly draw the book together, and it seems to me they are such things as fire in book two, water in book five ending with the corpse of the drowned sailor, earth in book six. This may not find favour as an instrument of analysis: it will not win prizes but it may amuse readers and reveal something of the mind of the poet. Virgil as we shall see in detail was a ruthless plunderer and improver of his own poems.

To begin a major narrative poem when you are over forty is to undertake a life-work. Virgil is supposed to have spent eleven years on the Aeneid, and at least this period of time appears to be true – except that he first spent two years or so of the eleven between 30 and 19 BC (when he died) in considering and planning his epic. Nine years means a book and a third a year, and they are anything from 705 to 952 lines long. Only the sixth book about the underworld is over 900 lines, until we get to the last three books, which I think may reflect the longer books of the Iliad as opposed to the Odyssey. Twelve hundred lines a year mean 100 lines a month, 3 or 4 a day of the final version. No doubt writing an epic is like walking a battlement with your head under one arm. It is the first step that counts. The shortest book in the Aeneid is the fourth with 705 lines, carefully cut in imitation of a Greek tragedy, with Dido speaking in the exquisite Hellenistic voice of Catullus (64 lines), which Virgil does not usually imitate.

There are innumerable passages where Virgil shows imitative genius in many different directions, such as that of the post-Homeric Aethiopis, but his voice is more generally the voice of Ennius, the great and the only serious example of Latin hexa-meter narrative verse. He is happy to take a word like *silvicola*, forest dwelling, from Naevius (Aen. 10, 551 of Faunus), but Naevius wrote mostly in 'Saturnian' verses: *superbiter contemptim conterit legiones*, proudly contemptuously crushes regiments. It is a fine, vigorous noise but it was an obscure and disused track in the forest of the past.

Ennius was a living force in Roman poetry, and some people preferred him to Virgil. His trumpets, at *tuba terriili sonitu tarantara dixit*, the trumpet sounded taratantara, are splendid. They were too famous for Virgil to imitate or he was shy of the word taratantara. He has a number of horns and trumpets in the Aeneid, including the fearful Alpenhorn that shakes the innocent snow from the Alps, but the signal for the final duel is *signa canunt*, the bugles sing. His Ennian archaisms, *Anchisa generate* and the rest, are used always for some precise purpose. A speech of Jupiter for example (10, 100f.) will be full of Ennian grammar (*fuat, infit*) and alliterations. The Sibyl is herself a piece of antiquity (6, 317f.) and Ennian language is noticeable in her habit of speech.[6] The Annals of Ennius had a long and numerous line of offspring, and epic annalists are, so to speak, two a penny in the not much trodden galleries of later Roman literature.

Virgil borrowed from the *Annals* of Ennius and equally from his tragedies certain traditional tricks of speech. We know that he had the habit of archaism from the time of the Eclogues, though there he may have intended only a rustic colour. He may well have been inspired in his treatment of the Fury Allecto in book seven of the Aeneid by scenes of which only fragments survive from the *Annals* of Ennius, where Discordia retreats underground. Fraenkel attacked Norden on this subject (*JRS*, 1945), which is one of sacred topography that aroused deep passions in him, with a vigour now alas long vanished from classical studies.

But Virgil's decisions about Ennius were limited by plot. The sulphurous and fuming waters of the Nar, which Edward Lear in his time thought highly picturesque may or may not have been an entry to the underworld for Ennius, but if so it was a rare coincidence. The place Odysseus visited by the Greek Acheron was no use to Virgil and his underworld must be connected with Roman prophecies: so it had better be Cumae for him.

On the Monument the climax of the boasts of Augustus was in his sixth and seventh consulate

> after I had put an end to civil wars and by universal agreement had total power and authority over all things, I transferred the republic to the will of the Roman people and their senate. By their decree I was named Augustus and the gateposts of my house were dressed in laurel, and a civic crown was hung above my doors, and a golden shield put in the Julian court, given to me by the senate and people for my valour, mercy, justice and religion ... The senates, the knights and the whole people in my thirteenth consulate called me father of my country.

That was the highest accolade August could come up with, because it meant that he was a second Aeneas. It had to be the climax of his monumental claims. 'When this was written I was in my seventy-sixth year'. Augustus had cleared the sea of pirates (25) and recaptured thirty-thousand runaway slaves whom he handed over to their masters to be crucified. He had penetrated to Meroe and Ethiopia, he had held world games (which Virgil's opening to the second Georgic imagines) and restored temples.

The honour of his title 'father of his fatherland' was conferred publicly in 2 AD after Virgil's death, but the grandeur of Augustus was a terrifying presence even to his friends, and Virgil trod as carefully as Horace. He was concerned to make the epic of Aeneas not just Roman but more widely Italian. That is why, when the ram's horn of the fury Allecto sounded near Lavinium (7, 512f.), it was heard in the Alban Hills to the east, and far away up the Tiber valley to the north. Allecto is Discordia, the very spirit of civil war. So in the Aeneid Italy is united if only by civil war, as the Catalogue like Homer's in the Iliad begins to suggest, and still more widely united when Aeneas goes to fetch allies from the Po valley,

132

from Mantua and from the Ligurians. Virgil is less interested in those foreign peoples who figure in the cloudier boasts of the imperial monument.

When Aeneas landed, he made his arrangements with Latinus, the king of the Latins, who knew by an oracle he must marry off his daughter to a foreigner. Latinus thought his neighbour Turnus would do, being foreign enough, but when he saw Aeneas he realised what was meant and that was how the trouble started, with plenty of help from Juno and her hellish herald.

But Virgil must also deal with the Arcadian influence on Roman origins, which was well-known to historians. The wolf-cult called the Lupercalia, the sacred dances and the Pan in the Palatine Cave were all thought to be evidence for Arcadia. Augustus even remitted the taxes of the Arcadian Pallantion, an antique and crumbling village in his day, because it was thought the Palatine Hill at Rome, which was Augustus's headquarters and so has given us the word Palace, took its name from the ancient Arcadian town.

So Aeneas goes to see the old Arcadian settler Evander, who shows him round his few hills, which will one day be the site of Rome. This bold stroke which Virgil follows through consistently does not appear to have raised any objections, and it may not have been original. Pallas the son and heir of pastoral Evander may be modelled on Daskylos the son and heir of King Lycus who was sent with Jason in Apollonius of Rhodes.

Evander had to take a step down in rank in order to enter the Aeneid. In Arcadia, at the ancient Pallantion, he was the son of Hermes and the nymph Themis, daughter of the river Ladon, and he was worshipped as a god; but as a man he had known Priam and Anchises, a connection which Virgil (8, 156f.) preferred to his doubtful divine glamour. His mention of Hesione sister of Priam and of Salamis where she gave birth to Telamon suddenly involves us in the obscurest of genealogies and of myths, which may have been a theme for tragedy, but may be meant simply to establish the heroic status of Evander in a Homeric manner, and to confuse all questions about him. At any rate, it establishes Evander's admiration for Anchises, and their 'guest friendship', and so helps to legitimate the presence of the Trojan Aeneas (and his Julian descendants) in Italy.

Livy has his own version of all these matters but it is probably a few years after Virgil's. He maintains that Latinus king of the Aborigines (pastoral savages who lived on the hills in villages without walls) resisted Aeneas; but they made peace and Aeneas did then marry Latinus's daughter Lavinia and Ascanius was probably their son. Turnus, the rejected fiancé, attacked them and Latinus was killed, but Aeneas got together all the allies he could, who were then named Latins. Still, he was then killed too, and buried by the river Numicius, and duly declared a god as *jupiter indiges*.

This narrative is much less use than Virgil's for an epic, though its existence as a version of history does explain why Virgil was put off the deification of Aeneas and the interesting role in that episode of Anna, Dido's sister and confidante.

The version of the story of Aeneas that is to be found in Dionysius of Halicarnassus is equally unhelpful. It is a complicated account in which the Latium of Latinus was an old aboriginal region from the Tiber to the Liris about a hundred miles south, and Romulus who founded Rome came sixteen generations after the fall of Troy, about 750 BC. He attributed a good deal to the help of Greeks, such as Oenotrus son of Arcadian Lycaon and his brother Peuketios the Iapygian (of whom you may read more in my Horace). He appears to be a daemon of the Pine-forest, and a mythic king in the far south of Italy, while Lycaon was transformed into a wolf. Troy never really fell in this version, because Aeneas held out in the acropolis, and his son Ascanius survived in Dascylitis until he returned to rebuild Troy. Aeneas moved to Orchomenos in Arcadia, and then Italy where he had a son Romulus. The odyssey this eccentric Greek source attributes to Aeneas explains more places in his mythology even than Virgil (or Ovid) mentions, and it is small wonder that it ends up suggesting that maybe Aeneas never came, or that it was a different Aeneas: the number of his burial places puzzled its author.

The Aeneas site that most surprises in the journey as Dionysius of Halicarnassus traced it from one to another is the racetrack or stadion of Aeneas and Aphrodite on Zakynthos, between a stop at Kinaithion and one on Leucas with a visit to Dodona, where Anchises left some bronze bowls. The island of Zakynthos was first founded by a hero of that name, who was a cousin of Aeneas, being a descendant of Dardanus.* The island is oddly innocent of archaeology, but the whereabouts of the racecourse are said to be known.

There were a number of these combined sites of Aphrodite and Aeneas in those waters, and several of them had athletic meetings of some kind, which were always coastal (Olympia itself was only a day's walk from the coast). Greek athletic meetings seem to have begun in the eighth century at the time the Homeric poems began to circulate. Relics like the bronze bowls of Anchises at Dodona can of course reason-ably be assumed to be phoney. But Kinaithion was an obscure site in the north-west Peloponnese now called Kalavryta, destroyed in 220 BC and refounded as a Roman colony, maybe by Hadrian (Paus. 8, 19, 1 with my note 138). It lay inland from Patras, which was a colony favoured by Augustus, but the connection with Aeneas, mythical as it is, must be earlier than the third century BC, so must the connection with Zakynthos, where one longs to know more. The only games Virgil has time for, after Sicily in book five, are

---

* Ancestor of the royal race of Troy.

the Actian games, which are significant to him for contemporary reasons (3, 280).

All the same, the Sibyl of Cumae is a strange intrusion in the Aeneid. We can see why Virgil was interested in her, if only for her romantic local sanctuary and her hallowed status as a Roman prophetess. But Dionysius of Halicarnassus thought of the Erythraen Sibyl in Asia Minor who told Aeneas to sail westwards, or else it was the oracle at Dodona. He felt that prophecy was a Greek monopoly I suppose and it does make more sense of the odyssey of Aeneas if it begins with divine commands from an Asian oracle.

But Virgil, having studied Homer, did not want it to make sense, because if it did then why the delays? Dionysius's Aeneas was told at Erythrae that after they had eaten their plates, as they did in Italy, they must follow a four-footed guide and make their city where it rested. This curious procedure is extremely common in Greek mythology and was so wide-spread that the army of Sparta for example used to follow a goat, and camp wherever it lay down to rest – a pleasing kind of journey no doubt. The Trojans were trying to sacrifice a sow (to Ceres I assume), when the intelligent brute escaped, and galloped away three miles from the riverside, then it flopped down exhausted. Aeneas heard a voice out of the forest telling him to build, or else he had a dream and next morning the sow had thirty piglets, so he knew he was building a settlement to last thirty years.

The care with which every bizarre variation of the myth was gathered and recorded does indicate how very carefully Virgil had to tread. One of his problems with Aeneas was the vast proliferation of his mythology, and another was how to fit this casual Greek wanderer exclusively into Rome.

What was to be done about the Greek cities of the south, so despised by Mommsen that he said their only contribution to civilised life was cooking, and boxing? It was lucky that they were Greek foundations and therefore later than the Trojan war. But Galaesus (7, 535), the peaceful farmer in the Aeneid who owned five flocks of sheep and five herds of cattle and a hundred ploughs, takes his name from the river that runs down from the moors at Tarentum – and Virgil speaking of its people (5, 575) still refers to Galaesus.

Once again, the important point is that the whole of Italy is involved. Horace (Od. 2, 6) like Virgil persistently refers to Tarentum as a pastoral place, which in his day of course it was.

> But if the Fates will not allow Tibur,
> Then I shall seek Galaesus with my flock

Horace's poem (Od. 2, 6) was written before Virgil's tribute to the vast wandering and returning flocks and herds of the southern moorlands, and to the phenomenon of transhumance south of Rome.

To Virgil it was partly a device to connect his Galaesus with Campania, where Galaesus could play his hopelessly peaceful part in the quarrel with Turnus. But Daunus hardly occurs: Turnus is carried away to his city (10, 688) and Aeneas speaks to Evander (8, 146) about the terrible Daunians making war, but that is all. He was too hot a potato to handle, and peaceful Galaesus is surely his substitute, and the substitute for Phalanthus, 'a country King' in Horace.

All the scenes of fighting in Latium are rearranged by Virgil as he chooses. Even the bronze bowls at Dodona and in southern Italy he ignores, though he likes the waterfall at Tibur, which is called Albunea (7, 81-91, and Hor. *Od.* 1, 7, 12). It once sheltered a Sibyl like some wild ecstatic nun in a painting by Magnasco, a spirit of the place incarnate, but Virgil makes it even more tremendous as an oracle of Faunus where a murky lake breathed sulphur and the priest slept on the untreated skins of sacrificed sheep (as petitioners did at Oropos in Greece) in the hope of interesting dreams. The fuming and sulphurous god of this water from the rock was called Mephitis, and was worshipped on the revolting, unreformed Esquiline in Rome, at Cremona and elsewhere.

It was through a place even more spectacularly nasty, and without the solemnity of the thunderous fall of water at Tibur, that Virgil has his nasty fury of discord, Allecto, disappear (7, 563f.) at the valleys called Amsanctus, 'the horrid cave and the wild breath of Dis'. The word for breath, *spiracula*, means a gas twisting as it rises, and is used by Pliny as the ordinary word for vent-holes of sulphurous emanations at Puteoli and elsewhere.

The consensus of scholars used to be that Virgil came closest to the traditional account of Aeneas and his wanderings in the third book, but that is to be examined. I have already said that I think the sixth book is the crucial one and the hinge of the whole construction, but in the third and fifth books there is a certain aimlessness, as there is in the corresponding part of the Odyssey, so I am not sure whether it matters that Virgil was in some way closer to a traditional treatment. After all, there really was no traditional epic treatment, only prose. Perhaps Virgil really did start by writing a prose account of what went into each book. Any writer would have to do something like that, if only in the form of notes. Virgil was not be free in the way that Homer had been, whose method of composing epic poetry we can scarcely understand and Virgil cannot have begun to grasp. He was condemned to write (I think) or at best dictate, as if he were a court official. He must have carried much more in his head than we do, because he had no reference books in the modern sense. That combination of imagination and memory, both sharper in condition than they would be today, in our world, is at the heart of his kind of poetry.

He did not give up his habit of patchwork, or of setting one patch most precisely against another, or his sense of an underlying sea-swell in the poetry which would carry it forward until when he got to the end of the Aeneid it overspilled from book to book for the last three books. He was a wonderful storyteller, and master of many traditional techniques, both classical and Hellenistic. He attended as a youth a course of lectures by Epidius given at Rome, but his recourse to rhetoric is sparse. The same lectures were attended later by Augustus and by Antony, but the three of them did not share any special secret about language, and the touches of rhetoric in the Aeneid seem to me to have come to the consciousness of Virgil by way of the stage, and what passes for poetry there. We are lamentably ill supplied with Latin verse drama, but Virgil did have access to Greek tragic poetry. He never saw a sober production, but at least he could read it.

As he grew older writing and writing, and spitting up blood from tubercular disease, as one must assume, he came to share the philosophic openness of Horace, and it is to be hoped that they shared many pleasures. They were a quirky old pair of bachelors, in middle age in the twenties BC. They stood on the margins of Roman life, and so did their patron Maecenas. It is true that Maecenas had a *froideur* with Augustus about the conspiracy of Varro Murena, and it sounds like an incestuous explosion, as many of the worst quarrels are, but in this case the surface never cracked. The tension was contained, and Maecenas remained on the friendliest everyday terms with his poets.

There were young poets growing up who must have felt overshadowed by Virgil and Horace. Tibullus was a true poet, and a simple, perfect writer of Latin, and Propertius was as inventive and brilliant, and perhaps as wilful and ambitious as anyone. Tibullus died when Virgil died, hardly beyond his first promise, and Propertius probably a year or two later, not much older than thirty.

> Yield Roman poets, yield Greek poets,
> Here's something greater than the Iliad.

This exaggerated praise of the Aeneid, which 'is being born', suggested an ironic overtone to Ezra Pound, a character to whom Propertius greatly appealed. And I have often suspected that Propertius showed his irritation with the older poet, since he is parodying the Aeneid (7, 45-6), and with more malice than justice. But his apparently magical touch depends on the magisterial style of Virgil as well as on exquisite fantasies and marvellously Greek noises.

Virgil's style in the Aeneid is one of steady command of the lifting rhythms

137

of his early verse and of the texture he wove from his many great examples in Greek as well as Latin. He was a learned writer in the sense that he was conscious of many wonderful and inspiring examples at once. He was like Spenser at his best, who drew his breath from the French Pléiade as well as from Catullus and Virgil. The reasons why Spenser failed to write an Aeneid are surely political. (Even his stanza form was not a completely disabling obstacle, though Milton had more intelligence. But Spenser's involvement in Ireland was a terrible mistake.) There was no Elizabethan epic possible that we could read today. The nearest I suppose was the Henry V of Shakespeare. It is curious to compare Shakespeare as historical dramatist with the problems of Virgil's Aeneid: I do not mean the plays that depend on Plutarch, but his English chronicle plays. In his lyrical youth he depends as much on Spenser as he does on Marlowe, but he does not suffer from the grandiose momentum and the dragging variations of Spenser's narrative verse. The texture and the underlying rhythm of verse depends on a force that we later call greatness, and not the other way round. A poet with the strong and sweeping wings of Virgil in the Aeneid must also have been a wide-ranging and precise critic, but the most illuminated, the most illuminating critic will not necessarily be that poet.

The force of the Aeneid is multiple. Certainly there is a feeling and a summoning up of Homeric epic, and Virgil comes closer to that than other contemporary or later Latin poets – yet still not very close except in details. But the force of all Virgil's poetry is a glimpse of hope that saw out his lifetime and Horace's. Fundamentally its force is his very unusual love of the whole of Italy.

The characters in the Aeneid hardly exist. They may be made of the best materials, but these materials are only like the March Hare's best butter that would not make a watch work. You could poke a finger through any of them, Aeneas and Turnus included. The elderly country kings are very nice, and there is something real about Juno, the demon queen, and about Allecto, whose disappearing act always reminds me of the devil's fart in Dante, which may be based on it.

The exception to this severe view of Virgil's characters in the epic is partly in the Boys' Own loyalty of Aeneas's companions (which can be matched in Robin Hood), but more I think in Nisus and Euryalus and possibly in Camilla and her grace. Nisus and Euryalus are the Hyacinthine young men who die and still look beautiful. They are 'both in the flower of their age', both Arcadians 'like the young men in spring' in the Eclogues. Aeneas's son Ascanius might have been such a young man, but Evander's son Pallas dies and he does not. He carries too great a weight of the future (12, 168) and is just another faithful henchman who must not get in the light of the hero, Aeneas (12, 385: Donatus was worried by this line).

If the position is as I see it, this bonding has more to do with Virgil's personal sexuality than with any model. The sadness of Orpheus and the bewilderment of Aristaeus seem for a few moments real, but Eurydice hardly begins to exist. The greatest exception to all this might be Dido, behind whom stands all the traditional power of romantic love. Yet in book four little is left of that except hysterical dramatic rhetoric, and I do not think one can believe in her. In the underworld she is only an image of guilt, an indignant shadow.

There is a rumour that reaches us through a grammarian who had heard from older men that Virgil's executors altered the order of books in the Aeneid, making the old book two into book three and the old three book two. If that is true (and it may be only the twittering of ancient academics I think) then the literary executors, Varius and Tucca, were quite right to make the switch. But it looks likelier that Virgil had considered it for himself. We do hear from Macrobius that Virgil had written to Augustus, 'I get frequent letters from you … As for my Aeneid, if I had anything worth your while to hear, I would certainly send it, but it is such a big thing to have begun, that I seem to myself I must have been mad to take it on, since as you know I must spend further and more powerful study on the work' (Macrob. 1, 24, 10-11). This must be from the letter or letters of reply written to Augustus in Spain. It is naturally only a polite excuse; the poet is not ready.

There is one fragment of Servius that indicates the kind of troubles Virgil had to contend with in planning the Aeneid. Two traditions about Amata are recorded (at Aen. 7, 51), either of which would make her a virago as appalling as Medea. She was the wife of Latinus, who had a daughter for Aeneas to marry (and so inherit) but Virgil says his only son had been snatched away in his first youth. Servius records that Amata blinded them or murdered babies to favour Aeneas. This extraordinary tale combined with her Bacchic madness (Aen. 7, 401-5 and 585) suggests that there was a Latin play about this tragic lady, and that Aeneas must have had some trouble twisting her story to suit the Aeneid (12, 54-80).

It is fascinating to see that Gladstone first noticed the strong and masculine quality of Virgil's women in the Aeneid as opposed to the shyer way women behave in Homer: 'they are agitated by violent passions and meet with violent ends'.[7] Gladstone had also noticed that a strength of character appears in Homeric heroines when they are recycled, to use a modern word, for the Athenian stage. It is a pity that we are so ignorant of the Latin tragic stage, as I have said. Yet I feel that whatever the plays were like, Virgil was more selective, more intelligent.

There is a clue worth following in the first book of Dante's *Inferno*, where Virgil reveals himself:

I was a poet, I sang of that just
Son of Anchises who sailed out of Troy
When Ilion the proud had burnt to dust. (73-5)

Dante calls him the honour and the light of all poets, and declares that his own prolonged study and great love of Virgil has been repaid,

Since you my author and my master are,
And it was from you only that I took
That lovely style that I am honoured for.

There are a number of reminiscences of the Aeneid in this encounter, including a sad reference to 'poor Italy for which the virgin Camilla, and Turnus, Nisus and Euryalus died' (108). We do not often think of Virgil as a writer of that kind, and he is not to us so thrillingly suggestive, so solidly glamorous. It may be worth trying for a moment to look at him through Dante's intelligent and awe-stricken eyes.

VI

HAPPY LANDINGS

Virgil looked like a tall, somewhat formidable countryman; not like someone from Rome, which was full of ex-slaves, but like someone who came into the market once a week in the square at Mantua, or the square at Florence in 1910, or someone who ran sheep from Perugia down as far as Tarentum in 1810. His work was massive reading and just a little writing: he was a poet of an old-fashioned kind. He wrote verse of an extraordinary balance and great intensity and in the end he was like a waterfall, like a great river of words, as Dante said – but only in verse, never in prose. Day after day he read, and he distilled, like a swarm of bees building up their honeycomb. He was as disciplined and in his intellectual journeys – which we have hardly touched on because they hardly show – he was as various, as far-ranging and as daring. As he worked at the Aeneid, he began to be old before his time.

Virgil may have begun to write anywhere in the twelve books. But he must have worked systematically through each one, so we should take them like that, in the order we have them. There is an objectivity about them that imposes itself, arising from the way he objectifies his own emotions in the material. You can seldom see him stand aside. He is now, in his middle age, not at all given to self-expression, but he is fascinated by his business, by Italy and by what he writes about. Sometimes he writes about a wilderness of antiquity, or a wonderland. His sea-coast of Africa is a wonderland that influenced Shakespeare in *The Tempest*. But these are shifting scenes, they lead into his enormously ambitious epic.

I sing arms and the man first from the seacoast
Of Troy ... (Aen. 1, 1-2)

Virgil's new book is about battles and fights and a journey, by which a fated exile or refugee came to Italy and the Latin coast, 'much tossed about by sea and lands, by the force of the gods and because of savage Juno's unforgetting anger. He suffered much in war to found a city, and bring his gods to Latium: hence the Latin race, the Alban fathers and the towers of high Rome' (3-6).

The language is terse, the phrases are weighty, the explanation is ambiguous.

But it looks quite clear. The verse at once proclaims a master poet who permits himself old-fashioned technical licence in his versification, from the second line on. He is not writing about Odysseus and his experience of sea and land and the minds of men, nor about Achilles and his rage. Yet it is obvious he will emulate both the great Homeric epics. His only problem is rationalist and theological. Can there be such fury in heavenly minds as Juno showed to religious Aeneas? It is a good Epicurean question.

Virgil does not answer his own severe question, but takes off at once on the story of Carthage, with the implicit answer that indeed there can be such divine fury.

Does he believe it? I greatly doubt it. But writing epic at all compels him to respect the convention that there are gods. He is most respectful to every belief and every ancestor of Augustus.

Juno is the Greek Hera, consort of Zeus, and at Rome she is the goddess of women and their sexuality. But Homer makes Hera savage, and Virgil, who needs a villain in heaven, more than follows suit. Her old image in Italy (at Lanuvium) bore arms and wore a goatskin cloak, and she had some connection with the Lupercalia. She was certainly one of the great goddesses, and Aeneas could not prosper until she changed her mind about him.

Virgil never loses sight of Hera's stubborn rage, or of her ultimate conversion. Her power is essential to the plan of the Aeneid, which is all but operatic. The roles of Iuturna, sister of Turnus, and of the fury Allecto are subsidiary to hers, and she has a real majesty, she is *Saturnia Iuno*, a most ancient goddess. The role of evil in this poem does seem to go beyond anything we would expect, and beyond what epic poetry inevitably demands. This theme would be worth a more specialised study.

There was an ancient city of the Tyrians, opposite Italy and the Tiber estuary, rich and very warlike (12-14). So far Virgil's account is true. Carthage was a Phoenician colony (from Tyre) that made inroads in western Sicily, southern Sardinia and Spain (Cadiz). He goes on to claim Juno loved it more than anywhere else on earth except Samos, the island sacred to her, and in fact it was refounded by Caesar as Iunonia. But she heard of the arrival of Trojans who would overturn the Phoenician towers of Carthage, and would now ruin Libya. So in fear of this and remembering the Trojan war, let alone her grudge over the Judgement of Paris and the Rape of Ganymede, she kept Aeneas storm-tossed and wandering the seas, far from Latium. So heavy a burden it was to found Rome (33).

It is almost as if it was Rome Juno dreaded, nothing else. She was insulted by Paris choosing Venus as the loveliest, and infuriated by Jove falling for a boy. So far the plot is neat. The overturning of the towers of Carthage by Rome had not

142

happened until 146 BC, but the goddess took a long and suspicious view. The Trojans were hardly out of sight of Sicily on their search for Latium when she brewed up a storm. She said to herself: should I give up, can I not turn them aside from Italy. The fates forbid me. But Athene smashed the whole Greek fleet, out of her rage with Ajax: she flung the lightning, ruined the ships and skewered him on a rock.

This fine and baroque scene of divine violence must come from post Homeric epic, and it is reflected here and there from Aeschylus onwards. In the Odyssey Ajax was merely killed by Poseidon while scrambling ashore. His sin was the rape of Cassandra at the altar, and the theft of the Palladion, a statue of Pallas Athene which was the Luck of Troy, so that Athene was a likely avenger. We are warned in a few lines of sizzling verse what the Homeric gods can do, before we come to a description of Juno's storm.

What makes the violence more interesting to us is that Accius in a play uses similar phrases, but Lucretius (6, 300) makes them an argument against the justice of the gods. Virgil evidently thinks that in a speech by Juno, his demonic Queen, he need not pay attention to this. In an epic the gods interfere on earth and they bear grudges.

Virgil must establish vengeful Juno before he begins his story, because her role is more coherent than any divine role in Homer and more terrible. She

> ... gripes the trembling Game,
> The Wretch yet hissing from her Father's Flame,

as Dryden puts it. But there modernity overcomes him and he has the goddess bind him to a rock whereas Virgil skewers him with it.

Juno rushes off at the height of her rage to find Aeolus, a god of winds in the Aeolian islands since before the Greeks discovered him there. That was long ago, and rumours of him reached the Odyssey. Odysseus has a wind tied up in a bag, but here there is something volcanic about the winds, as Ovid's explanation goes of earth-quakes like the pulses of human veins in which he thinks air circulates.

> Where in a spacious Cave of living Stone,
> The Tyrant Aeolus from his airy Throne
> With Pow'r Imperial curbs the struggling Winds,
> And sounding Tempests in dark Prisons binds.
> This way and that th' impatient Captives tend,
> And pressing for Release the Mountains rend ...

Homer's Aeolus was more civilised, he lived in a palace, and the winds

143

(Odyss. 10) were incidental to the story: Virgil's treatment is more barbarous, and they enter more intimately into his plot, reflecting Juno's nastiness. Lucretius has winds billowing in their cages which are clouds (6, 189f.) in a passage of splendidly cumulative power. In Virgil the metaphor is treated as real. It is Jove (60) who has contrived their prison, fearing how terrible they would be if they got loose. This is almost a different metaphor for civil war, but if Virgil thinks of that he suppresses it.

Juno bribes the old brute Aeolus with a nymph and he eats out of her hand. The winds are paraded and the storm produced (80-90) and suddenly Aeneas (92) is mentioned for the first time by name. It has taken 100 lines to create a back-drop of savagery and wild sea, so that he laments in fear of his life, recalling as happy those who died under the walls of Troy before their parents' eyes. He even wishes Diomedes* had killed him (2, 5, 297). It is assumed that readers of the Aeneid will recognise Diomedes as 'Tydeus's son' and Achilles as 'Aaiakos's son' in this Homeric lament.

There is indeed a certain experience of life as well as of literature in all this. The rigging screeches, where traditionally in Latin it hissed (87), and those who have heard that sound will recognise its authenticity. The terrific storm continues and makes the recollection of the heroic past feeble in contrast to it. They smash on hidden rocks called the Altars that really existed, though they lay between Sicily and Sardinia. Virgil has moved them, they are the kind of naturalistic detail that Callimachus had introduced to narrative verse.

The verse derives mostly from Homer, but its mastery is of a Hellenistic kind. That has often been said about Virgil, but here he is writing like the most dazzling late poet, like Callimachus himself: I mean a great poet whose poem has every virtue but greatness, every inspiration but that of the muse. All the same, Virgil's storm at sea frightens one, and leaves one very cold and wet and dizzy. Even Neptune sees what is happening and calls in the winds, rescues ships impaled on rocks, brings back the sun and opens a way through the Syrtes.

All this Virgil arranges with shameless brevity. The sea's raging dies, he says, 'as a rioting mob falls quiet at the voice of some great man'. So he really had been thinking about that deep-seated metaphor, which is convincing in everything but its conclusion (153).

Aeneas's people are tired out. There is an anchorage in a long bay where an island makes a harbour. We are in Africa (160) but Aeneas of course is lost in a suddenness of silence: he comes to a cave on the shore, and inside it 'fresh falling water, thrones in living rock' (167), a line that might have come from any Eclogue or from Theocritus, yet it takes its effect from the terrific tempest and

---

* Achilles's friend and a survivor from Troy.

the rock that skewered ships, the rock that impaled a man. The symbolism of the line is that of death, a place of fresh cool water, shadow and tranquillity, a phrase that transformed in time into the *refrigerium, lucem et pacem* for which the church still prays.

> Within a long Recess there lies a Bay,
> An Island shades it from the rowling Sea,
> And forms a Port secure for Ships to ride,
> Broke by the jutting Land on either side:
> In double Streams the briny Waters glide.
> Betwixt two rows of Rocks, a Sylvan Scene
> Appears above, and Groves for ever green:
> A Grott is formed beneath, with mossy Seats,
> To rest the Nereids, and exclude the heats.
> Down through the Crannies of the living Walls
> The Crystal Streams descend in murm'ring Falls ...

In this magical spot seven ships come together and ride without anchors. 'No haulsers, no bearded Anchors', says Dryden, 'no ropes no anchor's crooked bite' (169) says Virgil.

The Trojans come to the longed for sand and lay down their salty limbs. Suddenly in this landfall Virgil is not only the master we knew, but the great poet we hoped he would be. The moment (157-73) did not last long and this scene will dissolve as swiftly into another as if we were still in the fourth Georgic, but it has its place and function in the book and in the Aeneid. We are nearly a quarter of the way through book one after all, which is Virgil's first introduction: we shall have several. We can tell already that there is something tricky about this nymph-haunted place. The nymphs of Africa are too wild to be reliably friendly.

The sailors strike fire from a flint and make bread with the determined cunning of Boy Scouts (174-9). Aeneas climbs a cliff to look for survivors but not a ship is to be seen, only on the shore he luckily spots three stags leading their herds. First he shoots the three leaders with their high heads and branching horns, then tackles the others in the leafy woods, until he has seven for his seven ships.

Aeneas divides the wine Acestes gave them when they left Sicily and makes them a speech like one out of Horace, but a fine one: My friends, we are not innocent of evils, we have suffered worse, and the god will bring an end to this; you know the rage of Scylla, the sounding rocks, the Cyclopes, so call up your courage, perhaps one day you will remember this with enjoyment. We are heading for Latium, our quiet destined seat (198-206). But the speech rests solidly on the Odyssey (12, 208f.), and also it appears in Naevius, so one has no right to be certain of Horace's influence. Drink is an important ingredient I feel, in Virgil's as in Horace's ideas of the heroic mood.

Aeneas is sick with fear and anxiety and sad with losses, but Jove looks down and Venus weeps over Aeneas and his Trojans, who were supposed (236) to become commanders of land and of sea, and now look at them. Antenor has founded Padua beyond the mighty river Timavus. This argument is cleverly placed and rhetoric is not the least of Venus's wiles. Virgil had also taken lessons in the subject from Epidius. The poet had mastered enough rhetoric to put on a faultless performance for Venus.

Antenor has many and contradictory legends. He must be connected with the Timavus because of a connection with Enetica, and Croatia (Liburni), but Virgil assumes he was a diplomat who escaped from Troy by his merits. Polygnotos in his fifth century BC painting of Troy at Delphi showed Antenor's leopard skin on his door that guaranteed his immunity (Paus. 10, 27, 3). Why should he be more favoured than Aeneas? As for the Timavus, it was a famous natural wonder because it ran underground, and when the river re-emerged for its final gallop split up into numerous channels over a dozen or more miles of coast. Virgil had used it in the eighth Eclogue, and this was a final gratuitous few lines of waterworks.

Jove (254) smiles at this outburst from his daughter, and enjoys a few kisses (254-6). He then reaffirms his old promises and explains how Rome is to be founded. Three hundred years (not thirty) will bring Romulus nursed by a wolf, to beget the Roman people.

> To them I set no limit and no time,
> But empire without end ... (278-9)

Juno will change her tune and co-operate 'to nourish Romans lords of the world, a gowned people' (282). They will be citizens that is, and dress as gentlemen. (Is there not a burdensome undertone to this prophecy? All Italy in formal dress, a master-race in top-hats?) The time will come when they will take Greece, and Caesar's empire will reach the Ocean and his fame the stars: Julius named after Iulus the Trojan. He will come to you 'Weighed with the loot of all the Orient' (289).

The speech of Jove is as well constructed as that of Venus, and it makes an impressively thunderous noise, ending with the creak of the Gates of War as they shut. Augustus did shut them and was proud of the fact. Jove sends Mercury at once to arrange matters with Dido in Carthage. Dido and her people were to take in Aeneas and his sea-shaken companions (304).

Meanwhile Aeneas has passed an anxious night, and at dawn he goes exploring to see what coast this is. He leaves his fleet hidden under a hollow rock by the dark shade of overhanging trees (310-1), and away he wanders with his faithful friend Achates. Achates is a kind of Agrippa, not much use in an epic, although no leader should be without one, and in the antique age he can carry the weapons and run messages.

Who should meet them but Venus, pretty as a picture? She is dressed like a Spartan girl or 'Like Thracian Harpalyce who wore out / The horses of swift Hebrus in her flight'. The odd thing about this image is that Harpalyce is unknown. It is just possible she was a famous painting, or that Callimachus had mentioned her. She is a girl from the snow-rivers, like Eurydice, the picture of health of course, since she lived wild in the forest we are told. The river is the same as in the Georgic (4, 63).

Hey there (*heus*), says Venus, have you seen any of my sisters?

> ... Who crost the Lawn, or in the Forest stray'd?
> A painted Quiver at her Back she bore;
> Vary'd with Spots a Lynx's Hide she wore:
> And at full Cry pursu'd the tusky Boar?

We are whirled easily and lightheartedly from image to image and from style to style. Normally a picturesque epic fails for lack of speed, as I think Apollonius of Rhodes's does, but Virgil's careful needlework makes in the end a single web-like texture, and his poem is now rolling along at a pleasant pace.

Aeneas sees at once she must be a goddess, but she tells him where he is without lowering her defence. She cannot reveal herself as his mother without some difficulty to the poet, and to call Carthage Agenor's city is no real help. But it is genealogical and obscure enough to satisfy a taste we know existed and was deeply interwoven with Hellenistic verse technique. Still, it is a momentary lapse (338) and Venus decorates her tale with murders and treasures and ghosts with bleeding wounds to explain Dido's founding Carthage (367). The entire speech with its fabulous story and phoney Greek etymology (Byrsa, Bosra, the hide of ground Dido bought) is light entertainment. Virgil was fated to be an 'epic' poet when romances were already being written.

In return, Aeneas tells Venus his own sad story, and she sends him off to Carthage to find Dido and his lost friends, showing him the omen of a dozen swans. That is a lot of swans to see in Africa, but they are all part of the romance, 'They play with whistling wings circling the pole / And singing' (397-8).

Her pink neck shone, her ambrosial hair breathed odours, her dress flowed downwards to her feet, and she showed herself a goddess (402-5). Aeneas knew it was his mother but she had disappeared, as Dido would do, as Eurydice had done. Venus covered him in a mist so that no one could interfere with him, and 'away to Paphos flew, temple and home, / Where on a hundred altars Syrian grains / Burn smoking, and fresh flower-garlands breathe' (415-17). Are these delicious touches of the divine exotic not a preparation for Dido?

They saw Carthage from a hill (418). The mighty new city is tacked onto a memorable image of bees, left over from the fourth Georgic to which the swans also owed their origin.

This bee passage, typical of Virgil's re-used material, is better and looks fresher than ever. The activity and business of the bees and their honey that smells of thyme do not efface the building of the city all the same, the digging out of gates, the vast stones moved by hand, and the monolithic marbles for the theatre: Virgil has spoken of these things in the third Georgic. But also, he must, I believe, have seen Agrippa's enormous public works at Rome. Yet all that is left of the thunderous noises of building is the amiable buzzing, or if you like the serious buzzing of the bees. These are 20 lines (417-37) that Horace could not have written. It is a curious fact that for Yeats the faint thunder in the trees is the noise of pigeons, but bees occur in the same line: no doubt he has Tennyson in mind. Still however that may be, I have remembered these lines since I was ten or eleven, reading bits of a book of Virgil for the first time, and have always reread them with the same pleasure, although in 1942 I did not know what the smell of thyme was like, and still less how honey could smell of it. Bees are permitted in epic poetry because Homer admitted them (Il. 2, 82, 87f.), but Virgil's are his own (Geo. 4, 162f.).

Searching for Dido they come to a grove in the centre of the new city. This sounds civilised to us, but it is the site of the great temple of Juno patroness of Carthage. Suddenly Aeneas sees high on the walls a painting (?) of the Trojan war, such as there was in his day at Pompeii on Apollo's portico, and in Rome on a portico wall erected at the expense of Marcius Philippus, the consul of 38 BC, who appears to have been half-brother to Augustus. The Roman example was in a number of pictures by a Greek called Theoros, Pliny tells us. They may well derive from the strip cartoon illustrations of the Iliad, since Vitruvius suggests both the Iliad and the Odyssey as useful wall decorations.

Aeneas is amazed to discover the world-famous battles in which he had fought. He weeps, and speaks words that are the most famous and untranslatable that Virgil ever wrote (462).

Things do draw tears: mortality touches the mind.

He feels this fame will save the lives of his men. Yet now that I am elderly I cannot help remembering that Scipio wept over the ruins of Carthage, and quoted Homer. He was recorded by the Greek hostage and historian Polybius, who was with him. It is probable that Virgil knew the passage in Polybius, and that Scipio put pity and common humanity into his mind. This is a conjecture of course, yet it may be worth recording.

We see a number of famous and paintable scenes, including the white tents of Rhesus the Thracian prince who was murdered at night. Dryden underlines that his party were 'By their white Sails betray'd to nightly view', which is probably the reason why he has Virgil refer to 'the snow-white sails that were his tents'. But the sails are Dryden's invention. The story is not only Homeric (Il. 10, 469) and the poet of the tragedy *Rhesos* (who was not Euripides) has him betrayed by his horses which gleamed snow-white like swans (Il. 10, 437 suggests this). The white tents come from a painting, not from life or poetry. Horace pours scorn on the white mosquito-net rigged at Actium for the Queen of Egypt, but the tents of the Romans were black.

The poor boy Troilus is dragged by his horses and his spear scribbles in the dust. In the Iliad he was already dead, but almost no scene was more popular in the archaic period, in Italy as well as in Greece. Black Memnon the Abyssinian and Penthesilea the Amazon are still more picturesque decorations. No doubt they make up a body of legends that turn easily into verse, avoiding most of the better known tales from Homer? But Virgil does his best on the central scene, where Priam buys back the dead body of his son Hector, and it is moving, neither crowded nor banal.

Like the whole series of Trojan scenes, these lines are meant to stir grief as only Homeric epic can. It is a special property of Homer to stir us in this way, and does not depend on our being Greeks or Trojans, because it is the special work of all genuine epic poetry. Even in English we have one fragment of a lost epic, called the Finnsburh fragment, composed about 650 AD, which works in the same way. It was recovered from the binding of a book in the British Museum, and later lost by fire. The lament for Arthur O'Leary, or the Keen for Art Leary, is close to genuine epic, yet it was composed only about two-hundred years ago in Irish and lived on in the memory of Cork fishermen until it was written down around 1900. In all these poems it does not matter who one's ancestors are or what one's language is, they stir to grief. I doubt whether Virgil or anyone else in his time understood anthropology or epic society well enough to realise this truth. He may have thought the Romans had or might have a special sympathy by blood with the Trojans, and he certainly made Homer or rather the 'Homeric' tales (and not just the poems we know) into an important link between Dido and Aeneas.

149

So the coincidence of the paintings becomes a device of melodrama. And yet for a most moving moment when Aeneas wept and did not know why, Virgil did understand the impersonality of grief.

> It is the soft clashing of claymores you hear
> That they carry to the house.
> Soon shall be the cough of birds,
> Hoar wolf's howl, hard wood-talk,
> Shield's answer to shaft.

Dido comes with her crowd of young men and her mist of metaphor. She is taller than any of them, like a Spartan by the Eurotas, like Artemis among the Oreads, the mountain nymphs. She sat high on a throne in the temple shell (495) giving laws in the manner of Augustus, but there among her courtiers Aeneas spotted his old shipmates; he and Achates were still invisible so they observed while one of the sailors explained they were looking for a place called Hesperia, and could she help them? You may despise our humanity, but hope the gods remember right and wrong: Aeneas is our king if he is alive, and Acestes in Sicily our cousin. The other Trojans murmur in agreement. This speech (534 and 560) has two incomplete lines in it that suggest it had never been perfectly polished.

Dido offers help and wishes that Aeneas might be blown south by the same wind. She will send men to scour the sea-coast to look for him.

Aeneas and Achates are bursting to get out of their magic mist (580), but first Achates says only one ship is lost and that one we saw sink. (There had been twenty.) The mist splits open and there they stand like a conjuring trick, Aeneas with new youth and fire in his eyes, bright face and luxuriant hair. He looked like ivory or like silver or Parian stone treated with gold (593), and said: Here we are.

It is impossible not to mock this scene of revelation, which is in the most careful, elaborate, Hellenistic taste. It is like something from an epic by William Morris, written to be enjoyed with chocolates in Bedford Park. The ups and downs of the Aeneid are indeed remarkable, and in the first book Virgil is showing what he can do in several styles, some surely rebarbative. Can it be the influence of Apollonius of Rhodes shimmering across from Sicily (570)? Or have we in the new Aeneas the beginnings of the motif of sexual passion? The Odyssey is the remote model, yet the Aeneid is briefer, less elaborate and more luxuriant (23, 156 and 6, 229).

Dido is the first foreigner to treat the Trojans generously, so Aeneas (597-610) makes her a polite and courtly speech, and embraces his friends. Dido is amazed: Are you the Aeneas Venus bore beside the Simois? She remembers a Trojan (really it was the Greek Teucer of Salamis) who came to Sidon and was settled by her father Belus in Cyprus. This complex piece of genealogical explanation is not invented by Virgil to create another link with Aeneas. Teucer was exiled by his father for not bringing home his half-brother Ajax safe from Troy. The coincidence of his name Teucer with the Teucri, a name for Trojans, is confusing admittedly. But it looks intentional (624-6), because otherwise she is claiming a deliberately confused bit of genealogical history which ignores a well-known myth, just in order to make friends with Aeneas. Romantic writers are capable of such things, but we may hope that Virgil is not.

Let us go home, Dido invites, and they all follow her. She sends to the sailors twenty bulls, a hundred bristling-backed pigs and a hundred fat lambs with their mothers (635). Her palace is magnificent and decorated in gold with the deeds of her forefathers.

Meanwhile Aeneas sends Achates running back to the shore to fetch Ascanius his son, and some presents, a dress of Helen's given her by Leda before she eloped from Mycenae to Troy, a sceptre, a crown and a jewel. This childish mission is interrupted by Venus, who has thought up a plot to send Cupid in place of Ascanius to set light to the crazy Queen and twist his fire around her bones. Venus does not trust the Carthaginians with their two languages and uncertain loyalty. Terrible Juno burns and anxiety rushes in at nightfall (662). Apollonius of Rhodes had already played with the idea (already banal) of Cupid as a lovely boy, and here Virgil acknowledges him as master of this sort of material. He is not far from Theocritus in date or in theme after all.

Venus complains to her son about nasty Juno. Her theology as to Cupid's role is faultless – as Virgil's always is – but he no more believes it than Milton would. Venus puts Ascanius to sleep on Cythera (680) or maybe Cyprus and for one night only Cupid takes his place.

Love obeys, removes his wings, and rejoices to step out as Iulus (that is, Ascanius) (690), and soft flowers of marjoram and its breathing shadows wrap the real boy in sleep in the Cyprian mountains. That is the end of the poor fellow for now, because Virgil forgets about him and we are never told how he awoke or who brought him back to Carthage. *Amaracus* or marjoram is not a grand or luxurious plant, but just the herb we know, as the plant embroidered around Helen's dress was a simple yellow Arabian *acanthus*. Sergeaunt (1920), who is still an authority, thinks it was gum arabic, a plant I do not remember ever seeing grow. I would prefer it to be *acanthophylla*, a yellow flowering thistle that is an old friend from Greek mountains. Virgil probably went no further than Catullus for these modest embellishments.

The presents are a success and so is Cupid. Dido is most unhappy and will pay for her infatuation: she does not know how great a god is sitting in her lap.

151

When they have eaten they get ready to drink. The lamps are lit and the Queen calls for a pouring dish used by all her ancestors, heavy with gold and gems. There is I think a slightly ominous feel not only about the magic but the encrusted riches of the palace, its echoing roofs and huge lamps to challenge night. The court of Augustus near Boscoreale lived in less grandeur but more luxury.

Dido prays to Jove that this be a happy day for the Trojans and for her people, calling on Bacchus and on Juno. They drink and Iopas, a bard taught by Atlas, sings of the sun and moon and the creation (742-6), of the questions that puzzled Virgil in the second Georgic and of the mysteries revealed in the sixth Eclogue. They talked far into the night and Dido drank a long drink of love. She asked about Priam and Hector and how the son of Dawn (Memnon) was armed. She asked for the story of the fall of Troy and the long wanderings of Aeneas.

> For since on ev'ry Sea, on ev'ry Coast,
> Your Men have been distress'd, your Navy tost,
> Sev'n times the Sun has either Tropick view'd,
> The Winter banish'd, and the Spring renew'd.

Virgil ends his book less hopefully, For here's the seventh summer that carries you on, through all lands and all flowing seas (755-6). Dido sees Aeneas as a kind of Flying Dutchman and her disastrous attempt to rescue him from his wanderings can now unfold. Odysseus had delayed years with Calypso, and come home after a ten years' war and ten years' wanderings, but Aeneas cannot spend so long, and no nymph or Queen will delay him, whatever tricks the gods may play. Cupid as Ascanius contrives romantic passion by magic, yet Aeneas can keep his distance and his dignity for a book or two. With the opening of the next book we will come to Aeneas's story of the fall of Troy.

I have delayed a long time over details in the first book, to try to show how Virgil's patchwork technique develops very slowly into the long narrative haul of the Aeneid, and how his taste for variety flourishes even within one book. There are a few serious puzzles in the Aeneid, and occasional fallings off. In the first book the worst puzzle to me has been Dido's speech about Teucer or 'the Trojan'. The solution is that Teucer was the son of Telamon and Hesione, and 'Teucer' means 'Trojan'. Sophocles wrote a play about him, imitated by Pacuvius, that Cicero tells us was a familiar and well loved text to pupils of the law in his day. Virgil and Horace had a solid, old-fashioned kind of late republican education. That indeed is what separates them from their juniors; they certainly knew all about Telamon.

The smaller puzzles of book one are to do with its perfunctory romance plot, which is hardly worth taking seriously. It is in the second book that Virgil begins to show himself the great master of narrative verse that he became.

When Aeneas begins to tell the story his voice is deadly serious, and the gravity and grief intensify each other. Even a soldier of Odysseus would weep, he says, to tell this story. He does of course tell his own tale in Homer's Odyssey, at the court of Alcinous, where his tears betrayed him at the song of Demodokos the blind poet at the end of book eight. This starts off Odysseus, who goes on for four books.

But the weeping that betrays Aeneas is like a woman weeping over her husband's dead body who died defending her and she weeps as they hit her with spear-butts and drag her off to slavery. Virgil is still preoccupied as he was at the paintings, and at how things stir our tears. Any hard soldier would weep, Aeneas says, any Myrmidon or Dolopian. He goes further than Homer, who makes Odysseus weep at his own story depicted. He certainly knew Aristotle's Poetics, and there may be some intended sense in the Aeneid of 'pity and terror'. I do not know whether the terror (which Aristotle says is terror lest such a thing happen to oneself) is more than implicit.

But there is something human that is in common and is expressed by tears. It goes beyond romantic Apollonian narrative – and its preservation and later outbursts in simple romance requires a long discussion for which I have no time. Let me at least tell a true story, which I heard from a Greek American anthropologist in Monemvasia in 1963, who had been collecting the last fragments of a long tradition of folksong in the Mani. A woman had married into another village, her husband had been killed there in a quarrel and she had been insulted and mocked on her way home. She wept but kept quiet about it until her brother got the story out of her. He then shot his enemy who had his child on his knee. He escaped and many years later he went for shelter from a storm into a police station on Pendeli near Athens. Someone was singing a song from the Mani, and it was the song of his own story, and he wept. He went home because of the song, and was reconciled with the enemy family. The story was told by an old man who had been the child on his father's knee, and it was with him the murderer was reconciled. This kind of story underlies Homeric epic in an important way, and Homeric tears interest Virgil greatly.

As Aeneas begins to speak,

> ... Now dewy night comes headlong down from heaven,
> And falling stars persuade us into sleep. (8-9)

He begins with that dream-like object, the Trojan horse which the Greeks build and fill with men and pretend to go home in despair: but they hide on Tenedos. The Trojans open their town gates and explore. Some want to bring in the horse, a dedication to Athene, but others want to burn it or drown it, or open it up. The priest Laocoon says it must be full of Greeks, or a machine to breach the walls, or a spying machine. He sticks in a spear and the horse seems to groan.

At this moment the captive Sinon is brought in. This character was traditional, and appears (based on Odysseus) in the story told by Helen in the fourth book of the Odyssey, but here he claims he escaped from the nasty distinction of human sacrifice by the Greeks (115f.) and hid in a marsh (136). This part of the story recalls the narrative verse of Greek tragedy rather than the Homeric amplitude. It gathers power (171f.) as it goes on.

> The thing's believed, by tears and trickery
> We fell, whom great Achilles, Diomedes,
> Ten years, a thousand ships could never take (196-8).

Two bearded snakes or giant eels swim across from Tenedos while Laocoon is slaughtering a bull to Neptune, and kill him and his two young sons. This peculiar little anecdote or vignette is the subject of the ghastly masterpiece of marble sculpture, the Laocoon, that has survived in Rome. Pliny was thrilled by it, and in its polish, its vivid detail and its horrible subject and impersonal anguish it was just what the Romans liked. Virgil adds a further dimension of terror to the beasts with their bloody beards and fiery, bloody eyes, but nothing can make Laocoon live. The marble may be a copy of a bronze. It was carved by Rhodians while Virgil was alive or a few years earlier, but he was not swayed by it. The wreck of the sculptural group was found in the ruins of Nero's Golden House in the sixteenth century (in my own view it is a copy, and bits of the bronze are said to have been found).

The Trojans welcome the wooden horse into their city, and down go the walls to accommodate it. The Greeks crept out from Tenedos as the Trojans slept, the night was silent and the moon silent when the royal ship showed a flare, and Sinon let the Greeks out of their horse (259f.). The city lay buried in sleep and wine, the sentries were slaughtered and the gates opened.

At the time of first and deepest sleep, the ghost of Hector appeared weeping to Aeneas. This memorable and grieving spirit is the ancestor of many in the renaissance, and when Thomas Heywood introduced an entreacte of ghosts into the tragedies of Seneca in English verse, Hector was their model. Only Shakespeare in Hamlet laughed a little. Virgil's Hector is a distillation of Homer's, it is once again uncannily like Homer seen through Greek and then Latin tragedy, yet it is memorably vivid and genuinely moving. The monster snakes, who 'lick'd their hissing Jaws that sputter'd Flame', were too terrible to be quite credible, but the dream of Hector's ghost and what he says take hold of the reader.

> The Foes already have possess'd the Wall,
> Troy nods from high, and totters to her fall ...
> ... He said, and brought me from their blest Abodes
> The venerable Statues of the Gods:
> With ancient *Vesta* from the sacred Quire,
> The Wreaths and Relicks of th' Immortal Fire.

Aeneas takes into custody these holy objects, by which he must be considerably encumbered. Vesta is a symbol or incarnation of the Hearth, which was tended at Rome by virgins consecrated to the task. Hector has prophesied a new city and assured Aeneas that he himself was the only possible defender of Troy.

The scene begins not with ghostly moanings but first with the vision of Hector as he was in death, and bleeding, then a speech to him by Aeneas which is eloquent but direct enough to be moving. I can never finally decide about Virgil as a great epic poet, but he is certainly a great tragic poet, and his narrative is masterly. This stage of the poem began sharply at line 250 when heaven twisted and night came in a rush, a phrase that is certainly Homeric (*Od.* 5, 294) but at least the first half of the line comes from Ennius (Ann. 218) and it is probable that a deeper study of Ennius than is possible for us, since we have only fragments of him, underlies this whole scene.

I do not wish to exaggerate the dramatic nature of this part of the Aeneid, but it was in the theatre that the old Roman drama persisted into Virgil's lifetime. Ennius was performed in 54 BC, too early, but the Tereus of Accius and bits of Paeuvius in 44 BC; and Augustus favoured the old dramatic writers (Jocelyn, 1967). After many readings it seems to have been the vision itself that made the scene unforgettable.

> A bloody Shrowd he seem'd, and bath'd in Tears,
> Such as he was when by Pelides slain
> Thessalian Coursers drag'd him o'er the Plain.
> Swol'n were his Feet, as when the Thongs were thrust
> Thro' the bor'd holes, his Body black with dust ...

Aeneas in his dream imagines Hector has come home at last to help them, but suddenly when Hector has warned him

> Now peals of Shouts came thundering from afar,
> Cries, Threats, and loud Laments, and mingled War:
> The Noise approaches, though our Palace stood
> Aloof from Streets, encompass'd with a Wood.
> Louder, and yet more loud, I hear th' Alarms
> Of Human Cries distinct, and clashing Arms ...

It was like a harvest on fire, or a mountain river (an old and effective Virgilian simile) when 'the shepherd hears the noise from his high peak' (308). House after house burns, the shouting of men mingles with the blare of trumpets, and the sea glitters with flames, and one longs to die fighting (317). Panthus, Apollo's priest (319), is the first man Aeneas meets, and his words doom the city.

> Troy is no more, and Ilium *was* a Town!
> The fatal Day, th' appointed Hour is come ...

Virgil's words are longer, heavier and less excited, they are as ominously weighted as any words can be. And this is the turning-point, in so far as an inevitable tragedy has a turning-point, of this book, this story, this city and this lifetime. Book two of the Aeneid does carry touches of the romance, the adventure story, the historical anecdote, but it has a formal progression, it is one poem. That is important to notice, and must not be said lightly, since if it is true it is a huge step for Virgil to take, yet to see that it is true one has only to compare this style with the rather disjointed anecdotes of Livy, or the heroic lays of Macaulay.

Aeneas is whirled away into battle and flames (337) like a fury from hell, with a little crowd of friends, a motley company including an old man and a boy in love with Cassandra. Aeneas makes them a speech, because that is the epic custom. The gods have left, he says, we are protecting a city in flames, so let us die, despair is our one hope (354). They rush on like wolves, and dark night flies round them with its hollow shadows. The slaughter is terrible on both sides (361-9). Androgeos the Greek sees them and speaks, then sees they are Trojans and starts back as if from a snake. (Androgeos is a mystery, and Virgil took his name at random from forgotten reading: I will discuss him in book six.)

At first the Trojans do well. Cassandra's lover suggests they dress up as Greeks: he dresses himself as Androgeos, who conveniently is now dead. The other young Trojans follow suit, and they all fight so well some Greeks are driven back to the ships or climb back into their horse for shelter. They see Cassandra dragged out by the hair from the sanctuary of Athene but while her lover dies for her and the others help him. In the end the other Trojans attack them as

Greeks and the Greeks as Trojans. Athene's temple was in the Iliad on the heights
of the acropolis and Aeneas's named companions die in and around the temple,
most with short Homeric epitaphs. Aeneas with Iphitus and Pelias makes for
Priam's palace where there is shouting. Virgil has wrung every last drop of
excitement from the night battle and his defence of the falling palace is
splendidly ruinous (442-52), with the defenders rolling down the gilded roof-
beams on the Greeks. As usual one must suspect actual paintings rather than
experience of life inspired the poet.

Aeneas runs into the palace by an unguarded postern door and a private
gallery, up to a high tower where he could see all Troy, the Greek camp and the
ships, and there they pulled down crashing masonry on the Greeks (465-6). Here
he sees the breach in the palace and Pyrrhus like a glittering autumn snake and
Periphas (already dead in the Iliad). Pyrrhus as the son of Achilles has inherited
his father's charioteer as a soldier servant, a step down from epic to Roman
convention that Virgil does not intend. It is important to observe that this is the
climax of the night action and of the Trojan war and the poet's eye follows it as
if Aeneas were a camera, peering down from the tower in through the breach to
the private chambers of the palace. The murder of Priam is surrounded by formal
rhetoric as if in a Greek tragedy, his end is terrible indeed, and his epitaph
bizarre, because this is all a bird's eye view. The dead body has become
anonymous and the head is lost.

> I saw th' unhappy Queen,
> The hundred Wives, and where old Priam stood,
> To stain the hallow'd Altar with his Blood,
> The fifty Nuptial Beds ...

The antiquarian and exotic interest, the 'pillars proud with spoils and
barbarous gold flung down' (504) detain his fancy a line or so too long, but Virgil
deals with Hecuba and the shrieking wives like an experienced director. Priam
sees his last son die (526-33) and is killed (554-9), and only then does Aeneas
come to himself and resume his active role.

> Now die: with that he dragg'd the trembling Sire
> Slidd'ring through clotter'd Blood, and holy Mire,
> (The mingl'd Paste his murdered Son had made),
> Haul'd from beneath the violated Shade,
> And on the Sacred Pile the Royal victim laid ...
> ... On the bleak Shoar now lies th' abandon'd King,
> A headless Carcass, and a nameless thing.

157

The illustration to Dryden here is oddly operatic. Hecuba sings an aria on a stage in a pillared apse, the stage being the altar, and omens appearing as it were from the heavens above it, while Pyrrhus does his killing in the foreground, and a full chorus of women wail behind Hecuba. Meanwhile, all Aeneas's friends have died by fire or suicide and he remembers his own family.

Then follows a passage that appears to weaken this book. Aeneas sees Helen and being in two minds what to do with her leaves her alone (567-588). The episode is absurd, but it appealed to renaissance taste and was printed in the Roman Virgil in 1473. There is very little ancient manuscript support for it, and Servius and other late antique scholars in the fifth century AD guessed it was dropped from the Aeneid by Virgil's executors. But Virgil cannot have written it. How did Aeneas see her hiding in silence in a dark corner at night? The fire revealed her. 'The hell-cat of Greece and of Troy sat hated on the altar' (whose?) 'and fire flamed up in me'. Even Rupert Brooke's satiric sonnets 'Hot through Troy's ruin' manage Helen better. I have not supposed for many years these lines could possibly be genuine and do not admit it now. Jasper Griffin has pointed out in his *Mirror of Myth* (1986) that Homeric sufferings are direct but that Virgil makes them mental: Odysseus gets shipwrecked and has to swim, but Aeneas only suffers the sight of his friends drowning. Book two is a prolonged supper of horrors, yet Aeneas is as unhurt as a man dreaming. But someone was anxious to cram in every detail of the tragic night, so Helen must be seen just as Hecuba must be.

I do not believe it was Virgil who made it. Without these unhappy lines we move from the death of Aeneas's friends to the vision of Venus and her revelation that the gods themselves were destroying Troy: it was not Helen or Paris who was to blame (600-10). Neptune (god of earthquakes) was shown to Aeneas at his terrible work.

> Where yon disorder'd heap of Ruin lies,
> Stones rent from Stones, where Clouds of Dust arise,
> Amid that smother, Neptune holds his place:
> Below the Wall's foundations drives his Mace:
> And heaves the Building from the solid Base ...

The vision he sees is of all the gods combining against Troy, and Virgil's treatment is typically physical. Jasper Griffin notices that Aeneas is not only suffering mentally throughout the Aeneid, but he must suffer guilt, as he does over Dido and over the slaughter of Turnus, king of the Rutuli. Guilt must be among the feelings of so passive or comparatively inactive a spectator of the sack of Priam's palace and his death.

It is also true that Aeneas is a hero in that Greek sense which is clear in the worship of the late sixth century and the fifth BC: the heroes can do harm to the living as well as good, and they must be placated. Their terrible aspect is part of their real power, and it may be studied in the two naked bronze figures from the sea near Riace in south Italy, who represent I believe the old and suffering sailors of the Odyssey. They are the only ancient representations we have to convey this sense, and it is fair to say they alter the balance of ancient art at a stroke: Aeneas was such a man.

The vision of Venus is in stark contrast to the rest of this book and to the gods at work as Venus reveals them, and this of course is deliberate: it was a mistake to interpose the sleek Helen.

> Thus while I rave, a gleam of pleasing Light
> Spread o'er the Place, and shining Heav'nly bright
> My Mother stood reveal'd before my Sight.
> Never so radiant did her Eyes appear,
> Nor her own Star confess'd a light so clear,
> Great in her Charms, as when on Gods above
> She looks, and breathes herself into their Love.

One puzzle still remains: how to sew on all that follows, the retreat and flight from Troy, to the devastating account of the fall of the city.

It is done partly by Venus revealing the gods at work, partly by the flight of Aeneas through the burning ruins. Aeneas gathers his family in scenes of confusion, with the loss of his wife. Both his hands are occupied with his father and his son, on whom the gods send an omen of divine light (680). His father prays, the heavens thunder and his mother's star (or is it the Julian star?) shows the way west (694-5) as it sets behind the forests of Mount Ida.

They make for the ancient temple of Ceres and its venerable cypress tree: it is true that Demeter's (Ceres's) temples are generally in the country a mile or two from town walls, and they are often the pleasantest places to excavate or to visit. This temple will be where the refugees gather for the epic journey (716). Yet Virgil cannot resist another reference to the loot of Troy (763) and the division of the spoils and the slaves, all that being the material of tragedy: it was not for nothing that Virgil on his throne in the African mosaic sat between the epic and the tragic Muses. Finally Aeneas fills the streets with noise, yelling for Creusa his wife (767), but meets only her ghost who prophesies his arrival at the Tiber and disappears (791-3).

Suddenly a vast new crowd of friends arrives to be his companions and it is day. At first they take refuge in the mountains, because their fleet does not yet exist and the Greeks are still the winners, yet in a certain sense the rest of the Aeneid is now a foregone conclusion.

The story in book two is a wildly, perhaps a thrillingly, diverse patchwork of elements. In places it has the special momentum of great poetry, but in other places it seems too incredible, and the role of Aeneas as single eye-witness of all is not sustained without difficulty. Helen covers a tear in the canvas, and if she were not there we would not have looked for her. We do not after all hear about Cassandra, or the murder of Astynax, who was Hector's child. But the texture of darkness and fire is thrilling, so that if I am right in supposing that four books were based on earth, air, fire and water – an idea I first came to when thinking over the role of water in book five – then this book is certainly fire.

Virgil has re-used many stray phrases of his old work in book two, the ancient houses of the birds that fall as the tree falls in the Georgics serve for Priam's house, the Po valley floods in a metaphor for the Greeks bursting in, and so on. There are more half lines or unfinished lines than usual, often at the end of verse paragraphs, like patches waiting to be sewn together. It is arguable that Helen in the ruins was a mere sketch left unfinished. Venus forbids Aeneas to strike at her, and the idea that he should not is no more chivalrous than his evident dislike of dressing up as a Greek for the night fighting, and yet the attack on Helen is an account of something not done, an action not taken, so that it can hardly fit so close to Priam's death.

The book is picturesque from beginning to end, and we do not know what pictures of the events Virgil had seen. We do at least know that Polygnotos painted the Fall of Troy at Delphi in the early fifth century BC, though Virgil did not follow that enormous fresco in detail. Pausanias described the great work at Delphi a hundred and forty years or more after Virgil's death.

This book, the fourth and the sixth are supposed to have been chosen to read aloud to Augustus, in which case we must think again about book two being unfinished. My own view is that it lacks only a few trivial stitches, which Virgil thought of no more account than the occasional contradictions. He must have known when he wrote his account of Priam's death that the body 'by the shore' was intrusive. Is it possible that some Roman or Greek tragedy had produced Priam's ghost like Timon's bones on the beach, and that he accepted that version and tacked it onto his own? But this theory is doubtful, and it is likelier that he was influenced by an account of the fresco at Delphi or by some ancient commentary on Homer. Virgil was explaining why Priam's body could not be recognised and buried privately by some Trojan survivor. It was headless, and one among many.

We leave this book at sunrise, as we began it when '... the latter Watch of wasting Night, / And setting Stars to kindly Rest invite'. At the end of it, as the refugees assemble,

> The Morn began from Ida to display
> Her rosy Cheeks, and Phosphor led the day.

This is not magic time like the two periods of nine days that hedge in the Iliad, but it is the sign of new beginnings, the dawn and the morning star, which Virgil knew to be the planet Venus.

All that winter the Trojans built their fleet with wood from Ida and from Antandros, and in early summer they sailed. Whyever Antandros? It belonged to the Roman province of Asia and it was the northernmost of the Cyclades. Virgil knew this, or it was in some old source; no one knows. Delos is the essential oracle but Virgil fears it will overshadow the Cumean Sibyl, and when Aeneas lands there he will not name it. The god's 'noisy mountain', was only 150 metres high, and the heroes progress from Thrace to Delos and Mykonos and Crete in a straight line.

They land first on the coast of Thrace, intending to sacrifice a bull, but when Aeneas plucks greenery the bushes bleed and the voice or ghost of Polydorus warns them off. Polydorus was murdered and avenged in the *Hecuba* of Euripides: Aeneas was founding the city called Aenos and mentioned in the Iliad, but the legend is garbled, and Virgil has taken from it only this memorable little ghost story (that Dante remembered). At the end of it, we are nearly 70 lines into book three. The perfection of it and the banal moral (56) suggest he took it from Callimachus or Euphorion, the Hellenistic masters, both of whom treated the tale.

The next port of call is Delos, where King Anius reigns. They have passed Mykonos and a prison island the Romans knew called Gyarus, and come now to the prophet-king and Apollo's temple on its ancient rock, where the god answers them in bellowing from his mountain. He tells them to seek their ancient mother earth, and there they shall live and reign. Anchises says this means Crete, so off they go to Crete, where there is another Ida where their ancestors once lived.

> In humble Vales they built their soft abodes:
> Till Cybele the Mother of the Gods
> With tinkling Cymbals charm'd th' Idean Woods.

They sail away through the islands and land on Crete, where Aeneas founds Pergamum, and gets down to governing a prosperous settlement,

> When rising Vapours choak the wholesom Air,
> The Trees devouring Caterpillers burn,

so they return to Delos to try the god again, but this time the household gods come to Aeneas in a dream. They make him great promises and tell him of Hesperia and the Oenotrians, the place now called ITALIA (163-71). This was where Dardanus, the ancestor of the royal race of Troy, first came from, and there he must settle.

Aeneas tells his dream to Anchises who remembers Cassandra had raved about Italy, but no one paid any attention; Apollo gave her the gift of second sight, but also arranged no one would believe her.

The heroes are in sight of land when three days and nights of storm land them among the Harpies. These revolting creatures pounce on their food excreting and screeching: when they retreat a nasty brute called Celaeno perches on a cliff to prophesy doom. The islands are the Strophades or Wandering Isles, and since Virgil refers to Phineus he may have in mind a lost tragedy by Aeschylus about him. The monstrous creatures were wind-spirits or storm-demons in Hesiod and Homer, and sisters of the Roman *Dirae*. But they are beyond proportion in horror, which might, I take it, derive from what in Aeschylus was described but not enacted, like all the most memorable scenes in tragedy: those are the scenes chosen by the Athenian vase-painters, for example. But this scene or episode is so horrible that I do not recall ever to have seen it portrayed, though named Harpies do in fact occur on vases from about 600 BC. Their particular filthiness seems to be first recorded by Apollonius of Rhodes, and is said to be borrowed from the Indian fruit-bat. It is Virgil if not a painter who gives them women's faces. Celaeno warns the Trojans that they will get so hungry in Italy they will eat their dinner-tables.

This as we have noticed comes true. Celaeno flies away (258), and the heroes sail with the south wind past Zakynthos and the islands of the Adriatic, past Ithaca which they curse, and at last to Actium where they hold a little festival of Trojan games (280) to celebrate their safe passage round the hostile Greek cities. A year has passed and the seas are stormy again. Aeneas leaves a dedication at the temple with a verse inscription (288) of convincing antiquity.

They are beyond Corfu and passing the coast of Epirus when they come to Buthrotum, now Butrinto in Albania and uninhabited, but a thriving harbour in Roman times. Here they meet Helenus, a prophetic prince from the Iliad (6, 76 and 7, 44) who was part of the loot of Neoptolemus, who let him marry

Andromache. The story was known (Eurip. Andr. 1243) but not to Aeneas, who was pleased to meet old friends and be given a prophecy of his own, more comforting than Celaeno's. Book three makes up for its episodic character by silver trumpets as it were of Roman prophecy, and by an epic language that is well woven together, though we can often trace hints of Ennius, and even of Catullus whenever roars 'sweep the blue'.

Andromache is so moved by her own speech that she breaks off in mid-line to weep (340), but Helenus arrives to save her face. The scene is as neat as Euripides in its exploitation of a woman's predicament, and as unconvincing if taken as history. But Helenus is formidable, he knows the stars and the omens of the birds and Apollo's Asian oracles (359-61) and can warn Aeneas of the lakes of hell and Circe's island (386) and prophesies the thirty piglets with the enormous sow under the ilex trees on a river bank (389-91), with warnings of the numerous Greek settlements on his own coast. He has time also to lay down the rule of veiling the head at the moment of sacrifice (405) and to warn of Scylla and Charybdis (420f.), monsters from the Odyssey which had not grown stale.

Helenus's account of Cumae (441) sends a shiver down the spine: it is what Virgil must have felt when he saw the place.

> Arriv'd at Cumae, when you view the Flood
> Of black Avernus and the sounding Wood,
> The mad prophetick Sibyl you shall find
> Dark in a Cave and on a Rock reclin'd ...

The Cumaen Sibyl writes fate on leaves and puts them at the mouth of her cave, but the wind blows them about and then she loses her temper and sulks, so consultation of her calls for patience. She must be persuaded to speak and not to write, then she will tell you all about Italy.

This is all Helenus was allowed to say, presumably because Juno forbade the rest: she must have forbidden any prophecy affecting Dido. All the same,

> Bounteous of Treasure, he supply'd my want
> With heavy Gold and polish'd Elephant.
> Then Dodonaean Caldrons put on Board ...

There is a rich antiquarian list of the presents, as if one were going round the treasures of some great house full of antiques. Then 'Near the Ceraunean rocks our Course we bore' and sailed at once by the shortest route to Italy. Palinurus observed the stars and while it was still dark they sailed.

> And now the rising Morn, with rosie light
> Adorns the Skies, and puts the Stars to flight:
> When we from far like bluish Mists descry
> The Hills and then the Plains of Italy.

The first landing of the Trojans is at a temple of Athene on a hill, somewhere near Otranto no doubt, rather than Ancona.

It is dangerous country and no doubt full of Greeks, so that having taken note of a good omen of four white horses they set off again and come at once past the heel of Italy into the bay of Tarentum. They pass splashy Scylla and fuming Etna and the Cyclopes, and find a castaway from the ship of Odysseus called Achaemenides, a name borrowed from the Persian royal family, rather as Amyntas was taken from the Armenians. His rags come from a Latin tragedy Cicero knew. He had been forgotten in the cave of the Cyclops, which he now describes in gory detail.

> With spouting Blood the Purple Pavement swims,
> While the dire Glutton grinds the trembling Limbs.

Achaemenides has told his story just to the end when the blind monster appears and chases them out to sea, with all his tribe around him, tree-tall, mountain-tall and cloud-capped. This of course is the climax of horrors, and after it they skirt Syracuse and Arethusa's fountain, Gela and Acragas, like any tourist of the 1990s in a paddle steamer. From 'palmy Selinus' (the palm occurs on the Carhaginian coins from Sicily) they sail nearly to Palermo, but they halt at Drepanum, under Erice, where Venus had a famous hill-sanctuary that Apollonius of Rhodes celebrated. Now the hero's tale is over, and Aeneas retires to bed.

One can see how this book aroused Mommsen's derision. It is far from lasting seven years and, though it is peppered with patriotic prophecies, the ups and downs of the adventure do not always engage the reader. One remembers best the picturesque details like the white horses on the Italian foreshore and the smoke of Etna in the distance. The story of course was given and Virgil has done his best with it. Now perhaps it is best forgotten, since the fourth book is a single action, Dido's passion, her desertion and suicide: it is on a more serious level.

VII

SAND

In the fourth book of the Aeneid what happens is foreseeable, the story is complete in itself so that not only the book has a discernible shape, but the Aeneid itself begins to take on shape. Book four is the first in which Aeneas is not quite central and not the hero of an episodic romance. The form is very close to that of a Greek tragedy with Dido as heroine and the gods against her. But it does not over-balance into mere rhetoric, as Ovid's tragic situations so often do in the next generation. What rhetoric it displays belongs rather to tragedy, and may be found in the sharp incisions of Euripides, and in characters like his proud Medea. Its origins go back to Naevius and earlier. When Herodotus in the late fifth century BC explains the conflict of the Greeks with Persia in terms of Helen and of Troy no doubt he draws on tragedy, and Virgil's sub-theme of the conflict of Rome with Carthage, with the tragedy of Dido for its origin, shows a similar view of history. Indeed it is common in epic poetry in many of its forms for a woman to be found at the root of the tragic conflict: the prejudice is pre-literate, it appears.

It is particularly in virtue of the fourth book of the Aeneid that Virgil in his African mosaic sits enthroned between the Muses of tragic and of epic poetry. The poetry is magnificent, full of memorable phrases, and sustained by a long and rolling music. But it must be assumed that Virgil's world and its values, its views of marriage, of destiny, of faith and of religious duty, are quite different from ours. Aeneas and Dido are joined by magical and elemental power and the nymphs howl on the peaks when they couple, but they are not precisely married. From Dido's point of view, the story goes on to her rejection of her lover in the underworld in book six, a scene which is sad but inevitable. In this way as in many others the sixth book is pivotal, because after it Aeneas is free to concentrate on Italy and on the future. He must seek an Italian wife, which gives rise to the war in the second half of the Aeneid.

It is curious that his son by his dead wife Creusa, Ascanius, is his companion from book one onwards, and his heir, so that the Italian marriage seems unnecessary, but Virgil felt only a woman could be the adequate cause of the war. Ascanius was also called Iulus and the founder of that family, the *gens Iulia*, from which Augustus claimed descent. Livy records another version of these events, in which Ascanius was the son born in Italy to Aeneas and Lavinia. It is not clear why Aeneas failed to adopt that view, except that it falls outside the Aeneid, which ends like the Iliad with a death, not with the birth of a baby. At the same time, Virgil is never able to do as much with Ascanius as one expects. Anchises the father of Aeneas has a more important role. The claim to be descended from Ascanius, or the political usefulness of that claim, appears to have been about a hundred years old when Virgil was writing.

At the end of book three Aeneas fell silent, and book four opens with the Queen on fire, as it ends when that fire is out. 'She fed within her Veins a Flame unseen', as Dryden puts it. The body is volcanic, she feeds her trouble with her veins and a blind fire consumes her.

> Now, when the Purple Morn had chas'd away
> The dewy Shadows, and restor'd the Day
> Her Sister first with early Care she sought ...

The sister is called Anna, and her role is that of the member of a household in a Greek tragedy (they usually begin at dawn) to whom the heroine confides a dream. Anna has no part to play beyond this book in which she is intimately concerned with Dido's fate.

Ovid confuses her deliberately with Anna Perennis, a jolly goddess with an annual feast, also with a nymph daughter of Atlas, and with the goddesses Themis and Isis, and above all with the Anna who purified Aeneas after his last battle, and prepared him to become a god. These billowing and wonderful themes are not Virgilian, and if they existed before Ovid (Fasti 3, 611-650) then Virgil has taken care to suppress them, and his Anna is a classic human figure from a tragedy. The Aeneid is designed within bounds, and it cannot afford Ovidian extravagances. Varro a little earlier than Virgil maintained it was Anna and not Dido who fell in love with Aeneas and died by suicide. Probably Virgil could pick what elements he chose from the ramifications of tradition to make the classic form of his story. Book four is his if it is not Naevius's invention.

Dido coos like any pigeon about Aeneas. He is, as she confesses to Anna, the one man she would have married, had her life been other than it was and had she not forsworn marriage after the murder of her first husband Sychaeus by her brother Pygmalion (cf. Aen. 1, 343f.). As things stand, may she die, may she be blasted by lightning if she breaks her oath. Yet the phrase one remembers from her passionate speech is what Dryden calls 'the Sparkles of my ancient Flame', the traces of an old fire.

Anna replies (31) with generalised advice to think of children and of Venus's rewards. Is this how she cares for the dead? She has scorned many, Iarbas and others, but why scorn a man she likes? Carthage is surrounded by formidable enemies, and her own brother threatens war. Anna thinks Juno and the gods must have sent the Trojans this way. What a city and what kingdoms they might found together. She should ask pardon of the gods and delay the man, while winter rages at sea and wet Orion reigns.

These words 'added Fury to the kindled Flame'.

> Inspir'd with Hope, the Project they pursue;
> On every Altar Sacrifice renew;
> A chosen Ewe of two Years old they pay
> To Ceres, Bacchus and the God of Day:
> Preferring Juno's Pow'r: For Juno ties
> The Nuptial Knot, and makes the Marriage Joys.

Dido stands at the altar with a gold cup, and pours wine between the horns of a white heifer crowned with flowers, the priests pray and she offers incense. She anxiously inspects the entrails for an omen, but priests are useless (65) and no prayers can do her any good.

> A gentle Fire she feeds within her Veins
> Where the soft God secure in Silence reigns.

She raves and wanders like a deer hit by an arrow that runs to the woods and the glens of Crete, while still the arrow sticks. This figure of speech continues for only five lines (69-73) but it is memorably beautiful, and I think original. Dido takes Aeneas round the building works, she all but speaks and then falls silent. As day ends she gives another banquet and hangs again on the hero's lips as he repeats his story. At night she dreams of Aeneas, she holds little Ascanius – Cupid in disguise – on her lap for comfort. The picture we get of Dido in this nearly hysterical state of passion is highly convincing to this day. The city grows silent, no wall rises, no gate or tower or crane tottering against heaven (89).

When Juno sees what has happened she speaks at once to Venus (92) with biting sarcasm as if Venus brought it about. Venus realised Juno's wiliness and offered to give in to the will of Jove. Juno responded to this by outlining the next stage of the plan, which was a hunt in the woods.

> There while the Huntsmen pitch their Toils around
> And cheerful Horns from Side to Side resound,
> A Pitchy Cloud shall cover all the Plain ...

167

... One Cave a grateful Shelter shall afford
To the fair Princess and the Trojan Lord.
I will myself the bridal Bed prepare
If you to bless the Nuptials will be there:
So shall their Loves by crown'd with due Delights,
And Hymen shall be present at the Rites.

What she promises is more than a farce or a piece of comedy, though there is something masque-like about it, accentuated no doubt by Dryden. Virgil makes Juno as specious as a lawyer or a parson: I shall join them in lasting matrimony, and this will be their ceremony (126-7). Venus agreed and laughed because she detected Juno's trickery.

Meanwhile the Dawn left Ocean and arose, as she did in the Iliad (19, 1) 'from the streams of Ocean'. Virgil begins his eleventh book with the same pleasing phrase: Homer is enough and where dawn really breaks does not concern one in an epic. The young run out to hunt with the Massylian horsemen and the pack of sniffing hounds.

The lords of Carthage attend and the horse in its purple and gold chews the foaming bit while they await the Queen. She comes, with golden quiver, hair knotted up in gold, and a gold pin to her dress, and the Trojans join her, Iulus (Ascanius) joyful and Aeneas loveliest of all. The poem floats off in Hellenistic mood into trailing lines of beautiful Greek simile (143-150) from Apollonius of Rhodes, in which Aeneas is like Apollo among the Cretans and the noisy Parnassians and the painted Agathyrsi: the tattooed men of the remote north. This is a curious picture if one delays over it, but it means Apollo in spring, and the Cretans who founded Krissa in his Homeric hymn: the Alexandrians thought obscure learning one of the delights of poetry, they had been a generation of schoolmasters, and Virgil still carried that burden.

The hunt got up into the mountains and started wild goats and stags: one can hear the galloping feet. Ascanius is longing for a wild boar or a yellow mountain lion, when suddenly heaven rumbles (160), the sky clouds over and it hails. The hunt take shelter wherever they can, but Dido and Aeneas arrive at the same cavern. Earth and Juno of Weddings gave the sign, the heavens flashed fire and Nymphs shrieked on the topmost peak. That was the first day of death and the cause of evils to come. Dido was not concerned with rumour or appearance, she did not brood any longer on a secret love, she called it marriage and with that word covered up the fault (172).

The event had not lasted long apparently. In three unforgettable lines from Earth to the Nymphs sex was over, and the moralising had begun. Aeneas is neither blamed nor mentioned. And yet the lightning is also a metaphor for love, the rumbling and crashing noises, the streaming mountains and the screaming Nymphs offer a potent symbolism for the act of eros, if not for the longer drawn out affair we think of now as love.

Milton transforms Earth's signal to an earthquake, Dryden took a similar view, and commentaries a hundred or more years ago thought that might be what Virgil meant, but he is more likely to mean the peal of a trumpet. However that may be, those three lines are as powerful in their context as any in Latin poetry, and as compact. This was not the eros of Homer, Juno made no bed, no flowers sprang up beneath them, no golden cloud enveloped them.

> Then first the trembling Earth the signal gave;
> And flashing Fires enlighten all the Cave:
> Hell from below, and Juno from above,
> And howling Nymphs were conscious to their Love.

At once the personified Fame or Rumour, swiftest of all evils, ran through the cities of Libya, increasing in power. She was a daughter of Earth and sister of the giants, a frightful monster, with thousands of mouths and eyes and ears and feathers. She has 10 lines of physical description (180-90) and although she has roots in Lucretius (6,340) and even in Homer (Il. 4, 442) she is a Virgilian creation, turning all things to evil as the fury Allecto will do later on. She is the third irruption of a diabolic creature into the poem after Laocoon's snakes and Celaeno. Evil is an underlying theme in the poem and we shall watch its flowering.

What Fame does is to bring in Iarbas and tell him the news, which infuriates him all the more because he is a rejected lover of Dido's. Iarbas is the son of Zeus *Ammon*, an upper Egyptian god whose ram's horns Alexander the Great took over, and of a local nymph. Iarbas complains to Jove (206-218) and Jove sends Mercury to Aeneas, who is disappointing him. He was meant to reign in Italy, a land pregnant with empires and humming with wars, and in his descendants he was to subject the whole world to the rule of law (231). If the glory fails to move him, does he grudge Ascanius his Rome? What is he up to? Let him set sail (237).

Mercury put on his sandals and took his rod to control the dead and dreams, swam through swelling clouds and came on the top of Atlas that holds up the heavens, belted with dark cloud, his pine-forested head beaten with wind and rain. This is surely the passage Shakespeare remembered in *Hamlet*, 'In stature like the herald Mercury, new-lighted on some heaven-kissing hill'. Snow covers the shoulders of Atlas and his bristling beard glitters with ice. Here Mercury stands, then swoops like a bird after fish (255).

So Mercury flew, as a bird does between earth and heaven, cutting between the winds and lands. He found Aeneas gloriously dressed building castles, and addresses him directly with no pause, giving Jove's message and saying who sent it. Then suddenly he disappeared.

Aeneas was horrified, he could hardly speak and his hair stood on end. He burns to be away, to leave the sweet ground (279-80). What was he to do? He called his captains and told them to get the fleet ready secretly and get the crews to the beach. Meanwhile he would try to find the right time to tell Dido, and then join them; they obeyed at once (295).

But you can't fool your lover, so the Queen knew and feared what was coming. Wicked Rumour told her about the fleet. She ran about the city raving like a Bacchant on Cithaeron (303). In this rage she speaks to Aeneas (305) with the most passionate reproofs. The Libyans and the lords of the Nomads hate her, even Carthage is offended with her, all because of him, and she has lost her fame under heaven. Does he leave her to her brother Pygmalion or to Iarbas? If she had a child by Aeneas she would not mind so much (330).

He replies very briefly that he was not ashamed of her and would never forget her as long as he lived. He denies any deliberate trick and affirms his personal loyalty to his own past, if the fates allowed, he would rebuild Troy, but as things are Apollo has ordered him to make for Italy (346) and every night in the dark his father's unquiet ghost comes to him in dreams. He worries about his son's inheritance.

The speech began tight-lipped and cold, but the ghost added a certain warmth, and Mercury whom he now mentions (356) makes one shiver: I saw the god myself in open light / Enter these walls, I heard him with these ears (358-9). The words recall the poet's claim to have seen Pan in an Eclogue. But since this is an epic no Lucretian or Epicurean scruple remains:

> Stop setting fire to me and to yourself with your complaints,
> I make for Italy not by my own will (359-60).

With this half-line Aeneas ends. Dido can do no more than roll her eyes and answer him. We should remember that the early part of book four would have been a mere prelude in a Greek tragedy: this personal encounter would be the substance.

She calls him the faithless offspring of a Hyrcanian tiger spawned in the rocks of the Caucasus. Her passionate speech derives from Catullus (64, 154f.) where Ariadne reproaches Theseus, and now she is all fire, all fury. Whether one has a taste for them or not, these nearly hysterical speeches from ancient poetry can be impressive, and seldom more so than this one. If there is something a little stagey about it, that is because its mother was Athenian tragedy: so Dido is unanswerable, just as Aeneas was. She will follow him like an incarnate curse, like a hellish fury in dark fire expecting his death and his punishment. She breaks away (388) and leaves him:

> Abruptly there she stops: Then turns away
> Her loathing Eyes, and shuns the sight of Day.
> Amaz'd he stood, revolving in his Mind
> What Speech to frame, and what Excuse to find.
> Her fearful Maids their fainting Mistress led
> And softly laid her on her Iv'ry Bed.

Aeneas feels all the pains of a lover but he obeys the gods and makes for the shore. 'The oiled keel swims' and the sailors carry down wood from the forest with the leaves still on it (400). Between city and shore they swarm like dark ants.

> How Dido groaned upon her topmost tower!
> O wicked love, the things you drive us to!
> To weep again, to assault his heart again,
> To leave nothing untried for she will die!

She tries to get Anna to take a message and beg for his mercy; she is no Greek after all, no anti-Trojan. Why is he in such a hurry? She does not ask for marriage but only for time, for a delay, and then she will die.

They both weep. But Anna brings back no kindly message. It is like the blasting of an Alpine gale at an oak tree that has roots as vast as its branches:

> This way and that the Mountain Oak they bend,
> His Boughs they shatter, and his Branches rend;
> With Leaves and falling Mast they spread the Ground,
> The hollow Vallies echo to the Sound:
> Unmoved, the Royal Plant their Fury mocks;
> Or shaken, clings more closely to the Rocks.

If this is Aeneas, it is interesting that 'his branches reach to heaven, his roots to hell' (445-6) but his loyalty is not in our sense hellish. He is rooted in the past, they reach to the underworld of his memory, and for that reason he is not fit for marriage until after book six; that at least is my reading of Aeneas, that he is a man who cannot escape from the past. His mind's unmoved, the tears roll emptily (449).

That a man in real life could be so affected by war and defeat in war must have been common knowledge in Virgil's lifetime, and the Roman civil war left scars that took many years to heal. I do not think that Virgil has Augustus in mind, though for him too the wars had been bad enough. But a man whose mind scraped at heaven and at the future yet whose roots fumbled at the dark past, a man in a way not unlike Horace, must have been easy enough for Virgil to imagine.

> The wretched Queen, pursued by cruel Fate,
> Begins at length the light of Heav'n to hate:
> And loaths to live ...

Omens accumulate, wine turns to blood, and milk thickens as she sacrifices, and at her private temple her dead husband summons her to the grave. The solitary Screech Owl strains her Throat: / And on a Chimney's top, or Turret's height, / With Songs obscene disturbs the Silence of the Night. Her dreams are terrible, they are the worst dreams of tragedy, the illusions of Pentheus and Orestes.

Dido seeks now for the time and means of suicide, and of course she turns to Anna (478). She tells her in a thrilling bit of verse of a remote and magical sanctuary in the Atlas. Nigh Ocean's limit, next the falling Sun', lives the old priestess of the Garden of the Hesperides, who calmed the ancient guardian snake for Hercules with opium and honey.

> The yawning Earth rebellows to her Call;
> Pale Ghosts ascend; and Mountain Ashes fall.

Dido pretends by her advice she is entering into love magic. It is kill or cure, and she will either win Aeneas back or lose him altogether: the mysterious priestess is half-way between the backstreet witch Moeris in the eighth Eclogue and the Sibyl of Cumae. Dido wants a bonfire made of all the relics and arms and presents Aeneas has left, including their marriage bed.

Anna thinks this no worse than Dido's grief over Sychaeus, so she agrees.

> The fatal Pile they rear
> Within the secret Court, expos'd in Air.
> The cloven Holms and Pines are heaped on high
> And Garlands on the hollow Spaces lye.
> Sad Cypress, Vervain, Eugh, compose the Wreath
> And every baleful Green denoting Death ...

172

VII. SAND

The priestess comes with loose hair to call on the death-gods, on Night, Erebus, Chaos and Hecate, sprinkles 'feign'd Avernian drops' of water, and

> Culls hoary Simples, found by Phoebe's Light,
> With brazen Sickles reap'd at Noon of Night,
> Then mixes baleful Juices in the Bowl:
> And cuts the Forehead of a new born Fole,
> Robbing the Mother's love. The destin'd Queen
> Observes, assisting at the Rites obscene.

She held a cake and stood with one foot bare, her dress 'girt up' and her hair loose: she called on the stars and all those powers that avenge the injuries of love (521). Night fell when men and all beasts of the wilderness were silent but the Queen's troubles, her raging love and furious anger had all re-awakened (532). What is she to do, marry a Nomad or follow the fleet? It is not a thinkable solution. There is no likeness by the way between Dido and Cleopatra, intended or unintended. She must die, that is the only solution. One cannot live like an innocent animal (551).

Meanwhile Aeneas was asleep on the poop of his ship, ready to set off, when Mercury appeared in his dreams. How can you sleep in such danger, the god asks, can you not feel the favourable wind? The Queen is bound for death and raising all kinds of trouble. Get out while you can, by dawn the beach will be full of burning torches and the sea of shipping. Be quick, *la donna è mobile*. And he mingled with the darkness of night (560-70).

Aeneas was terrified by the sudden visitation and woke his sailors. With a quick prayer to whoever the god was, he cut the rope with his sword and they were off (580). They twisted the white foam and dug the blue sea. Now Dawn sprinkled the earth with new light, leaving Tithonus (her husband) and her saffron bed (585).

When the Queen saw the light brightening and the fleet at sea with no ships left, her speech (590-629) was more eloquent than any that Ovid, who shamelessly imitated it, ever wrote, and longer than usual. She then calls on an old nurse, as is usual in Greek tragedies, and makes her arrangements (634-40). She has prayed or rather cursed to the Sun, to Hecate of crossroads, and the Furies, and she wants Aeneas to lie unburied on the sand, as Palinurus will be: she has even ordered the Carthaginian war to take place. As Dido dies on the still unlighted bonfire, she speaks her own obituary list of achievements (653-8). This is how to die, she says, and the Trojan will see the fire.

As she dies her people find her and the noise and horror sound like the fall of Carthage or of Tyre, with fire in the rooftops of gods and of men (671). Her sister rushes around beating her breasts and tearing at herself: she flings herself on the dying Dido.

Juno puts an end to this extreme scene (693) by sending Iris, dewy and yellow-winged, to take a lock of Dido's hair to the King of Hell, since she died before her time. This surprising passage is Hellenistic in feeling and very pretty. Its ancestry by Catullus out of Callimachus is venerable enough. It is brief and has a certain freshness. The whole of the fourth book has been a set piece that will not be repeated, and the fact that a Hellenistic border is boldly fitted to a more ancient, blood-stained and deadly serious tapestry should not surprise anyone who has entered into the poetry of Virgil and his method of composition.

The fifth book begins with the fleet at sea. The south wind speeds him over the dark water, but Aeneas can see the fire at Carthage. He does not know what it means but he fears and suspects what has happened. Then there is no more land, only sky and sea and bad weather (11). Palinurus calls out from the high poop asking what Neptune is up to. He warns Aeneas they will never make Italy with such a sky. The wind has altered and now Palinurus feels the best hope is Eryx in Sicily. He knows this somehow by the stars, though they do not seem to be shining (25).

The fleet turns east, which pleases Aeneas because his father (3, 710) Anchises was buried there. It is Acestes who sees them while he is out hunting on a mountain top dressed in a shaggy African bearskin, and he welcomes them to land. He is the son of a Sicilian river Virgil calls Crinisus and a Trojan girl, we are told, and remembering his parents he offers 'country wealth'.

When day has put the stars to flight, Aeneas makes his men a speech from a tump of ground (45). This is the anniversary of his father's death and burial. Wherever he was he would observe the day, but much more so here at the old man's grave. Everyone can join in, because Acestes is offering two cattle to every ship. If the ninth dawn is fine, Aeneas offers a prize for the fleet, for foot-racing, javelins, archery and boxing.

They crown themselves with myrtle and set about celebrating (72-4). He pours wine, milk and blood on the earth and strews purple flowers; he prays, and at once a huge snake comes out of the ground glistening with many colours. The tump where he spoke was his father's tumulus. Aeneas wonders if this is the Genius of the place or his father's servant: he slaughters a pair of sheep, a pair of swine and a pair of bullocks. They all join in and get down to cooking.

On the ninth day (104) the games begin. They are very fully described and they are the main subject of book five. To the Romans they had the fascination of popular entertainment, an antiquarian interest like Homer's games, and the glamour and glitter of great contemporary poetry: for us, these attractions have largely faded. We must imagine the crowd of locals, some ready to compete, the prizes set out and the trumpets from the mound in the middle. (The snake has sensibly made himself scarce.)

Four chosen ships are to race, one under Mnestheus founder of the Memmii as Varro had recorded in his Trojan Families, Gyas, Sergestus of the Sergii, and Cloanthus of the Cluentii. The ships must row round an offshore rock where the cormorants (?) like to sun themselves. Aeneas has marked it with a green branch. The captains wear gold and purple, the rowers gleam with oil and wear crowns of poplar.

At the sound of a trumpet, they are off (140) and the sea is torn open with oars and the beaks of ships. They are swifter than a chariot race and the hills roar again with the applause. Gyas is winning, Cloanthus is too heavy to catch him. But Gyas yells to his steersman to go closer to the rocks, as Cloanthus takes this dangerous course: the boy Gyas weeps and he flings his steersman overboard. The poor fellow climbs onto the rock where he sits dripping. The Trojans laughed to see him fall, to see him swimming and to see him vomiting up the sea-water. Sergestus and Mnestheus gained the hope of overtaking Gyas and coming second. The battle is hard fought but Sergestus smashed his oars on the rock and Mnestheus beats him, like a dove fluttering from a cave and then gliding quietly to rest (217). The race nearly ended in a draw but Cloanthus won it with a prayer.

> The Quire of Nymphs, and Phorcus from below
> With Virgin Panopea heard his Vow;
> And old Portunus with his breadth of Hand
> Push'd on, and sped the Gally to the Land.

The race has been so dramatic as to be implausible, but the description is as lively as it could be, the rowers sweat in rivers and the similes are not banalities, indeed they are more memorable than the action. Maybe this is all a kind of foreplay for the epic treatment of war itself, and if so it bodes well. And yet there is something that generates ennui in all this boyish good fun.

The prizes are elaborate and weigh heavily. The first is a dress embroidered with the rape of Ganymede described like a real event, but the words drowsily recall Lucretius (2, 500) and his gleam of Thessalian sea-purple: the boy seeming to pant as he runs after deer, the cruelty of the eagle and the howl of the dogs add a disquieting touch of homosexual realism (252-7). The second prize is some preposterously massive gold-crusted armour that gave a phrase to the British coinage under George III and Elizabeth II, *decus et tutamen* glory and security: two servants could hardly carry it. The third prize was silver and bronze, and they all wore crimson ribbons when at last Sergestus came to shore, his ship like a snake run-over in the road or half-killed by a passerby. He came in under sail and Aeneas was pleased his ship survived, so Sergestus was given a Cretan slave girl called Pholoe and her twin babies (285): the prize is Homeric (Il. 23, 705). Is this bad taste, or a joke and so even worse taste? The German scholar Gossrau pointed out that an American of his day would not find the prize surprising, but things have changed since his day. My own feeling is that Virgil's mind has gone into some wrong gear from Ganymede onwards.

Aeneas moves from the shore to the green field of a natural amphitheatre (286). Here Nisus and Euryalus, whom the poet loves, are to compete in the running, Euryalus 'splendid in shape and fresh youth' (295) and Nisus 'for his holy love of the boy' (296). There is no link of kinship as there would be in the Iliad between such a couple. Everyone running is to have a prize and there are three first prizes with olive crowns: a horse, an Amazon quiver with a gold baldric, and an Argive helmet. The race is swift and dramatic when Nisus in the lead slipped on some bullock blood, which is much what happens in the Iliad (23, 763f.), and Euryalus who was lying third wins in his place. Salius protests, but the crowd favours beauty. Aeneas rewards Salius, who was (5, 229) an Arcadian from Tegea, with a lion-skin. Nisus says: What about me then? showing his filthy face, so Aeneas laughs and gives him a wonderful shield. In the course of a lifetime I have nearly never reread all this nonsense, but it belongs with the rest. The shield was torn down by Greeks from a temple of Neptune (360), and how Aeneas came by it we have no idea.

Now comes the boxing match, always a damaging contest even at Olympia, brutal in Homer, and here exaggerated beyond our tolerance with massive and dangerous metal-studded gloves (405). An old champion agrees to fight a baroque younger boxer. If you think these gloves are bad, says the old man, you should have seen the ones Hercules wore (411). They fight with more normal and equal hand-thongs, but the emphasis is still on strength, and the model is Apollonius of Rhodes. The old man loses his temper and half murders the Trojan so Aeneas stops the fight, but the winner to show what he could do then murders the bull which is his prize with one solid thump, breaking in the animal's fore-head. He then retires from the boxing ring for ever (484).

The shooting of arrows follows. For this they tie a dove to the top of a ship's mast. Hippocoon draws the lot to shoot first: being a son of Hyrtacus (9, 177) he must be a brother of Nisus, but Virgil does not really care about this. Mnestheus shoots wearing his olive crown from the regatta and Eurytion and Acestes shoot third and fourth. The first hits the mast, the second the knot and sets the bird free, and Pandarus's brother Eurytion kills the poor bird anyway.

Acestes produces a magic firework. He fires into the air and his arrow bursts into flames and disappears (524-8) like a meteor or a falling star. Everyone prays at this amazing omen and Aeneas makes a little speech. The climax has been unexpected and the verse faultless.

Aeneas now orders a cavalry exhibition led by Ascanius like one of those young princes who were *dux iuventutis*, leader of the youth of Rome in succession under Augustus. There are three troops each of a dozen riders in this display, under Polites, Atys of the Atii, the family of Augustus's mother, and young Iulus, all ancestors of great families. The prettiest horse is a chestnut and white Thracian pony such as the Riders rode at Athens: they were inspected every year, and they are the horses on the frieze of the Parthenon. The Trojans are pleased to see boys looking like their fathers.

The tracks they follow are like the Labyrinth (588) and they sport like dolphins (594). Ascanius passed on this tradition to Alba Longa and so to Rome: and the boys are now called 'Troy, the Game of Troy'.

At this happy moment, Juno takes a hand. The storm has already shown she was still actively hostile, and old Anchises is rather a hero, and a Greek hero at that to judge by ritual, than a god. Juno's plan is to send down Iris as an old woman, invisible at first, as the wind bears her down the rainbow (609-10) to where the Trojan women are lamenting over Anchises on their own and gazing gloomily at the frightening sea (617).

Iris takes the form of Beroe wife of Doryclus and she persuades them to burn the fleet and settle where they are. She tells them Cassandra advised her in a dream (623-40). She is first to fling fire, but Priam's old nurse Pyrgo recognises her as a goddess by her flashing eyes (648).

> ... the Matrons, seiz'd with new Amaze,
> Rowl their malignant Eyes, and on the Navy gaze.
> They fear, and hope, and neither part obey:
> They hope the fated Land, but fear the fatal Way.
> The Goddess, having done her Task below,
> Mounts up on equal Wings, and bends her painted Bow.

Her Task was all too easily done. Although one may regret Virgil's view of women – and question whether it would be quite so low in another context – there is no doubt that here he expresses near-contempt.

The women are possessed by some divine craze, and break out into mad riot, setting fire to all the ships. Yet it was certainly Juno who possessed them, and when the Trojans arrive in alarm, the women scatter and hide in caves and woods, and Juno's possession is over (679). That does not put the fire out of course, until Aeneas prays to Jupiter, who sends torrential rain and saves four ships.

Aeneas is still in doubt whether to sail on or to settle in Sicily when old Nautes, who learnt sailing from Athene herself, gives him advice. Let him leave the old men and women behind, let them live in a town here called Acesta (later Segesta) with Acestes, but let all the young and brave make for Italy (718). In this way Aeneas transforms his trailing refugees into the young heroes necessary for the rest of the story, so the brief appearance of Nautes is of some importance. Varro says he was the founder of the Nautii, and brought away the Palladion (the Luck of Troy) from the ruins of Troy. Aeneas does not go quite so far (the word *nautes* is the Greek for a sailor).

Night falls at once, so that Anchises can address Aeneas in a dream. He comes by Jupiter's orders with the same advice as Nautes has just given, but he adds that Aeneas must first visit the underworld, and seek out his father who is not in the gloom of Tartarus but the holy Elysium: Here the Sibyl with much blood of black cattle shall lead you, there you shall learn the story of your race, and see your walls. And now farewell, dewy Night turns her course, and the rough Sunrise breathes with panting team (735-9). So he spoke and fled like smoke in the air.

Aeneas longed to go on with this conversation, he stirred up the fire and made offerings to Vesta and the household gods, then he woke Acestes, who luckily agreed with his requests. They repaired the ships, while Aeneas marked out the new city with the plough (755). That was when he founded the temple of Venus Erycina on top of Mount Eryx which is he says a neighbour to the stars. It is still worth visiting when free of clouds, though little is to be seen but the site, which when I saw it was an overgrown garden. Anchises got a priest and a sacred wood.

This book has been a strange amalgam, and so far it appears to lack momentum as romances do, as the chapters of the Apuleius's *Golden Ass* often do for example. The women possessed by Juno are a mere sketch of something that will happen in Italy, and so is the fire in the fleet. But the ending of book five is extraordinary and thrilling.

For nine days they feast, a magic touch from the Iliad,[1] then the fleet sets out, paying three calves to the hero Eryx, and a ewe-lamb to the Tempests, whose cult was real in Rome and is noticed by Horace. Aeneas flings the guts of sacrifice into the sea (776) and the right wind blows. Meanwhile Venus conciliates Neptune, who is (799) *Saturnius* as Juno is *Saturnia*, a member of the older and most powerful generation of the gods. The god gives a brief apologia which applies interestingly to Homeric poetry and agrees to take just one more victim. One head for many shall be sacrificed (815).

Neptune then harnesses his horses with gold and shakes their foaming reins, his blue car speeds lightly away, the sea-swell falls level under the thundering axle, and clouds flee across heaven. His troop follows him, and Virgil lingers over their wonderful Greek names. We are not told where Neptune is going or where Venus met him, it is all sea-glitter and sea-spray; if this is Hellenistic verse adapted from Homer, then the trick had never been better done.

The fleet sets out under sail, tacking together, with Palinurus in the leading ship. Sleep slips down from heaven bringing evil to you, Palinurus, and sits on the high poop like the hero Phorbas: Palinurus son of Iasus, he says, the sea is carrying the fleet, the winds blow evenly, it is time for rest, lay down your head and I will watch for you (846).

Palinurus replies that the sea is dangerous, he clutches the rudder and keeps his eyes on the stars. But the god holds a branch dripping with Lethe water, and drips the power of the Styx on both the sailor's temples: he shuts his struggling eyes, pulls away the superstructure of the poop, and drops Palinurus in the flowing sea. They are near the rocks of the Sirens, white with seamen's bones, when Aeneas wakes, corrects the ship's course (how?) and laments his friend's death. Too trusting in the peace of heaven and the sea, Palinurus, you shall lie naked on the unknown sand (870-1). So the book ends, with one of those curiously touching epitaphs that make us sense the humanity of Virgil, and which he manages so well in the later books.

The sixth book is Aeneas in the underworld. It is modelled on the underworld visions of Odysseus and it has something in common with the great painting at Delphi described at length by Pausanias, and it builds on Roman and pre-Roman tradition which we can see in the 'Cave of Orcus', and which surfaces again in the medieval doctrine of Hell and Purgatory and in the vast fantasy of Dante. Where it touches on philosophy it is wonderfully eclectic.

There is no doubt that the Romans of Virgil's time found it intensely moving. I said earlier there survived a mysterious and unlikely tale that Virgil or his editors shifted the order of the earlier books – and certainly a phoney opening attached itself like a clam to book one – but no one has ever denied the strength of books two, four and six, and we know that Virgil, who read in public only when he needed reassurance, read book six to Augustus and his family: the mother of Marcellus, who had just died at that time, fainted when she heard him commemorated.

The literary source for Virgil's roll-call of the ancient Romans was Varro's Images, as Nicholas Horsfall has pointed out, but for Marcellus he used the Emperor's speech at the young man's funeral. There is indeed some character of a public monument about this book of the Aeneid, though the springs of its grief are personal. The only modern analogy is *In Memoriam* as Tennyson first planned it, nine poems of five stanzas each, every poem a single sentence, about the ship that brought Hallam's dead body to England. Yet In Memoriam as we have it is an overgrown garden, and there are some curious features to be noticed in the construction of the sixth book of the Aeneid too.

Earlier I already hinted at the function of book six as the hinge of the poem, and the necessary precondition of the entry of the new Aeneas into Italy and of his mission to found Rome and the Roman people, two very different entities. Augustus found Rome brick and left it marble, a fact emphasised today by the survival of so much imperial brick once faced in marble that has long ago gone to the lime kilns. Virgil does not linger over the praises of Rome as a city, because in his time it was a vast urban agglomeration, constantly increasing and inhabited largely by ex-slaves of mixed race. Even the senate was a ghostly assembly, and the attempts of Augustus to revive so many of the institutions of the republic were not all obviously victorious. Virgil was more interested in Italy, the Italian ('Roman') race of tough and dour farmers. It is that wider and rather new version of Rome that Anchises would show Aeneas in the underworld.

It takes Virgil nearly a third of the 901 lines of this book to get Aeneas into that dark and ghostly place. He must first make his landing at 'the Euboean shores of Cumae' as he calls it (2) or 'the Hesperian coast'. It seems to have little to do with Italy, it is part of the odyssey of Aeneas as Sicily was: the true landing in Italy will be in book seven. Cumae was founded perhaps in Homer's lifetime in the eighth century BC, but its traditional date was in the eleventh BC, and it was from Cumae that the Greek settlements spread on the west coast of Italy for two or three-hundred years. In 474 BC it helped to overcome the Etruscans in Campania, though it was taken over soon afterwards by the Sabelli, an expanding Italian people who talked Oscan. The coinage of Cumae showed a formalised Triton's horn and a bud of barley bursting open. The shell is probably the fishermen's instrument, which was still used to call fishermen together when a shoal appeared, as late as the nineteenth century when it was observed in use by Edward Lear. At this venerable place the Sibyl's cave is still an impressive object of pilgrimage, and Colin Hardie has shown it to be highly probable that the cave system behind the Sibyl's cavern was a centre of underworld mysteries and strange rivers of the dead. Virgil's antiquarianism has for this reason a strong religious colouring here, which began to emerge perhaps in Sicily.

The young Trojans scatter along the beach unknowing, they seek the seeds of fire that lurk in flints, fell trees, and explore rivers. But Aeneas looks for the acropolis where high Apollo presides, and the Sibyl's terrifying hiding-place, in a vast cavern where the god inspires his priests and opens the future.

Aeneas enters the groves of Hecate and the golden roof (13). This is where Daedalus dedicated to Apollo 'the oarage of his wings' when he came to land, escaping from Crete, and built the mighty temple. On the doors the death of Androgeos is worked in bronze, for which death the Athenians had to pay seven boys a year to the Minotaur. He was a son of Minos and Pasiphae, murdered at some games in Athens, but he shares the name of a Greek hero who died at Troy in book two.

Virgil does not mind. He only wants to describe this fine piece of mythological antiquity, which if we see it as an archaic bronze, as other 'works of Daedalus' are in Pausanias, then it may well have been seen by Virgil at Cumae. And yet the way he ties his account to the wickedness of Venus, the passion of Pasiphae for the bull, and so to the Minotaur and the unfollowable windings of his labyrinth, does suggest this is only a literary invention foreshadowing what is to come. Certain touches of landscape (23) and the string in the labyrinth seem to rule out archaic bronze-working. And it is a strange fact that Androgeos had an Altar of the Hero in the harbour at Athens and his wooden figure was carried on the poop of ships. He is oddly close to Palinurus son of Iasos, another hero-name, and it is possible that in researching Palinurus, whose name suggests a wind and who has a stormy cape named after him, Virgil may have stumbled on the similar Androgeos.

Aeneas sees how Daedalus had tried and failed to represent Icarus with the others, when suddenly his friend Achates brings him the Sibyl. There is no time for gazing about, she says, bring seven bullocks and seven sheep (37-8); and she summons them inside the sanctuary.

The cave has a hundred entrances, a hundred doors, and booms in a hundred voices. On the threshold she throws a prophetic fit (46-51) as the god takes her over. She demands vows and prayers at once if the doors are to gape open.

A cold shiver shakes the Trojans, and Aeneas prays. He has searched and laboured to catch the fleeing coast of Italy, now he demands the help of all the gods for a new start, and above all the help of the Sibyl. At this point one should emphasise that Sibyls existed all over the eastern Mediterranean, and the Romans were obsessed by the fragmentary books of their prophecies, which were like leaves blown about in the autumn: as numerous and as unintelligible. Those that survive to this day are mostly Jewish: but Virgil names his Sibyl, and such prophetesses of Apollo really existed, just as early records were really written on leaves and only later on leaf-shaped clay tablets.

Aeneas promises Hecate and Phoebus a temple of solid marble with feast days in honour of Apollo. He begs the Sibyl not to write her prophecies on leaves which will blow away but to chant them (76). The wild priestess riots in her cave trying to shake off the god, but the great doors swing open. She prophesies worse trouble on land than he met at sea, wars and the Tiber running blood, a second

Achilles and Juno's enmity. The trouble will be over a woman (as it was about Helen).

> Yield not to evils: go more boldly on
> Where Fortune shall allow. You will be saved
> By a Greek city, which you don't foresee (96-8).

The Sibyl sings her terrible riddles and the cave bellows back. When she quiets down Aeneas tells her he has well considered all these labours, but all he asks is, since this place is the door of hell, to see his dear father (108). He claims the same as was granted to Orpheus and Pollux and Theseus and Hercules.

She tells him the descent is easy and the gate open day and night, but the trouble is retracing your steps. A very few by virtue and divine blood or because Jove loved them have managed it. The centre is forest and black Cocytus (river of wailing) flows around it. If you are so crazy as to cross the Stygian lake twice and see Tartarus (hell) twice, this is what you must do. There is one golden bough on a dark tree that all the grove and shadows cover in the folds of ground. This golden branch is holy to Juno, and it must be carried to the Queen of hell, Proserpina (125-42).

For many years I wondered if this golden bough meant mistletoe, but we do not know how much Virgil knew or believed about that, though Pliny knew something. Nicholas Horsfall offers a corrective to anachronism in such matters, and the golden bough must remain, like the golden fleece or the golden apples of the Hesperides, something from a story undatably old. When you pluck the golden bough another grows in its place: if you are fated to 'descend' it is easy to pluck, otherwise impossible (148).

Aeneas and Achates depart wondering whom she means, but find the dead body of Misenus the trumpeter, drowned by Triton for challenging him on the conch. That must be an old story, given the coins of Cumae, and Virgil does say 'if it is to be believed' (173).

Again the axes crash in the ancient forest, tall house of beasts, and they burn Misenus, whose name is that of a landmark. Aeneas is worried by the immense forest, and prays (187) to be shown the golden bough. Luckily white doves appear: a word to Venus, and they lead him to the stinking jaws of Avernus (201) where they fly up and settle on the boughs of the green tree with the golden glitter. It is just like mistletoe in winter (205) and the gold tinkled in the wind. Aeneas swiftly took it home to the Sibyl (210). Cato and Cicero knew mistletoe, and Virgil mentions it innocently in the first Georgic as *viscum*; so here it is only a simile: it is metallic and like mistletoe, the amazing foreign growth which is so

182

striking in bare branches in the winter. It grows even in Gloucestershire where hell has no entrance, and there is no golden bough.

Misenus is burnt with full ceremony and tears, and Aeneas builds his mighty tomb, a landmark for ever (235). He then goes to a vast cavern hidden by lake Avernus (that no bird can cross because it is so sulphurous) and by dark groves. They slaughtered four bullocks there, and Aeneas a black ewe lamb and a barren heifer to the underworld gods, whom Virgil summons in wonderfully dark and rolling syllables (247-53). The ground bellows under their feet, the trees are shaken and they see the dogs howling in the shadows as the goddess comes.

The Sibyl warns away the uninitiated, and tells Aeneas to draw his sword (260) as he follows beside her.

> Then Earth began to bellow, Trees to dance,
> And howling Dogs in glimmering Light advance ...
> ... Ye Realms, yet unreveal'd to Human sight,
> Ye Gods, who rule the Regions of the Night,
> Ye gliding Ghosts, permit me to relate
> The mystick Wonders of your silent State.
> Obscure they went through dreary Shades, that led
> Along the waste Dominions of the dead:
> Thus wander Travellers in Woods by Night,
> By the Moon's doubtful and malignant Light ...

At the jaws of hell they come upon abstractions, sorrows and diseases, then Famine and Want, Death and his half-brother Sleep, Strife and the Furies. Gradually these mysterious forms take on a reality and the mythical mingles with the vague and night-marish. Sleep roosts in an elm tree whose leaves shelter dreams, then come chimerical creatures like the hydra and the gorgon and centaurs. Aeneas made to attack these visions but the Sibyl warned him they were insubstantial. In hell, Virgil is impressionist and misty.

They come to where Acheron runs into Cocytus and to where the ghastly old man Charon stands as ferryman with his pole and his punt, aged but strong (304). Here the bank is crowded with the dead, like the leaves fallen at the first frost of autumn or like migrating birds (310-2). They stand begging for a crossing, stretching out their hands in longing for the other bank, but the old sailor picks and chooses. Aeneas wonders why.

These are the dark lakes of Wailing (*Cocytus*) and the marshes of the Styx, which even the gods fear to swear by and deceive (323-4), he is told. These are the unburied: those the ferryman takes have been buried and the water carries them. The rest wander a hundred years and flutter round this coast, and then they can cross over.

Aeneas pondered their unequal fate, he saw among them Leucaspis and Orontes who died at sea, and then Palinurus who tells the story of his death: he was murdered by wreckers on the coast at Velia (*portus Velini*) after surviving three days and nights in the sea, and Aeneas should seek his body there and bury it. The Sibyl tells him not to worry, he will be buried and honoured for ever by the shore, and his grave marked with miracles. Alas Velia is lost now, but there is still a Cape Palinuro, an afternoon's journey south from Paestum.

Charon is churlish about taking them across (388f.). The place belongs to ghosts, dreams and sleepy night, and Charon still regretted carrying Hercules and Theseus and Pirithous. One tried to steal the dog of hell and the others the Queen of hell.

To this the 'Amphrysian priestess' replies. By this obscure title Virgil means the Sibyl. Apollo was the shepherd of Amphrysus in the third Georgic (2), but here Virgil seems deliberately to recall an earlier and Greek descent into the underworld that does not survive (398). Charon is shown the golden bough, which he has seen once long ago (no one knows when) and takes them, though the punt groans under the solid weight of Aeneas (413).

The other bank brings them to Cerberus, the three-headed guard dog, barking with all three heads in his cave. His hair has snakes in it which look angry so the Sibyl flings it a bit of drugged and honeyed food (Apollonius of Rhodes had Jason do the same, 4, 152f., in similar words). Now Aeneas hears laments and the cries of babies, those who died early and suicides. The souls of dead children become in medieval doctrine the souls of unbaptised babies: Norden explains all such puzzles of the history of doctrine. Minos is the traditional judge of the dead. There is a grove of women famous for tragic love stories, all Greek of course (444f.) except that among them glides Dido (450). Aeneas sees her like a moon in clouds, he addresses her passionately but she will not look at him. She goes back into the wood to her old lover Sychaeus (474) and leaves Aeneas to weep on his own.

At last they come to the far meadows of heroes famous in war, that is Greek epic heroes, though not at first those of Homer. First came Tydeus and Parthenopaeus and Adrastus, and then the Trojans out of Homer he remembers. When the Greeks see Aeneas glittering in arms they are terrified (491), some turn and run as they ran once for their ships, some squeak because they cannot scream.

Here Aeneas found Deiphobus mutilated by the Greeks, that is Menelaus personally and Odysseus, because he was found as the husband of Helen, who betrayed him. This is an episode of lurid horror, but it ends in pathos. At this moment (535) the night was half over, and the Sibyl hurried the hero along.

'Night rushes and we pass its hours in tears'. The road divides (540), one way to Elysium and the palace of Dis, King of the underworld, and the other to Tartarus and hellish punishments: belief in punishment in hell was already old and deeply rooted. Deiphobus says his humble goodbye and returns to the dark.

Aeneas can now see Phlegethon, the river of flame, and Tisiphone, chief torturer of the wicked. He can hear the groans, the lashes and the clanging chains (558). The Sibyl knows that region because Hecate showed her round when she was first put in charge of the Avernian groves. Rhadamanthus rules there, the Hydra is inside, and Tisiphone and her nasty sisters do the torturing. Hell is twice as deep as the sky is high above Mount Olympus (579). Here live the Titans of mythology (580) and famous sinners like Salmoneus of Elis who pretended to be Zeus, and Prometheus for ever eaten alive by a vulture. Here also are the Lapiths, Ixion and Pirithous. Theseus, who abandoned his friend and was rescued by Hercules, is not mentioned, and the old commentaries suggest the text is faulty: Tantalus has been left out, and yet the next line (602) refers to him. 'Over him the dark flint falls or seems to fall', but the Oxford text with some manuscript excuse prefers to read 'Over them ...' Tantalus and his rock were in the painting Pausanias describes at Delphi all the same. Yet if Tantalus and his rock were mentioned at all it should have been before line 601. Aeschylus on the fate of Prometheus is also ignored.

We then hear of worldly sinners at a dinner they can never eat, and of typically Roman sins (608-13), of those who roll great rocks or hang on spokes of wheels, and of Theseus who sits and will sit for ever. There was an embarrassing legend that he was rescued but that he left his bottom behind on the rock that had grown into his flesh. John Barron has pointed out an Athenian vase painting of the rescue where he was sitting on his cloak, as if in denial of this painful story, and was summoned to arise, not tugged off the rock like a tooth by Hercules (617-8). But Virgil takes a sterner view. Phlegyas (Ixion's father) gives a dreadful warning (620), and the list of sins continues with the sins of tyrants, such as corruption and incest. With a hundred tongues Virgil could not declare them all.

The Sibyl hurries him up past the workshops of the Cyclopes to leave his gifts at the gate and enter (638) the happy lands, the meadows of delight, the fortunate woods. They have their own sun and their own stars. Some heroes play games, some dance and sing, and the Thracian (Orpheus) plays for them. Aeneas sees the oldest of Trojans, their ghostly chariots and grazing horses (653-5). He watches the paean sung by those who died for their country, the chaste priests and the good poets in the sweet-smelling grove of bay, where the Po (659) or Eridanus of childhood runs down through the trees. He sees the public benefactors and all who wear white brow-bands. Here the Sibyl notices Musaeus, and asks after Anchises. But she is told they have no houses, presumably they just

185

wander about and sleep where they like: the travellers have only to climb this hill, and he will show them all the glittering meadows.

Anchises (679) is in the next valley inspecting souls who have still to live, his own dear descendants. When he sees Aeneas (684-8) he greets him with tears and open arms, but Aeneas tries in vain to embrace him, the ghost eludes him like a light wind or a winged dream. Here Aeneas sees Lethe, the river of forgetfulness, and the great throng of people like bees on a summer day among the flowers. He is terrified and asks for an explanation, and Anchises (713) explains they drink forget-fulness and await reincarnation, but now he wants to number his own with Aeneas, so that they can be glad together over Italy (718).

Aeneas thinks the appetite for life is terrible, so Anchises explains that one spirit occupies the entire material universe: hence men, animals, birds and creatures of the sea. Sparks of heavenly fire are in them but bodies weigh them down, so they know fear and desire, grief and pleasure. When they die, not all the evil vanishes at once, but traces have grown into them, so they suffer, some hung in the empty winds, some under the seas, some burn. We all suffer our own ghost, then are sent to Elysium and a few of us live here until the long circle of time has destroyed our ingrained fault, and leaves our heavenly sense and simple fire. After a thousand years the god brings us to Lethe again and to the upper world (724-51).

This strange Pythagorean passage (724-51) which is so convincing as an ancient creed, and so moving, so pregnantly phrased and memorable, is in its place simply in order to explain how Anchises can show Aeneas Romans not yet born, who were history or myth in Virgil's day but the merest futurity in the Aeneid. The device is entirely successful, and the touches of antique colouring in the words add to its effect. We hardly believed in the hell of the Aeneid, but this one we might believe in for an hour, and the extent to which Virgil dabbles in the solemnities of Plato does not affect us.

The three of them now view the coming generations from a mound, a tump or a tumulus. Anchises will expound the glory of the Italian race (757). The first is Silvius, Aeneas's posthumous Italian son by Lavinia (760-6), the King of Alba Longa. Then Procas, Capys, Numitor and Silvius Aeneas. They will name Nomentum, Gabii, and so on (773-6), of which at least Gabii was a deserted, ruined place in Horace's time. Romulus and his descent from Mars is noted, though barely so. At last we come to Rome with its seven hills, first defined by Varro it seems (783): Rome like the Phrygian mother goddess (often shown crowned with towers on coins), and to Caesar (789) and his clan. Here is Augustus Caesar who will bring back the age of gold to Latium. He will rule Spain and India and lands beyond our stars.

Beyond the Solar Year; without the Starry Way.
Where Atlas turns the rowling Heav'ns around:
And his broad shoulders with their Lights are crown'd.
At his fore-seen Approach, already quake
The Caspian Kingdoms and Maeotian Lake.
Their Seers behold the Tempest from afar;
And threatning Oracles denounce the War.

The heightened language in which Virgil (and Dryden) now speak is that of prophetic and oracular books with which the Romans must have been familiar, as we are with the Revelation of John. The triumph will outdo Hercules, and Bacchus returning victorious from India. The triumph of that god is fully described only by Nonnus, a later Greek poet, in a baroque catalogue in which Sleep sits as he does in the elm tree beneath all whose leaves are dreams.

We return to the praises of Roman heroes which go on about 35 lines. It is splendid (809-46) but there is something statuesque about them, and they recall the inspiring statues Augustus was to put up to them. Numa the founder of the laws is too famous even to need naming here: the description is enough. Tullus and Ancus, the Tarquins and Brutus follow, with a strong plea for liberty (820). We descend from mythic to legendary and so historic times, and to Caesar descending from Monaco and the Alps, and Pompey in the east (830-1). They are adjured to drop civil war, and we return to the list in historical order, which Virgil has deliberately discomposed: the point to which we return is the conquest of Greece, Hannibal and Spartacus being shameful episodes. We are to recall Cato and Cossus and the Gracchi. Cossus was a hero in a fifth century BC war, and Livy records that Augustus was interested in him, otherwise he is harder to explain than Caesar coming down 'from Monaco and the Alps'. But the mixture of characters cannot seriously be sorted out: we go back to the Scipios and to a bit of Ennius about Fabius Cunctator (846) as if the riches were never ending.

The end of all this is the resounding advice of Anchises on the mission of Rome.

Let others better mold the running Mass
Of Mettals, and inform the breathing Brass:
And soften into Flesh a Marble Face:
Plead better at the Bar; describe the Skies,
And when the Stars descend, and when they rise.
But Rome, 'tis thine alone, with awful sway,
To rule Mankind, and make the World obey,
Disposing Peace and War thy own Majestic Way.

To tame the Proud, the fetter'd Slave to free,
These are Imperial Arts, and worthy thee!

Then (854), as a climax of this book, comes the praise of Marcellus who might have inherited the empire but at the end of 23 BC he had died, at the age of twenty-one, and it is possible that the lines which follow were inserted in a book already written, probably in 24 BC, but I doubt it. His mother was Octavia the sister of Augustus. Propertius (3, 18) also wrote of his death, Octavia named a library after him, and Augustus a theatre which survives as the renaissance palace of the Orsini family and is still inhabited.

Anchises points first to the great Marcellus of an earlier generation who died near Horace's Venusia, but Virgil notices the sad young man beside him and wonders who he is, and why 'Shadow and dark night hover round his head' (866). Anchises replies with deep melancholy about the deaths Rome will suffer.

It seems to me that this dark ending is essential to the book as a single and coherent poem. Virgil praises him as a soldier, a horseman, loyal and religious, almost as Yeats praised Major Robert Gregory: but Virgil is interested in his funeral, because Augustus buried him in his own mausoleum by the Tiber and spoke the funeral speech.

What groans of Men shall fill the Martian Field!
How fierce a Blaze his flaming Pile shall yield!
What fun'ral Pomp shall floating Tiber see
When, rising from his Bed, he views the sad Solemnity!

He will be Marcellus, and Dryden exaggerates a little how Anchises ends his speech. Give lilies from full hands, I will sprinkle purple flowers, and give my descendant's soul this empty gift at least (883-6). Dryden says

Full Canisters of fragrant Lillies bring
Mix'd with the Purple Roses of the Spring:
Let me with Fun'ral Flowers his Body strow,
This Gift, which Parents to their Children owe,
This unavailing Gift, at least I may bestow!

When Anchises had shown his son all these things and fired his mind with Elysium, he prophesied his own fate and brought Aeneas to the gate of horn where visions come and go, and the gate of ivory where false dreams pass. Through that door he dismissed his son, who went straight to the ships, sailed away from Cumae, and anchored at Caieta nearer the Tiber.

VII. Sand

In the course of writing about the sixth book I have not dared to become entangled in the learned controversies there are about it, which often depend on small muddles and can sometimes be blown away like cobwebs. I have scarcely referred to the genius who mostly illuminates it, Norden, or to the mass of secondary scholarship about book six, though I had reserved some minor matters I was itching to discuss more fully, from the cult of Phrontis at Sounion and Androgeos at Mounyehia to the vast elm tree where Sleep lives beside rivers. But these matters are too light, they lack substance. The tree must be folklore, it is deciduous, dark and creaky, a shade tree. It used to grow by the Severn as it did long ago in fields where Virgil might sleep as a boy: or the peasants might say you dream if you sleep in shade so heavy; and this is not the only intrusion from childhood, because the Po (Eridanus) runs in the Elysian fields.

VIII

ITALIAN EARTH

Virgil as a narrative poet is used to dealing with the unexpected and to delaying his climax even where it is foreseen. In the second half of the Aeneid, he has the further problem that from now on his epic story has a more or less single, coherent plot (Aeneas's arrival in Latium) and the result is that he is driven to the wildest variations and concatenations. Book seven begins with antiquarianism and book eight is the locus classicus of that. When Gibbon visited Rome he noticed how it had gone back to the state it was in when Aeneas first inspected the site: a romantic exaggeration, but not wholly unjustified. Virgil was impressed by the kind of history Livy tells and many of us may confusedly remember from the schoolroom and the poems of Macaulay: Virgil has given us an unforgettable though still a cloudy impression of the past in book six, and in the antiquarian visions of book eight he will do it again. But his heart is not in Rome, it is in the landing of Aeneas on Italian earth, and in the river winding through trees and the noise of birds. There is something deeply satisfying about the poetry of the seventh book, almost the suggestion of another Georgic.

The linking passage is a brief epitaph for Caieta, named after Aeneas's nurse, who was supposed to be buried there and was remembered in a temple of Apollo and Caieta near Formiae on the borders of Latium and Campania (Livy 40, 2). Aeneas buries his nurse and the sea being calm he sails on northwards. The wind goes on blowing at night and the shivering sea glitters in the moonlight (8-9). They pass Circe's estate, the smell of her cedar fires and the roars and howls of the beasts into which she likes to transform her visitors. 'Circe's island' was now on the mainland Varro thought, because of the draining of marshes, and the cedar fires Homer mentions were in Calypso's cave not Circe's palace in the woods, but what does it matter? Neptune sent a strong wind to blow them past. Circe's reputation was extensive on that coast, and Caieta was also called Aiete after her brother Aietos. Legend maintained that her son by Odysseus Telegonos founded Tusculum. It does not suit Virgil to go into this, because he needs to give just a taste of Aeneas at sea, before the waves redden and yellow dawn gleams in her rose-coloured chariot (25-6).

The Trojan from the Main beheld a Wood
Which thick with Shades and a brown Horror stood:
Betwixt the Trees the Tyber took his Course,
With whirl-pools dimpl'd, and with downward Force,
That drove the Sand along, he took his Way
And rowl'd his yellow Billows to the Sea.
About him, and above, and round the Wood,
The Birds that haunt the Borders of his Flood,
That bath'd within, or bask'd upon his Side
To tuneful Songs their narrow Throats apply'd.
The Captain gives Command, the joyful Train
Glide thro' the gloomy Shade, and leave the Main ...

It is here that Virgil announces the theme of what is left to write of the Aeneid (36-44), the arrival in Latium and the war that followed. The climax of this invocation of Erato, his antiquarian muse, is his reference to 'a greater order of things, a greater work' (43-4) which Propertius, followed by the much funnier Ezra Pound, parodied.

Apart from the formal salute to the Iliad, the important point here is Latium, and here lies the importance of his Aeneas's nurse Caieta, who overshadows even the exotic Circe. She marks the border of Latium with Campania, where Virgil chose to live and which he saw as still largely Greek. We often think of the Greek part of Italy as the sole of Italy's foot, but the one of Greek settlement extended far to the north, and in Virgil's time visibly included Campania in the west and Ancona in the east. When Aeneas comes to Latin ground and the Roman Tiber, he plunges inland among the still untroubled forests: it is as if he wants to roll like a dog on Italian earth. This part of the Aeneid must begin (45) with Latinus the old king of Latium, son of Faunus and Marica, a Laurentine nymph. Faunus* was a son of Picus, son of Saturn, the father and god of the golden age.

But this old peaceful Prince, as Heav'n decreed,
Was bless'd with no Male Issue to succeed.

His only son had died and his daughter, Lavinia, being beautiful and an heiress was much courted. Her mother the Queen favoured young Turnus,† but the omens were against the match (58). So far the poet is happily telling us a fairy story, but the omens are already alarming.

* An oracular god of the woods and wilds, sometimes identified with Pan.
† King of the neighbouring Rutuli.

192

Deep in the Palace, of long Growth there stood
A Lawrel's Trunk, a venerable Wood,
Where Rites Divine were paid, whose holy Hair
Was kept, and cut with superstitious Care.
This plant Latinus, when his town he wall'd
Then found, and from the Tree Laurentum call'd:
And lost in Honour of his new Abode
He vow'd the Lawrel, to the Lawrel's God.
It happen'd once (a boding Prodigy),
A swarm of Bees, that cut the liquid Sky,
Unknown from whence they took their airy flight,
Upon the topmost Branch in Clouds alight:
There with their clasping Feet together clung,
And a long Cluster from the Lawrel hung ...

This meant a foreign Prince was coming to Latium to reign and prosper. But another omen followed which was even more startling: when Lavinia stood beside her father at a sacrifice,

Strange to relate, the Flames, involv'd in Smoke
Of Incense, from the Sacred Altar broke:
Caught her dishevell'd Hair, and rich Attire;
Her Crown and Jewels crackl'd in the Fire:
From thence the fuming Trail began to spread,
And lambent Glories danc'd about her Head ...

This means Lavinia will be crowned[1] but war will follow. Old Latinus goes off to consult his father, Faunus. He lived in the shadows near the Albunean spring, which was white and sulphurous: Albunea was the Sibyl of Tibur (Tivoli) and her water tumbled into the Anio. In this passage Virgil makes it a place of oracular dreams, where the priest sleeps on the skins of offerings and sees and hears the unearthly buzz of ghosts: 'a swarm of thin aerial Shapes'. Latinus sleeps on a hundred black sheep-skins and hears the divine voice warn him that Lavinia must marry the stranger, who is about to arrive.

And suddenly, here he is (106) as Fame caries the news of the oracle. Aeneas and pretty Iulus and the others eat their frugal country picnic, the bread they used for plates (pizza?) and all as was prophesied, to their delight (116f.). They know now that this is their new country. Aeneas prays to Earth, to the Nymphs and rivers, Night and the rising stars, and Jove thunders three times (141). Next morning they explore the marshes of Numicus, a stream, the river Tiber and

Latium. Aeneas sends a hundred orators (or diplomats) crowned with olive to the king while he makes his camp by the shore (157-9).

The Trojans meet the Latin youths at exercise and are summoned to meet old Latinus in the ancient temple of Picus. It rises on a hundred columns, and the portraits of his ancestors in cedar stand in the forecourt: Italus and father Sabinus planter of the vines with his sickle curved, old Saturn and Ianus with two faces; Old kings and those that suffered wounds in war (182). Arms hang on walls,

> ... curved axes and the captive chariots,
> The crests of helmets and the locks of doors,
> And spears and shields and the beaks torn from ships.

There was the antique Picus with the rest whom Circe loved and made a bird, sprinkling his wings with colours (191). This whole antiquarian passage about Picus's temple in the terrifying grove (170-191) sound almost real, but it ends with Picus himself with augur's staff and purple-striped toga and the iron shield on his left arm like a figure designed for instructing children. The cedar figures are all more instructive than beautiful, yet the musty old sanctuary is somehow unforgettable, and the king who disappears into the magpie makes a thrilling impression on readers.

The Aeneid is not set in legendary time, all the same it is hard to know to what extent the period after the Trojan wars in which the Aeneid is set was regarded by serious Roman antiquaries as a time of legends, subject to entertaining manipulations by poets, or to what extent it was taken more seriously. There were local religious links with that past, such as the grave of Romulus in Rome in the Forum, the cave under the Palatine Hill, the cult at Ostia that seems to commemorate the landing of Aeneas, and the strangely persistent miracle of the sow and her piglets at Lavinium, let alone the shrine at Cumae where the Sibyl once prophesied. Some of these Virgil gently sidesteps or ignores, others he follows religiously. Certain Roman families claimed to trace their ancestry to the same very early times, and Virgil pays many of them lip-service. There was a continuous framework of dates, at least since the fall of Troy, that was generally accepted, but Virgil is playful with the generations.

In the case of Hercules, whose heroic narrative is legendary and exaggerated, he makes what he chooses of the stories, but without disrespect, because Hercules is an ancestor of the *gens Iulia*, the family of Augustus. Virgil's determination to tie Roman origins to Aeneas and the heroic age of the Illiad has many consequences, and on it the entire Aeneid depends. He could not have taken that decision had his not been an age of antiquarian enthusiasm with an appetite for poetry as well as the past.[2]

Latinus now tells the Trojans his people do not follow laws but still live as Saturn did. Yet he remembers how Dardanus set out from Latium to Troy and Samothrace and is now a god (so they are all cousins). Ilioneus, one of Aeneas's followers, replies (212) with equal politeness about the divine origin of the Trojans and their desire to settle (249). Latinus is thinking of the omens and his daughter's marriage, and agrees. He gives them all horses (274) and a chariot for Aeneas, with a pair of heavenly origin breathing fire, and proposes the match with Lavinia.

At this moment Juno (286) comes back that way and observes to her fury that Aeneas is happy and ready to build. She curses (293-322) at some length and assesses what strength she can summon from the underworld (312). She summons the fury Allecto (325) whom even her father Pluto and her sister furies hate. Allecto's name is Hellenistic and her genealogy a botch of similar date, but her nature is as ancient as Homer.

Allecto squats on the roof and flings a snake into the Queen Amata's bosom. The snake slips between her breasts, becomes a massive gold necklace and a trailing ribbon from her hair (351). Amata is already mad with anxiety and the snake speaks venomously to her heart. The Queen wails over her daughter marrying a Trojan (359). She goes raving around the city (378) whizzing like a boy's top (383). She runs off like a Maenad into the forest. The religion of Bacchus was sternly disapproved of by the Romans, and the order of the senate for its repression is one of the earliest Latin texts in continuous prose. The fine little bronze tablet was framed like a picture in the renaissance and may be seen in the imperial collection in Vienna. The craze spreads now, and other women join Amata in singing a wedding song for Turnus (398).

Allecto's next visit is to this daring young Rutulian at Ardea (409-11) where she appears as the old hag Calybe, Juno's priestess. The Rutuli were Latins and Ardea was some three miles from the sea and its temples belonged to the whole league of cities in which 'Latium' can first be traced. It was once a port, but malaria finished it and under the late republic it was a prison and under the emperors an elephant farm. Virgil speaks of Ardea as a place once glorious, now a relic (413). Here 'Calybe' appears to the young prince and makes trouble over the marriage – the Aeneid at this stage has turned to mere fantasy and unhistorical romance. Allecto loses her temper with Turnus's coolness and shows herself in full horror, to his surprise (417). She carries war and death in her hand and flings a dark flaming torch into his breast, which terrifies him (459); and he boils up with military vigour like water in a cauldron (466) and decides to attack

Latinus. He appears in arms with the beauty of youth and the grandeur of his ancestry (474).

Allecto then seeks out the Trojans on Stygian wings, and finds Iulus hunting, so she sets the dogs after a stag brought up tame by the peasant Tyrrhus and his daughter Silvia, who used to groom the stag and wash him and put garlands on his horns. The charming scene (488-92) might come from an Eclogue or from Daphnis and Chloe. But Allecto has the stag shot by Ascanius. Silvia weeps, and calls the peasants from the woods, and Tyrrhus is panting with rage, and Allecto settles on a high roof and blows a blast on the pastoral horn – I think the Alpenhorn. It is heard as far away as Hecate's lake and the sulphur springs of Nar (which Ennius mentions) seventy miles across country. The grove trembles, the forest resounds and mothers shiver at the hellish voice and hug their children (518).

These few lines are terrifying, and here for the first time Virgil reveals what he can do with Allecto, and we are convinced. The war begins terribly, Almo the eldest son of Tyrrhus is first to die and then Galaesus, the richest farmer once and the peace-maker (with Homeric irony and brevity). The goddess flies off to Juno promising to spread the fighting (551). Juno congratulates her but says she must not wander out of hell, and Juno herself will see to matters now (559-60). Allecto dives down to a valley in central Italy called Ampsanctus where the water is deadly and hell breathes, and she dives into this hole and disappears.

The place existed and impressed a number of writers after Virgil's time, and Fraenkel in an article and Nordern both discuss it, but the awful fact is that when Allecto has disappeared and Juno has taken matters into her own hands, the poem begins to flag. This turns on another piece of antiquarianism, the Gates of War. Augustus was proud of the fact that these impressive gates had stood open hundreds of years until on three distinct occasions he personally shut them. These ancient gates were those of a temple of Numa, so Plutarch says (Numa 19), or of Janus and of War and they were so sacred that Virgil had to bring down Juno herself to force them. He precedes her with a lecture, and a Roman senator, and fills several lines with references to the empire's wars under Augustus: I find all this historical paraphernalia less impressive than the crude boldness of Allecto.

Readers must judge the passage for themselves:

> The Roman Consul their Decree declares,
> And in his Robes the sounding Gates unbars.
> The Youth in Military Shouts arise,
> And the loud Trumpets break the yielding Skies.
> These Rites, of old by Sov'reign Princes us'd,
> Were the King's Office, but the King refus'd ...

VIII. ITALIAN EARTH

... Then Heav'n's Imperious Queen shot down from high,
At her Approach the Brazen Hinges fly,
The Gates are forc'd, and ev'ry falling Bar,
And like a Tempest issues out the War.

Divine intervention is too swift and too sudden to be convincing, and the antiquity of the custom itself is of less interest to us than it was to Virgil's first audience. Verse written three-hundred-and-fifty years ago about the Speaker's Mace in the House of Commons would be just as faded today. All the same, in these lines Virgil is like a man chewing iron (620-2).

What follows is sufficiently terrible, first a list of towns of the Latin league that commanded Latium (630-1) and their armaments, then with an invocation to the Muses based on Homer, a list or catalogue of the leaders and their troops, something like a Homeric catalogue elaborated. Auden used to remark on the persistence of lists in poetry. He felt it was bad taste to dislike them, and no doubt he was right. Nonetheless, this list, being written by a homosexual poet who comes late in the day, is too pretty at first, dwells too long on the lovely youths and their fine bodies, and uses too often the word *pulcher*, beautiful, which becomes counter-productive. In fact he has somehow strayed for a while across the borders of myth and legend into those of romantic fiction. At least the device like Helen's view of the Greeks in the Iliad serves to introduce a handful of heroes who will figure in the war.

First comes wicked Mezentius who despises the gods, then Lausus, the loveliest in body except for Turnus, unhappy in being the son of Mezentius. Aventinus lovely son of Rhea and lovely Hercules comes next in his impressive lion-skin with the white teeth. It was thought in late antiquity a lesser poet would have called them snow-white. The twins Coras and Catillus came from Tibur like cloud-begotten centaurs. Caeculus of Praeneste came too, trailing as the others do wonderful scraps of exotic, and all but Tennysonian topography, 'ice-cold Anio and the stream-sprayed rocks' (683-4).

Virgil delights in the regional oddities of arms and armour: now that 'beauty' is forgotten a more touching innocence takes over. Messapus tamer of horses is a son of Neptune whose men came from the heights of Soracte and the most ancient villages, singing about their king like the snow-white swans in Homer, when the mountains resound and the river and the marshes re-echo (699-702). This remarkable bit of verse is a climax, and ends in a half-line.

Yet it begins again on a slightly different tack. You would never think they were bronze-clad regiments in such a swarm, but a flying cloud of raucous birds blown inland from the sea.

Suddenly we are back in the Georgics, and here one can see how the old

197

material is reworked, because the reworking has for once been left unfinished. Italy itself was most deeply Virgil's subject, in spite of the epic trimmings of this poem. The lines about the raucous sea-birds contain a pun on *aeratas* (bronze-clad) and *aerias* (air-borne) which must be old.[3]

With the Sabine Clausus founder of the Claudian family, whose monument was found not far from Horace's Sabine villa, we enter into deeper Roman mysteries (706f.) and the towns of the upper Tiber. The noise of shields and the tramp of feet are in contrast with the wildness of the scenery and the baroque richness and power of the elements (718-22). Halaesus, the Greek, yokes up his horses to join the swelling scene. Every name now trails a stranger more romantic story than the last: Oebalus son of a nymph (734), Ufens of the mountains with his forest hunters (745f.), and the priest Umbro with his helmet wreathed in olive, whose songs and stroking hand put snakes to sleep. He could cure snake-bite but not the Trojan spear that killed him (757), and the lakes wept for him. The irony is Homeric but it must be admitted that with Virgil grief has entered into the Roman countryside. The line about the lakes (760) is unfinished. It is like a few words from an Eclogue.

We are in a mood by this time to believe any legend, or any lie if you like, and Virgil tells us how Hippolytus returned to life (Horace *Od.* 4, 7 says he did not) and lived 'inglorious in the woods of Italy' (776), disguised as his son Virbius, protected by Artemis. No horses were permitted in that grove, because of the death Hippolytus had died (dragged by horses), and yet now Virbius trained horses, and he rushed to war (782). This story has a touch of real myth to it, but the knots of comparative mythology take long to untangle, and this one in particular has vast and unexpected ramifications into Asklepios the god of medicine and various other tales about resurrection from the dead. Greatly as I relish them, I do not feel they are necessary knowledge for readers of a life of Virgil, or strictly relevant to the Aeneid, but it is most interesting that the line about living 'alone in the Italian woods inglorious' should have so strong a resonance in the second Georgic (486) and at the end of the fourth. Virgil must in some way see himself in the character Virbius in the impenetrable grove, perhaps because medicine is a science, and the progress of science was his first ambition. We do not know and it is an indulgence to raise such unanswerable questions.

Turnus all but finishes the list of heroes. His arms and the paternal grandeurs of his territory are elaborately described. It is an essential device of Homeric poetry that the heroes are never really described, but that we are encouraged with similes to build up our own ideas of what they looked like. Virgil comes perilously close to deserting the convention here by his dwelling on the decorations of the weapons. Turnus's helmet sounds like something operatic, but Virgil swiftly transmutes to places, which is the strength of this whole ending of book seven.

It may be that Virgil saw his Turnus in some way lacked sparkle, and that is why he gave the final position (803) to the warrior girl Camilla, who could outrun the wind and run over crops so lightly she never even bent them underfoot. She could run over the waves of the sea without wetting her feet. The idea is absurd but the words are splendid and she adds all the qualities that brute Turnus had lacked. Her only disadvantage is that she has no territory, she is a fantasy racing out of sight.

The last part of book seven has led us deeply into the intricacies of Latin topography, and the heart of Virgil's obsession with Italian earth. Even the rich Latin farmer Galaesus is named after the river in the south. And we shall see that the theme of Italian earth is not to wither away at once. In book eight we return to Aeneas and his ships near the estuary of the great river.

The preamble is like a news bulletin on the tense situation in Latium, but Aeneas (18) soon brings us to the book proper (26). It was night and the animals slept, when Aeneas lay down on the river-bank and the god Tiber rose from the water to speak to him. This thrilling and surprising scene is introduced with a few lines (22f.) about the wavering of reflected light and the penetrative powers of moonlight. They are subtle as well as beautiful and we are to observe that he intends no disloyalty to Epicurus:

> Then, thro' the Shadows of the Poplar Wood
> Arose the Father of the Roman Flood;
> An Azure Robe was o'er his Body spread,
> A Wreath of shady Reeds adorn'd his Head:
> Thus, manifest to Sight, the God appear'd ...

He was as such gods were depicted in painting, otherwise we would not recognise him and nor would Aeneas. 'This is thy happy Home!' he says, and the river-god promises Aeneas a comforting omen:

> A Sow beneath an Oak shall lye along;
> All white her self, and white her thirty Young.
> When thirty rowling Years have run their Race,
> Thy son, Ascanius, on this empty Space
> Shall build a Royal Town ...

This means Alba Longa. There will be lasting peace, Juno will relent, and all

will end happily. When Aeneas wakes he must pay Juno her sacrifice, and expect
help from Evander the Arcadian, whose town in exile is called Pallanteum (like
the Arcadian Pallantion) and is threatened as Aeneas is by the Latins.

> The God am I whose yellow Water flows
> Around these Fields, and fattens as it goes:
> ... In Times to come
> My Waves shall wash the Walls of mighty Rome,
> He said, and plung'd below, while yet he spoke:
> His Dream Aeneas and his Sleep forsook.

It was dawn. Aeneas found the sow and offered her to Juno with her litter,
then the Trojans took to the water again, knowing the river would lead them to
Evander, their natural ally, and the focus of many Roman legends. There can
never have been a more magical arrival in Rome:

> The following Night, and the succeeding Day,
> Propitious Tyber smooth'd his wat'ry Way,
> He rowl'd his River back, and pois'd he stood,
> A gentle Swelling, and a peaceful Flood.
> The Trojans mount their Ships, they put from Shoar
> Born on the Waves, and scarcely dip an Oar.
> Shouts from the Land give Omen to their Course;
> And the pitch'd Vessels glide with easy Force.
> The Woods and Waters wonder at the Gleam
> Of Shields, and painted Ships, that stem the Stream.
> One Summer's Night, and one whole Day they pass
> Betwixt the green-wood Shades, and cut the liquid Glass.
> The fiery Sun had finish'd half his Race,
> Look'd back, and doubted in the middle Space,
> When they from far beheld the rising Tow'rs
> The tops of Sheds, and Shepherds' lowly Bow'rs ...

It is hard to pause even here. One day it will all be marble, Virgil assures us,
as if by magic he had obliterated the city and substituted a small town of
shepherds and of sheep.

The river journey begins early in book seven and ends here (100). Dryden was
enchanted by it, though the Latin runs rings round him, so I have quoted him
here at extended length. As always with poetry, one is led to ponder the deeper
themes that underlie it. Rome is Arcadian, and it arises like a mirage from the

river, with its beneficent god crowned with stiff green rushes. Augustus famously found it brick and left it marble: another transformation scene. And the war to come will be a replay of the Trojan war no doubt, but also Greeks or Trojans, Homeric and civilised soldiers, against the magically powerful native Italians: the only solution must be their amalgamation. I mean the only political solution, because the themes of poetry, of which grief and defeat and burning to ashes are among the strongest, and the regeneration of nature almost equally strong, have no solution.

Evander was sacrificing to Hercules outside his town with his son Pallas. The town council offered incense and the warm blood smoked. The tall fleet with its silent oarsmen slid towards them through the dark forest. Pallas called out the questions still usual in the Mediterranean, 'Where are you off to? Where from? Who are you? What are you doing on this unexplored road?' Aeneas on the poop offers an olive branch meaning peace, and says his men are Trojans persecuted by the Latins (118). He seeks alliance with Evander. They are welcomed into the sacred wood and leave the river (125). Speeches follow of diplomatic importance and mythological interest. Dardanus was grandson of Atlas and so was Mercury, father of the Arcadians, so they are cousins. And Evander once knew Priam and Anchises when they visited Salamis and Pheneus (near Stymphalos not far inland from Corinth). They now resume their Herculean picnic (172-83). Evander points out the cave of the wicked giant Cacus who stole the cattle of the hero, and tells the story of how Hercules found his lair. If this was – as I imagine – the style of folktales told to children it was more than impressive.

Can this be a learned, Hellenistic style copied from Greek poets? I doubt it. The ground gapes like an underworld of caverns and ghosts (242-6). Evander and his people (269) still celebrated the happy day, and Livy confirms (1, 7 and 9, 29) the ritual and the family names Virgil introduces. The people wear crowns of poplar as they drink at the Ara Maxima, the Great Altar which still stood when the Aeneid was written (270-9), and the Salii, the ancient guild of priests (from whom the Romans claimed they learnt Arcadian dancing: *salire* means to leap) sang and leapt (285f.).

Yet, there is a sense in which Virgil's Roman antiquarianism had Greek origins. Any reader of Plutarch's Theseus and of his Romulus will observe that the Roman monuments are an attempt to rival those of Athens, and in the fragments of the Greek historians (Jacoby, 1940) we can observe that the earliest of the investigations into ancient or mythical monuments were Athenian. People like Varro imitated the curious and specialised type of learned literature that Athens had generated, applying the method to Rome, where of course it was even more needed to dignify a state whose dignity was new. By setting the speculations in verse and in an important book of the Aeneid, Virgil dignifies the discussion still further. The song of the Salii was in his day a venerable document, and the college called later the Fratres Arvales recorded their grandeur and solemnities on stone: the inscription has survived.

From this point, the Ara Maxima, Aeneas must be shown the future city of Rome, about which Evander must prophesy, as Anchises prophesied in book six. The praises of Hercules (287-302) are the climax of the ritual and I suppose the remote example Aeneas must follow. Now Evander leads Aeneas and his son into what will be the city itself, chatting away like any guide except that he is also a prophet.

Evander's description of an earlier Italy makes no attempt at detail, but it is stronger on atmosphere. He shows them where the forest groves of the Nymphs and the native Fauni stood, and men who knew nothing of agriculture until Saturn came from heaven into exile (320). Saturn named the place Latium because he hid there (*latuit*). That was a golden age, but of course it deteriorated, as golden ages will. Invasions followed and kings, and the giant Tiber after whom the river was named – alas we know nothing worth recording about this pleasing character. He is not the river-god who appeared in a dream to Aeneas. And here the powerful Nymph Carmentis and Apollo installed her son Evander in exile. Not much is known about Carmentis, who sounds like a close relative of the Camenae, the nymphs of water-springs who became the Roman muses. Evander merely points out the altar and gate named after her (339) and recalls her prophecies.

They come to the wood where Romulus hid, and the cave called Lupercal under the cold rock, named after Lycaean Pan (344). The cave, restored by Augustus, with its Greek statue of Pan was a famous monument, but Virgil calls him Lycaean after his mountain in Arcadia while deliberately suppressing any memory of the nasty rites that still took place there in his time. Virgil needs to explain the Greek Pan whose statue stood in the cave, that is all, so he calls Pan 'Parrhasian', a smaller but more respectable origin for the god.

He passes on to the Argiletum, where Cicero owned some shops, the Tarpeian rock (with no mention of its use for execution) and the Capitol: in modern terms the hill between the Forum and the Via Veneto, above which perches the Ara Coeli, the most living link with Roman antiquity that still survives today. The organisation of this brief flood of allusions or information in the form of a guided tour of Rome is a Greek convention that survives in Pausanias,[4] but we have examples of it earlier than this.

There have been attempts to make the adventures of Aeneas in the old country of Dardanus a sort of replay of the return of Odysseus to Ithaca and even a foreshadowing of the return of Augustus to Rome in 29 BC.[5] These are wild suggestions, but much recent Virgil scholarship has been wild. K.W. Gransden goes so far as to suggest that Evander and the visit of Aeneas to his rural settlement is some kind of equivalent of Odysseus landing on Ithaca and spending the night with the old swineherd Eumaeus. The two cases are utterly unlike each other.

The reason for the link with Evander is simply the very popular idea of a mythical connection of Rome with Arcadia. When after the grandeur of the Saturnian Janiculum (358), they turn to Evander's farm, and hear the cattle lowing where the forum and the public orators would one day be, we are back to memories of Hercules. Aeneas sleeps on leaves and a bear-skin (368): the contrast between antique simplicity and poverty and modern grandeur, like that of the Augustan gold roof of the temple and the shaggy thickets of the past (348) on the Capitol. (Nonetheless, Gransden is right in his useful structural analysis of this book.)

We are now about half-way through it, and what follows concerns the forging of the arms of Aeneas (like those of Achilles) and their delivery to him in a valley near Caere. Each of these two last sections of the book is further subdivisible into three as if Virgil was deliberately straying into the structure of Horace's version of Pindaric lyrics, a strange but not impossible analysis suggested by Gransden though he does not invoke Horace.

Venus arrives suddenly as soon as her son Aeneas is asleep (370). She is off to see Vulcan, saying she did not worry him over the Trojan war; but now that Aeneas has come to the Rutuli she implores Vulcan's help and offers love to her old husband, who agrees and falls asleep (406).

At midnight he gets up and goes to work in his factory on Lipari (417) where he works underground in the volcano which is also that of Etna, where the Cyclopes make thunderbolts for Jove. (It may be worth pointing out that meteorites were the first source of iron ever used by man, so that much magic long attached to iron-working.) The craftsmanship of the Cyclopes must now be turned to arms. The Greeks and Romans could of course make steel though they did not know what it was or what carbon contributed to it. The process of making steel swords remained secret and magical for many centuries after Virgil's time, but bronze or iron swords had steel edges as early as the fifth century BC.

The metals flow molten in their channels; bellows, anvils and water work their effect until Evander and his dogs wake with the dawn (455) at cockcrow, and he tells Aeneas to set off now (479) for the Lydian city which we know as Etruscan Caere. Mommsen thought it was the great rival to the rise of Rome and its tombs are still famous for their richness and beauty. The city lies some thirty miles north of Rome, at Cerveteri. Mezentius was its tyrant who tied the living to the dead. When the people rose against him he escaped from them to be Turnus's ally; and now Aeneas must lead the Etruscans against this wicked king. Evander was invited to the same role by Tarchon of Mantua (506) but feels too old; his son Pallas would go but he has a Sabine mother and is not eligible (510), so Aeneas can lead the Italians (513) and Pallas can go as an apprentice (519).

At this moment Venus flashed a signal from heaven with claps of thunder, trumpets and visions of arms. Aeneas knows he is being called from heaven by an agreed signal (535) and the coming slaughter weighs on him (540). He and Evander pray and sacrifice, and he goes to his ships and chooses soldiers. Fame runs through the city, while Evander, who is more like Nestor than Eumaeus, remembers how he killed Erulus at Praeneste. He prays and says his goodbyes to his son Pallas.

Aeneas and his party (385) set off for the new adventure, with Pallas looking like a dawn star rising from the Ocean. The hoof-beats of the horses make their famous noises (596) to the wooded hills of Caere, the grove of Silvanus (600) and the camp where Tarchon waited. To this spot, in a hidden valley, came Venus with her present of arms to Aeneas, giving him an embrace and laying them down gleaming under an oak tree.

> He lifts, he turns, he poises, and admires
> The Crested Helm, that vomits radiant Fires ...
> ... But most admires the Shields mysterious Mould,
> And Roman Triumphs rising on the Gold.
> For those, emboss'd, the Heav'nly Smith had wrought,
> (Not in the Rolls of future Fate untaught)
> The Wars in Order, and the Race Divine
> Of Warriors, issuing from the Julian Line.
> The Cave of Mars was dress'd with mossy Greens:
> There, by the Wolf, were laid the Martial Twins.
> Intrepid on her swelling Dugs they hung,
> The foster Dam loll'd out her fawning Tongue.
> They suck'd secure, while bending back her Head,
> She lick'd their tender Limbs, and form'd them as they fed.

The mythical images are charming, and the she-wolf is exactly like the bronze one now in the Capitoline Museum which was found near the cave in the renaissance.

But the historical series of events is deliberately different from the shield of Achilles, which by being impersonal seems to me more magically effective. The shield of Aeneas has an order and a climax that I find absurd or intolerable. The

100 lines of legendary history read like Livy illustrated, and are well enough. The palace with its straw thatch and the Silver Goose whose cackle saved the State are charming, so are the Gauls with their long Alpine spears (661), and even the white foam on the blue sea does somehow suggest a work of art.

But the trouble is the Battle of Actium, in which the action is unhistorical, the role of Augustus more than mildly ridiculous, and the defeat of Antony and Cleopatra with the dog-faced Anubis barking in vain against the classical gods (698-9) goes beyond the boundaries of the baroque. We have fragments of another Actium epic by a lesser poet which is worse still.

It appears to me that the convention is at fault in the first place, and that any glorification of Augustus in verse must falter as this one does into frigidity. The end of this book in a kind of apotheosis of the Empire, and a triumph frozen for all time only makes things worse. Horace had more than once taken similar risks, but I do not feel that he failed. There is no point in criticising Virgil's perform- ance in more detail, some of the lines are delightful, some of the images memorable – Dryden handles them all with relish, operatic as they may be.

When book nine opens we are ready for the battles to begin, and so they will, but we must also face the catalogue of the allies just as we have already had the catalogue of Turnus and his men. In these lines Virgil perfects the powerful poetry he had invented in the Georgics, but they do not come at once. The reason is that Aeneas must be away for a time and arrive only at a critical moment to rescue his Trojans and win his battle: while he is away Turnus all but triumphs, just as Hector all but overcame the Greek army while Achilles was away. Achilles was detained by his own bad temper and affronted honour, and Romans learnt at school (as we know from Horace) what bad behaviour that was: Aeneas cannot be guilty of it. He must, therefore, wander off on his mission towards central Italy so he can summon the tribes to fight on his side, and this of course is close to Virgil's heart.

The last stages of the war will begin only when Aeneas in person commands, and fights a duel with Turnus, which Aeneas will win. Turnus is not quite Hector, and the Aeneid cannot end with his burial as the Iliad does with Hector's. He cannot be spared or shake hands either and he cannot commit suicide like Cato and Antony, since it must be clear that Aeneas is the hero and Turnus is not. It is important to understand this machinery of argument because it will not be stated, though the plot of the Aeneid depends on it.

Juno sent Iris to Turnus where he sat in the holy valley of Pilumnus who was his ancestor and one of the three obscure gods recorded by Varro who help women in child-birth by chopping, sweeping and pounding to keep away Silvanus, a god of the badlands and perhaps a baby-snatcher. Virgil does not intend to characterise him very accurately; here he is just a grandfather of the Rutulian champion as he is in book ten (69). Yet Virgil's knowledge of gods is encyclopaedic, in the same few lines he refers to Iris as Thaumantias, daughter of Thaumas who was the father of the Harpies in the *Theogony* of Hesiod. Did the name attract him because *thauma* means wonder or miracle?

Iris tells Turnus his day has come, because Aeneas is usurping Evander's authority and raising the Etruscan peasants, so now is the time to attack his camp. She then whizzes up to heaven on her wings, leaving only the rainbow to mark her journey. Turnus says she has torn heaven open and he sees the stars (20), but he obeys, drinks water from the spring and burdens the aether with his prayers (24). His army takes the field rich in horses, coloured clothes and gold, Messapus in the van and the sons of Tyrrhus urging on the rear (being peasants). To the Trojans they appeared like a dark cloud, like the Ganges or the Nile in flood; and they defended the walls of their camp as Aeneas had warned them to do, while Turnus (52) flung the first javelin.

The Rutuli are like wolves around a sheepfold: so they attack the ships moored under the walls with fire (70). Luckily the Great Mother of the gods had the agreement of Jove that these ships, whose wood came from a holy grove of hers on Ida, should now be transformed into goddesses of the sea. They swim away like dolphins and the Rutuli stand stupefied (123). The story is well told and not long. It is an interlude of 45 lines of which one does not tire. Messapus found his horses in confusion, the river roared, but Turnus did not lose his head. He assured his troops that the portent showed the Trojans could not run away. He refers to the Iliad. He does not need arms made by Vulcan or a thousand ships to take this shivering camp, there will be no need for a wooden horse (152). They make camp, set sentinels and settle down to dinner and drink. The Trojans watch them from the walls.

Now comes the episode of Nisus the Trojan huntsman and his friend the beautiful boy Euryalus. They were lovers and together guarding a gate (182-3). The feeling of their story is Greek and indeed Homeric, but Virgil takes things further. Aeschylus makes Achilles and Patroclus lovers but Homer is not so explicit. Virgil has adapted the night expedition of Dolon from the Iliad for its deadly ending, and there is, and is meant to be, a particular pathos about his two young men. We met them as athletes in book five, but Virgil now ignores that episode. Here their motive is simply to get news to Aeneas and bring back help.

> Then Nisus, thus: Or do the Gods inspire
> This warmth, or make we Gods of our desire?

Nisus feels an adult ambition, but Euryalus insists on sharing the expedition because he despises life and has an appetite for glory, as they both have (206-7). They argue in a high-minded way but the discussion does not last long, Euryalus has his wish (223). They both go to the Council of War which is still in session. Iulus admits them and tells Nisus to speak. He unfolds his plan to get news to Aeneas in Pallanteum (Rome). They will return with loot and kill many, they know the ground well from hunting: it will be easy.

At this they are promised exotic rewards (263-6), outgoing Homer in lavishness, including Turnus's horse and arms, a dozen captives, and Latinus's own estate. Euryalus commends his old mother to Iulus and the Trojans weep. Beautiful Iulus promises to adopt the old lady and give her the same rewards if her boy dies. He gives Euryalus a sword and two of the others give Nisus a helmet and a lion-skin (306-7). The whole crowd sees them off.

But we are told (313) they will not get through:

> ... And Messages committed to their Care
> Which all in Winds were lost, and flitting Air.

They find the enemy asleep and drunk, this has been emphasised a number of times, and slaughter commences (325) with Rhamnes, augur and king, but his augury did him no good. A gambler was killed who would have done better to play on until dawn (338). Nisus raged like a hungry lion and Euryalus was as bad. Rhoetus hid behind a great mixing-bowl but Euryalus killed him vomiting blood and wine. The scene is described in repellent detail, because that was felt to be part of Homer's great attraction. They saw horses eating as they do in a famous passage of Homer, looted a little and gave up for fear of light (355) so they escaped (366).

But at that moment three-hundred armed riders came from Latinus with a message for the camp, and Volcens their captain saw the gleam of the helmet of Euryalus. The young men were hunted down in a dark, overgrown wood which is eerie enough to have figured in the *Inferno* of Dante, first the boy weighed down with loot and then Nisus who kills Volcens and is killed, falling across the body of his friend. They both die impossibly noble deaths, Nisus trying to take all the blame on himself, and saying of Euryalus,

> His only Crime (if Friendship can offend)
> Is too much Love to his unhappy Friend.

Blood streams down him and his snow-white shoulder falls on his breast, like a flower cut by the plough,

> Like a white Poppy sinking on the Plain,
> Whose heavy Head is over-charg'd with Rain.

The simile is an old one that Catullus took from Sappho, but when one first reads it as a boy sentiment reigns, and it seems supreme poetry. Virgil is better than Dryden in detail. In Dryden the blood is purple, but in Virgil it is the flower, and the poppy is not white (435-7).

> Fortunate both if my poems have power
> You never shall be lost to memory
> While the house of Aeneas lives on
> Round the still rock of the Capitol,
> And Rome's father reigns ... (446-9)

This episode has lasted nearly 300 lines and we are now more than half way through the book. It is in heavy contrast to the serious fighting that will follow, but it has dark tones that prepare in however romantic a manner for the war. Yet, the shorter episode of the Great Mother turning ships into goddesses seems to me more memorable.

But now Fame spreads the news and the women lament. The Trojans take Euryalus's old mother indoors, the trumpet sounds for battle (503) and heaven echoes. The Volscians attack the walls and the Trojans roll boulders onto their heads.

In Homer there are only seven or eight things that can happen in a fight, and they do not all occur together except in the grandest conflicts, but Virgil writes more like a historian. Still, the fighters are soon at one another's throats, and with a prayer to the Muse (525) he plunges in. Turnus attacks a tower, and kills a Trojan as an eagle takes a hare or a swan (!) or a wolf a lamb (566).

There are lovely concatenations of names and fascinating details about individuals. The son of Arcens in his Spanish embroidery for example, whose rivers and groves and gods make him even more mysterious (585). Ascanius shoots a kinsman of Turnus in mid-boast about Italian toughness and Trojan luxury (600-20). Part of his boast was a sneer at the Great Mother. Ascanius prays to Jove, who responds. At that moment (638) Apollo happened to be watching seated on a cloud. He congratulates young Ascanius and transforms himself to Butes, an old retainer, to come down to earth to talk to him. As he vanishes (660) they recognise him by his rattling arrows. He has warned Ascanius to withdraw.

So the field will be open for Turnus to have his moment. Two young men like trees or like their native mountains guard a gate, tempers are lost and battle blazes. Turnus (691) hears the gate is open and rushes to the attack. When one hero falls the earth groans and the hero's shield thunders – after Homer and like many improvements, one for the worse (709). The fall was like the crash of some construction into the sea at Baiae in a swirl of black volcanic sands (715), making the islands tremble. Mars urges on the Latins and puts Panic into the Trojans. But Pandarus whose brother has been killed goes for Turnus, who jeers at him, and Juno turns aside his spear (745) so Turnus kills him and earth shakes at the mighty weight.

The last part of this book, by its need to improve on the Iliad and compress it, reads like a compendium of Homer exaggerated. But if one can forget Homer the story is gigantesque, superhuman and in its way awe-inspiring. Juno (764) gives Turnus strength and courage – Virgil does not understand the subtler role of Athene, nurse of all heroes. The killing gets faster and more furious. Amycus the huntsman is hunted down, and a friend of the Muses dies (774-6) who sang of wars and battles. The Trojan leaders rally their men and make for Turnus to mob him as he takes a rest by the river (790). Juno can give him no more help as Jove has sent her a stern warning by Iris (802-3), so Turnus, his helmet ringing with weapons (809) and his body a river of black sweat, dives in full armour into the yellow river, which washes him and returns him to the shore. This scene brings the book to a sensational ending and makes a pause.

Book ten begins with a Council of the Gods (copied from Ennius) which the preceding divine interventions were sufficiently grave to have provoked. Homer has them in the Iliad: this is less functional, it is only a relief from the scene on earth.

Jove makes a brief speech, Venus replies at length (16), and in the course of argument refers to Diomedes threatening an attack from 'Aetolian Arpi' (28) which was a town in Daunia (Roman since the third century) where presumably the Homeric Diomedes had landed from Aetolia in north Greece: but this explanation is as puzzling as the conundrum.

Diomedes has been forgotten since book eight, obviously because he was a hero too formidable to fit into the Aeneid, as Venus observes. She wants to take Ascanius away for ever to live in her sanctuary in Cyprus if he may not be king. And now Juno replies (62). Both are eloquent in the manner of schools of rhetoric as the elder Seneca describes them. The gods murmur like a forest, but at Jove's voice (100) they are silent: 'The Clouds dispel; the Winds their Breath restrain; / And the hush'd Waves lie flatted on the Main'. 'Jove decided to leave it all to fate, / And shook the sacred Honours of his Head', that is he nodded and the mountain shook around him.

So much for divine intervention. Since fate of course is that power which decrees that what happened was bound to happen, it is the most essential ally of the Augustan settlement, and therefore of Virgil in the Aeneid. We get a new though brief catalogue of some surviving heroes, though they read uncannily like obituaries. Only Ascanius, beautiful and bare-headed, seems secure.

Meanwhile Aeneas has reached Tarchon by sea (though he set out by land, 8, 555), and has secured his help. Virgil prays to the Muses (163) and begins a list of Aeneas's new allies: Aeneas and young Pallas lead the ships; Massicus in the Tiger leads a thousand; Abas with six-hundred from Populonia and three-hundred from the island of Ilva, famous for its mines; Asylas the augur led a thousand from Pisa,

> Who Heav'n interprets and the wand'ring Stars:
> From offer'd Entrails Prodigies expounds,
> And Peals of Thunder, with presaging Sounds.

Astur followed from Caere, ancient Pyrgi and Graviscae in the fens; and Cunerus (186), the Ligurian with his crest of swans' feathers: Your fault O Love, sign of his father's shape (188). This compressed line is fully explained:

> Cycnus in grief for his loved Phaethon
> Among the poplar leaves, his sister's shadow
> Consoling his sad love with his music,
> Sang his way soft-feathered to white old age,
> And leaving earth pursued the stars with song.

Cunerus was rowed in the mighty Centaur threatening the sea with its rock. Then came Ocnus son of: Prophetic Manto and the Tuscan river, / Who walled you Mantua, gave his mother's name, / Mantua rich in blood: not of one race, / But three peoples live there under a fourth: / A queen of peoples, strong by Tuscan blood: / Five-hundred armed against Mezentius / Whom Mincius shadowed in his native reeds / Grey from Benacus marshalled in his pine. (198-206).

Aulestes follows in the Triton with a hundred oars and a blue trumpet-shell. Below his wild breast mutters the white wave (212). Yet it is clear Virgil loves these ships that are almost people, and suddenly (219) a company of the old ships transformed into sea-gods comes swimming among the fleet. Cymodocea addresses Aeneas. Hoist sail, she says, we are the holy pine-trees of Ida, we are your fleet (228-9). This baroque extravagance may be from Aristophanes or Catullus (4); it may carry traces of Hellenistic Greek poetry, but the verse is fresh and original, and the conception charming. They give Aeneas news, tell him to arm, and give the ships a push from behind (247). Aeneas utters a prayer and day breaks.

The Trojans see them from the walls and fling spears like a migration of storks. Aeneas's crest flames and his shield vomits golden fire (271) and he comes like the deadly dog-star bringing famine and disease (274). In Homer it is the spear-point of Achilles that glitters like the deadliest of stars (Iliad 22, 25). It does not depress Turnus. The landing is dramatic and punctuated by speeches. This may not be disciplined but nor is the resistance. Tarchon's speech was out of Thucydides (4, 11).

Trumpets sounded (310) and Aeneas began the slaughter, and after 50 lines of it the spotlight falls on Pallas (365), because this is his moment, his *aristeia* as the Greek critics of Homer call it. Pallas meets his match or his equal in age and beauty (434-5) in Lausus, but they will not meet. Does Virgil plan to make Pallas and Lausus in book ten a vignette to match Nisus and Euryalus in book nine? It is possible, but these are not isolated or highlighted by their adventure and the battle rages on around them in Homeric confusion.

Turnus has a sister Iuturna (439) though she is not named until book twelve (139) who for no obvious reason now joins in the fighting as charioteer, where Pallas and Turnus confront one another. Turnus is like a lion spotting a bull. Paris prays to Hercules, who weeps. Jove tells him everyone has their fatal day: my son Sarpedon died (in the Iliad) and so will Turnus. They fight, Turnus wins and makes a boast (490) jeering at Evander to bury his son, but removing Pallas's sword-belt, an ill-omened act we are told (504).

Aeneas takes eight captives, sons of Sulmo and of Ufens, whom he will later sacrifice to the dead (519-20) and kills a man begging for mercy, refusing ransom (536). He kills a priest of Apollo and Hecate and a son of Faunus and Dryope. The process goes on episode by episode from nastiness to nastiness, without excuses. He kills the ruler of Amyclae, which lay between Caiete and Terracia (thought to be a Spartan colony) and raged like Aegaeon who had a hundred arms and fifty mouth and belongs to folklore.

He rages mercilessly (439-605) until Jove addresses Juno, observing that Venus is making her side win. Juno wishes she could save poor Turnus for his father Daunus: after all Pilumnus the god was Turnus's ancestor (619). Jove allows her to save him for the time being, but that is all. She makes a ghost like Aeneas to draw Turnus away and into a ship, into which Turnus jumps:

> The guileful Phantom now forsook the Shrowd
> And flew sublime, and vanish'd in a Cloud.
> Too late young Turnus the Delusion found,
> Far on the Sea, still making from the Ground.

Turnus prayed for death, and contemplated suicide, but Juno circumvented him at every attempt. At length she landed him on his native coast and restored him to the arms of Daunus in south Italy.

Mezentius took Turnus's place in battle (689) as Jove planned, and defied the Trojans like some vast rock in the angry sea (695), and this being his moment he did some killing, and gave Lausus the arms of the dead (700) some of whose stories go almost beyond Homer in mysteriousness (704-5). He is like a wild boar from the Laurentian marshes living for years on the reeds of the forest, trapped at last but foaming with fury: no one dares meet his just rage (714).

This word rage (*ira*) has come a number of times into these books, and Galinsky is surely right to point to it as a key to the closing stages of the Aeneid, and to Virgil's disapproval of it as a philosopher: and yet I am not sure that Virgil has worked out his philosophic position in all its consequences: he thinks war is hellish and battle passionate and terrible, yet he is not a Quaker. Mezentius is a lion. He kills the Greek Acron of Cortona who has run away from marriage, and his heels beat the ground (731). He ignores Orodes in flight but fights man to man (734) and kills him face to face. You will go the same way, says his enemy. Jove will see to me, is his reply. Mars raged on both sides equally (755), no one ran away, and the gods pitied the vain rage (*ira*) of both sides, Venus this way and Juno that, while the pale fury Tisiphone raved between the ranks.

Mezentius was like great Orion whose head scrapes heaven, but Aeneas had spotted him. First Aeneas offered Lausus as a trophy to the gods. He caught and finished him with a sword. Antor, the friend of Hercules, had just been killed by mistake (780) and died remembering sweet Argos.

There is an atmosphere of pathos and Virgil begins to distance Aeneas from his blood-lust of battle-fury. Lausus dies weeping and remembering his father Mezentius (790); he is killed trying to save his father's life. Mezentius is wounded but he mounts his beautiful horse (858). Aeneas has been infuriated, though he shelters behind his shield like a farmer from bad weather and as Lausus dies (820) Aeneas feels genuine pity for the young man (822), as Achilles did when he killed the Amazon (Virgil has altered the sexes). He leaves the dead Lausus his weapons (where Turnus had stripped and put his foot on the dead Pallas) and himself takes his body in his arms (831) while his weapons are left on the ground.

Lausus is much lamented by Mezentius and his friends. Mezentius of course intends vengeance and Aeneas answers the challenge (872), so Mezentius is killed, begging to be buried with Lausus.

Aeneas has felled the horse with a spear:

... with all his Force
Full at the Temples of the Warrior Horse
Just where the Stroke was aim'd, th' unerring Spear
Made way, and stood transfix'd thro' either Ear.

The horse reared and then lashed out with his rear feet and crashed down on his master, whom Aeneas finished with his sword. One feels the same sorrow at the fate of Lausus as one does at that of Paris, but little at the unlucky death of Mezentius: more for his horse.

Yet Aeneas because he pities Lausus ends with his *pietas*, his human decency, restored. The entire tenth book does not perfectly hang together as a single tapestry: if it did it would be a masterpiece that Virgil was not born to write.

With the eleventh book we approach the end of the Aeneid, but slowly and through a field strewn with sad fantasies. The quality of mere romance that so shocked Mommsen in the Aeneid was essential to Virgil's approach to 'epic' verse, and could scarcely be otherwise. After the phenomenal success of the Eclogues he did show remarkable development as a poet, but the reality on which his grasp was tight was that of the country, and the Aeneid so far entered almost more deeply than the Georgics into the Italian landscape and its meaning. The eleventh book is taken up with funerals, the felling of trees (out of Ennius but one never forgets it and it foreshadows the death of Turnus); the speeches including the tribute of Diomedes to Aeneas, of the Iliad to the Aeneid as it were; and the brief triumph of the Amazon Camilla like the flight of a dragonfly.

The dawn rises yet again from Ocean, and Aeneas prayed to the dawn god as it rose, dressing an oak tree with the spoils of Mezentius (8) to the god of war. He tells his men in ceremonious lines they must go now in procession to Evander's city with the dead body of his son Pallas. He spoke weeping (29) and the ritual lament followed (38). Aeneas (42-58) made a funeral speech and the procession formed:

Of oaken Twigs they twist an easy Bier,
Then on their Shoulders the sad Burden rear.
The Body on this rural Hearse is borne:
Strew'd Leaves and funeral Greens the Bier adorn,
All pale he lies, and looks a lovely Flower,
New cropt by virgin Hands, to deck the Bower:
Unfaded yet, but yet unfed below,
No more to mother Earth or the green Stem shall owe.

Dryden has omitted the line 'soft violet or fainting hyacinth' (69) and so diminished the recollection of dead Euryalus. The Trojans offer clothes and horses and loot of some grandeur, and Aeneas's captives (81) are led in the procession to their death. Poor old Acoetes, Pallas's tutor, walks behind, and behind him come the bloody war-chariots. The horse Aethon follows weeping (his name is Homeric (8, 1-85) but we have never heard of him before in the Aeneid); with his armaments put off he dampened his face with big tears.

Now the Rutuli send an embassy to beg for the bodies of their dead: Aeneas not only agrees to this, but gives them a severe lecture about the unjust war; he says Turnus should agree to a duel. Drances who hates Turnus replies for the Rutuli (123-4). A truce is agreed for twelve days and for that time (122-31) Trojans and Latins wander on the hills and

> Loud Axes through the groaning Groves resound:
> Oak, Mountain Ash, and Poplar spread the Ground:
> Firs fall from high: and some the Trunks receive
> In Loaden Wains, with Wedges some they cleave.

Virgil's was the great age of road-building, in which roads were pushed through the virgin forest that had covered Italy. Virgil has not only read Ennius, he has seen and heard the devastation; in the Georgics he had already lamented it.

As the procession with Paris dead approaches, the Arcadians come to meet it with funeral torches alight, and: The Fields are lighten'd with a fiery blaze, / That cast a sullen splendour on their Friends. Evander hears the shrieking and flings himself on the corpse, and at last speaks (151) in bitter resignation and at some length (161-181). The reader notices that speeches have somehow taken over book eleven, and that Virgil is masterly in their decorum. Evander now lives on only to see vengeance strike Turnus. Next morning,

> Their Friends convey the dead to Fun'ral Fires,
> Black smould'ring Smoke from the green Wood expires;
> The Light of Heav'n is cloak'd, and the new Day retires.

The circling procession, the offerings and sacrifices are described in detail, though not the death of the captives. The same on a lesser scale is done for the Rutuli, though Paris is not the only dead man on Aeneas's side. After three days the ashes of the dead and the unburnt bones are covered over with earth. In the city of Latinus the women curse Turnus, and Drances promotes this (220) demanding a duel.

At this point the embassy sent to Diomedes returns (226) and a debate follows (234) convened by Latinus in distress. Venulus is the first to report (243). They have been to Argyripa in the fields of Iapyx to see the lord of Mount Garganus, that is Diomedes, survivor of the Iliad, on a spur of Apulia well-known to Horace. It had been granted to Diomedes by Daunus for help against the Messapians or as a dowry for his daughter whom the Greek married. This is in the wonderland of legend; Diomedes does not see why these happy peoples should emerge from their golden age (252-4).

We Greeks were punished, Diomedes says, for the Trojan war: and the list of disasters he offers may owe something to a lost tragedy, Virgil's rhetoric being usually or always that of Euripidean tragedy. His companions are lost and have turned into shearwaters.

> Hov'ring about the Coasts they make their Moan,
> And cuff the Cliffs with Pinions not their own.

Dryden takes them for chuffs and Virgil for river-birds, but they had no such reference book as D'Arcy Thompson on Greek Birds.

Diomedes warns the embassy that Aeneas is too formidable a foe for them and advises peace. When Venulus ends his speech the council bursts into comment like a river over stones until Latinus himself speaks (302). He points out the hopelessness of the war, and suggests terms on which the Trojans may settle, or if they choose withdraw. He offers to build ten or twenty ships for them.

Then Drances speaks (336) and we are told again how he hates Turnus. He is rich and a good speaker but no soldier. He wants to give in, but his speech is only a foil for the next, by Turnus who now re-appears (376). Turnus's speech is vigorous, furious, and astute. We hear of Aufidus running backwards (405) and of Camilla (432): Drances is scornfully demolished by this natural bully, and we know what to expect next.

Meanwhile Aeneas (446) is on the march: the noise of panic is like the rough-voiced swans on the noisy marshes of the Po (457). Turnus (459) shouts to his allies, and the war-trumpet sounds (474). He rushes gleaming from the citadel like a stallion set free in meadows and familiar rivers (495) and meets Camilla and her Volscians. The horse is by Ennius out of Homer (Macrob. Sat. 6, 3) but Virgil here at least is best, and outdoes even the Georgics.

Camilla wants to lead against Aeneas but Turnus proposes an ambush, the first sign of tactics in this war. The landscape is now wilder, with hillsides dark with dense leaves (523) and cliffs (529) and uneven forest country (531). Artemis calls the nymph Opis to say she is worried about Camilla, whose history we are told in full. Camilla is named after her mother Casmilla and her father wrapped her in cork, tied her to a spear, and flung her into Campania across the Amasenus, dedicating her to Diana who loves her as her manner is. Her father was a hunted exile from Privernum of the Volsci, where the cork-oak still grew in the seventeenth century. All this obscure information perhaps suggests that Varronian genealogy may have connected her with the Roman family of Camilli. *Libro* (bark) and *libraus* (balancing) within two lines of each other (554-6) are probably carelessness rather than a pun (though Virgil does make puns). Camilla's father dedicated her also to Hecate, another title of Diana, and she lived alone on the mountains suckled by a mare.

Virgil makes her a romantic child wearing a tiger-skin and shooting cranes and swans. Women in the Etruscan towns wanted her to marry their sons but she preferred virginity (583) and Diana. The goddess regrets Camilla's involvement in this war, but she entrusts to Opis magic weapons to avenge her at her death, whoever kills her. With this Diana disappears (596). She is the goddess of wild country, and of hunting, so she is Camilla's natural patroness.

The Trojans are coming with all the Etruscan leaders and their squadrons of horse. Against them Messapus moves with his brother Coras and Camilla's wing (604). The shooting is like a snowfall, the shouting and the noise of the horses increase. The Trojans under Aconteus (615) win at the first crashing encounter: they were close to the city gates and the Latins turn the soft necks (622) of their horses. They were like a tide, twice flooding to the walls, until the third time (630-5) the fighting was hand to hand. Another horse dies and also a strong man, weltering in blood and corpses, to set off the Amazon Camilla (649) with javelins, axe and bow, and her girls around her (655). They are like the Amazons of Thermodon, Hippolyte who attacked Athens or Penthesilea whom Achilles slew. Virgil undoubtedly knows them as works of art, and there is a tinge of Greekness about them; he does not know the stories told by Turkish nomads about Kyg Kala, from which the Amazons derive, the mythical city of warrior virgins in the steppe.

Camilla does a lot of slaughter until Virgil has almost run out of names: Liris (670) is a river-name, Tereus (675) is famous from the story of the nightingale, Iapyx is a wind or a person but her an Apulian horse (678). Butes occurs twice, by mistake (695 and 9, 647). She downs Orsilochus of the Apennines (700) with an axe. And the son of Aunus the Ligurian (701) fails to escape her by his Ligurian craftiness (716). She takes him as easily as an eagle takes a pigeon.

Jove sees all this going on and sends of the Etruscans Tarchon into action. He rallies his men (730) and says some nasty things to them about their talent for sex and revelry. He then attacks Venulus, sweeps him from his horse and carries him off, arms and all (*arma virumque ferens*, 747). Is a joke intended (1, 1 *arma virumque cano*)? I *suppose* not. He is like an eagle fighting a snake, a scene beloved by the Greeks, dating from Hesiod and early illustrated in a tradition that has survived in manuscripts.

The old man has encouraged his Lydians (Etruscans; 759) and now Arruns is stalking Camilla. Chloreus, priest of Cybele and beautifully dressed, whom Camilla was herself stalking, opened an opportunity as she was intent on him and incautious. Arruns saw this and prayed to Apollo of Soracte, who half heard his prayer and let Camilla die (804). But Arruns hid like a wolf that has killed a shepherd or a steer (811). The dying Camilla made a dying speech to her friend Acca, with a message to Turnus to come. Her life fled angry to the shadows, like that of Turnus later (831).

The Arcadians, Trojans and Etruscans rushed on, but Opis saw and lamented Camilla. She went down from her mountain to the grave-mound of an ancient King covered by a vast ilex tree (851), where she soon saw Arruns on the run, and almost ceremoniously shot him dead. There is some reference to Amazon meaning papless or breastless, making them better archers, a view based on the Greek word Amazon which Virgil does not take.

Camilla's wing now leads the retreat, the horses thunder like hexameters (875), a dust-cloud thickens round the walls, and the town looks like falling. Turnus gets the message in the woods (896) and Acca tells him the extent of the disaster.

> He leaves the hilly Pass, the Woods in vain
> Possess'd, and downward issues on the Plain;
> Scarce was he gone, when to the Streights, now freed
> From secret Foes, the Trojan Troops succeed.
> Thro' the black Forrest, and the ferny Brake,
> Unknowingly secure, their way they take.

The plan Turnus made had gone wrong, but it had kept him out of the way while Camilla blazed and died.

Aeneas was mysteriously absent too. Virgil does exploit the landscape, and that is important for the whole Aeneid, so that we finish this book with our heads ringing not only with war and blood and battles and horses, but with the silences, the hills and the trees. The armies are now face to face, and Turnus 'hears th' approaching Horses proudly neigh', but the day is over, and 'westward to the Sea the Sun declin'd'. The next morning must surely be the last. So far the deadliest fighters have been the most doomed, particularly in book eleven, but no doom hangs over the head of Aeneas, he is an Achilles who is not going to die in this war or, for all we know to the contrary, he may never die.

217

In book twelve, Turnus 'rais'd his haughty Soul, to meet his Fate'. He was like a lion pursued who turns on his pursuers when he is wounded.

> So Turnus fares; his Eye-balls flash with Fire,
> Thro' his wide Nostrils Clouds of Smoke expire.

He offers Latinus to fight Aeneas in a duel for Lavinia. Latinus says there are plenty like her in Latium and the gods make it plain Aeneas must succeed – while Turnus has kingdoms of his own.

But Turnus (45) insists on the duel, though he must now behave worse and worse until any lurking sympathy for him is gone. Yet this is not a simple process. He refuses to withdraw to the distant kingdom of Daunus, or even his nearby stronghold at Ardea, it seems. Latinus argues the position at some length, but Turnus just goes on getting wilder. The Queen breaks into the argument which has by now become somewhat operatic (55). She is going to die; the fact that a character is marked down for death, like Tarchon (11, 706), need not be elaborated, but the Queen (12, 595f.) has suicide already in mind, it is part of her desperation, and Turnus (57) is her only hope. She begs him not to fight. Lavinia (64) does not have a great deal to say but she blushes, and Turnus sees this and addresses her mother.

Turnus sends a messenger to suggest a duel at the first blush of tomorrow's dawn. He then goes indoors to see his horses, given to Pilumnus by Orithyia, a Greek goddess: perhaps they were immortal? The grooms are petting and combing them (85-6). He arms and puts on a sword the divine armourer gave to Daunus and makes a speech to his spear. His eyes flash fire and he bellows like a bull about to fight (103). These 3 or 4 lines are nearly an exact repetition of the Georgics (3, 232-4), but an improvement, 2 lines being the same. It is curious that there Virgil reports these fighting bulls in the far south of Italy, not far from the kingdom of Daunus.

> Thus while he raves, from his wild Nostrils flies
> A fiery Steam, and Sparks from his Eyes.
> So fares the Bull in his lov'd Female's sight;
> Proudly he bellows and preludes the fight;
> He tries his goring Horns against a Tree
> And meditates his absent Enemy:
> He pushes at the Winds, he digs the Strand
> With his black Hoofs, and spurns the yellow Sand.

It is not a simile that makes Turnus more acceptable as a human being, but there is no suggestion he is outside human nature.

Aeneas (107) is just as savage, working up his own rage (108), but he cheers up his friends and comforts his fearful son.

Another wonderful day dawns and the battle-ground is prepared under the walls, with grass altars in the centre, ritually decorated. The Italian regiment marches out, and the Trojans, armed as for fighting. Mnestheus, Asilas and Messapus, the leaders are dressed in purple and gold, and at a trumpet the soldiers take their places, the people perch on walls and towers and gateways. Juno sees all this from the Alban hill (134) and at once spoke to Turnus's sister Iuturna (146), whom Jove made a nymph as a reward for her lost virginity. Her name was that of a river a few miles away, but Virgil promotes her to power over all lakes and rivers.

> Then thus the Goddess of the Skies bespake
> With Sighs and Tears the Goddess of the Lake ...

Juno tells Iuturna her brother must die, and since she must no longer intervene she stirs up Iuturna to break the truce, create tumult, and somehow snatch Turnus away.

> And now in Pomp the peaceful Kings appear:
> Four Steeds the Chariots of Latinus bear,
> Twelve golden Beams around his Temples play
> To mark his Lineage from the God of Day.

A priest begins the sacrifice, Roman rather than Greek, and Aeneas vows to the Sun, the Earth of Italy, the Sky-god and the Queen of Air, the War-god and all springs and rivers, all gods of the sky and the blue sea, that if he is beaten his son will retreat to Evander's town, and if he wins Italians and Trojans will live together in peace (189-91). Latinus swears in similar terms. No day shall break this peace in Italy (202). The victims were slaughtered and their bowels drawn alive (214), an operation which as you would expect the revolting verse tragedian Seneca gives in more elaborate detail in his *Thyestes*.

The Rutuli felt sorry for Turnus, and Iuturna in disguise as a soldier spread rumours and created a mood of serious resentment (239). A sign in heaven: an eagle taking a swan (250) but the eagle was mobbed and dropped the swan in its river, so the Rutuli were cheered by this omen (257) and Tolumius the augur was delighted. He shot an arrow at the enemy and a spear struck one of nine brothers, sons of Arcadian Gylippus by a Tuscan. The survivors (277) fought back and the truce was over.

If the spear was not from Tolumius was it not from Iuturna? We are not told, though in the Iliad we know exactly who breaks the truce and why.

The altars are torn down, and Latinus flees, Messapus fights, Corynaeus takes fire from the altar (300) and it appears we are in for another battle scene. Aeneas calls to his men to control their rage (314) but an unknown hand (Iuturna again?) hits him with an arrow.

The moment Turnus sees Aeneas wounded and retreating, he leaps into a chariot like bloody Mars leading the winter winds of Thrace with Terror, Rage and Ambush in his train (336). He lashes horses smoking with sweat and their hooves scatter a dew of blood. He kills some Homeric and antique names, including Dolon's son, snarling dark humour at the dead.

Aeneas goes back to camp in pain where Iapyx son of Iasos (and brother of Palinurus?) whom Apollo loved and taught medicine was ready to heal him. It is said of Iapyx that he rejected augury, the harp and shooting, Apollo's other skills, but preferred to know 'the power of herbs for healing and to practice wordless arts unhonoured' (397) which recalls again Virgil's longing to know science at the end of the second Georgic.

Iapyx took the arrow out 'with healing hand and the god's powerful herbs'. Neither Fortune nor Apollo helped, but evil was near and the battle raged closer (407-10). Venus was grieved and brought dittany from Crete (412-3), a herb used by wounded wild goats (the kri-kri, 415). It sounds to me like 'mountain tea', of which sixteen varieties were for sale thirty years ago in the covered market at Chania in Crete. Having performed a quasi-miraculous cure 'with scented All-heal and ambrosian juice' (419). Iapyx sends everyone back into battle (425). A brief moralising to Ascanius, 'My boy, learn courage and hard work from me: / The rest from others', and Aeneas is off (435-40). His enemies see him coming and they tremble. Iuturna is terrified (448). A little more than half the book remains, yet the duel has not begun.

Aeneas comes upon them like a storm: Tolumius the augur is among the first to die, but in the chaos Aeneas seeks only for Turnus (466). Now Iuturna takes over from Metiscus as her brother's driver, like a swallow diving through a rich man's house for food. But she will not let Turnus engage (480). All the same Aeneas is tracking Turnus until Messapus enrages him and he starts slaughtering, thinking of the oath. He lets go altogether of the reins of rage (499). The slaughter is fearful on both sides. How can Jupiter have wished such a conflict between peoples who were to live in peace (504)? Among the more pathetic of the dead is Menoetes, who hated war to no purpose, an Arcadian, who fished the rivers round Lerna, a poor man.

Like fires roaring through a wood or rivers roaring down a mountain, Aeneas and Turnus rush through the fighting wild with rage (527). The Trojan war seems to a reader to have begun again, and the poetry has a strong taste of Ennius and has something Homeric about it (550).

Venus now gives her son one of those good ideas so rare in the battles of the Aeneid (554) and he calls on his generals to make an immediate assault on Laurentum which is no sooner said than done (576). It is like smoking out a swarm of bees (cf Geo. 4, 44) from a rock (592). The Queen hangs herself, Lavinia lacerates herself, Latinus tears his clothes and dirties his white hair.

Turnus (614) begins to tire and hears the noises from the city. Iuturna in disguise tries to keep him where he is, but Turnus says I knew it was you who broke the armistice, my sister. He will not turn his back, he prays to the underworld he hopes to impress by his death since the gods are against him (647). A mounted friend calls him to help against Aeneas. He accepts the challenge (680).

With this re-entry of Turnus the climax of the Aeneid – which is a piece of story-telling and subjects itself to the laws of story-telling – clearly begins. The story has grown more interesting and more surprising with every twist and turn. It is no good at this stage looking for anything deeper or more deeply poetic. Turnus abandons Iuturna and sets off for his death, like a rock falling from a mountain top. The soldiers withdraw at his command and leave him a space (696) for the duel he now contemplates. Aeneas is delighted (700), the phrase *laetitia exultans* is like Biblical Latin, and his arms thunder like Eryx or Athos or the very Appenines (703).

The spectators crowd and gape, earth groans, shields clang: swords clash and chance and courage mingle. They are like two bulls in the south, the herdsmen have fled and the cattle await the issue (Geo. 3, 219). This time the simile is 8 lines long, and Jove weighs their chances (725). Turnus breaks his sword: he was using his charioteer's (Metiscus's) sword by mistake.

> Surpriz'd with fear, he fled along the Field
> And now forthright, and now in Orbits wheel'd.
> For here the Trojan Troops the List surround
> And there the Pass is clos'd with Pools and marshy Ground.
> Aeneas hastens, tho' with heavier Pace,
> His Wound so newly knit retards the Chase.

The chase was like an Umbrian stag-hunt: the simile is a long one and gives the fighting an immediacy and a vividness. No one interferes for fear of Aeneas (761) and they circle five times. A wild olive tree sacred to Faunus grew there

(Iliad 22, 145), venerated by sailors who dedicated their clothes to Pan after shipwreck. (I take this monument to be real. Theophrastus records that arms were found under the bark of a wild olive, that the tree had overgrown, as you still find barbed wire deeply embedded in willow trees. However that may be, the Trojans had cut it down, but later the tree grew again around Aeneas's spear and would not let it go.) Turnus, crazy with fear (776), prayed to Faunus: the tree held and Iuturna (as Metiscus) rushed to help her brother, bringing him his own sword (785). Venus was furious and tugged out the spear for Aeneas.

So after this breathing-space they began again. But Jove had been watching and addressed Juno. His speech was cogently reasoned (791-806) and Juno submitted on terms (808-38). Aeneas and his men must adopt the Latin language and dress (835-74). Jove then sent one of his *Dirae*, his pestiferous attendant ladies, to frighten off Iuturna, the Dira whizzed down like a Parthian poisoned arrow (800). The apparition is splendid, recalling the great days of Allecto, Turnus is terrified and his sister runs away and hides in her river in tears (886).

Aeneas asks why the delay? This is not meant to be a race but a fight (890). Turnus sees a mighty rock twelve modern men could hardly move, a field boundary, and flung it like a man falling in a dream: the Dira frustrated him (914). The spear glittered and came at him like artillery, like a thunderbolt. It hit him through the thigh and pinned him to the ground. His people groaned, and the mountains and deep woods re-echoed (929). Turnus begged for his life for his father's sake and admitted defeat: he even gave up his claim to Lavinia. Aeneas was on the point of relenting (910) when he saw the sword-belt of the boy Pallas which Turnus wore. His rage was terrible (*ira*, 946) and he killed him in the name of Pallas.

> The streaming Blood distain'd his Arms around
> And the disdainful Soul came rushing thro' the Wound.

That is the end of the Aeneid, with less of deep grief than the Iliad: but it is certainly dramatic.

IX

ASHES

It must be clear to any attentive reader that the Aeneid was never quite finished, that it contained contradictions and set problems beyond Virgil's intention. It is tempting to ask whether the whole vast construction had a single meaning or a dominant message, but I doubt that, since it does not appear possible for a poem written over so long a period. If it is true as Suetonius reported that Virgil wrote first in prose, that would give him only the outline of his intention. The first and most important choice was Aeneas. Virgil chose to write about the only Roman hero who meshed with the Iliad and the fall of Troy: he chose to imitate and adapt the works of Homer in a Latin form, relying on Ennius for an epic flavour in his verse more pronounced than before (though this antique colouring had been introduced instead of dialect into his Eclogues long ago). I have spoken also of his passion for Italy itself, which was like a love affair. To show that civil war was futile and wicked, and that all Italy should be felt as one place, which it had recently become, and which Julius Caesar's and Augustus's policy favoured, was certainly central to his aims.

The question remains what is to be made of his preoccupation with Rome and its future: Jove says in the first book that he has granted Rome never-ending command, unlimited empire, *imperium sine fine dedi*. In the vision of Anchises in the sixth book and in the shield given to Aeneas in the eighth (656), Virgil takes a triumphal stand about the Roman empire, and there is no doubt that Augustus was pleased.

Yet there is also a sub-text, because Virgil seems to hate battles and wars, and to nourish a personal horror of that passionate rage *(ira)* without which there would be no fighting. This is more obvious towards the end of the Aeneid, where the complex feelings of Virgil about his material lead to a text of some complexity. Augustus accepted this: the narrative is in the past as Juno's malice is in the past. Nicholas Horsfall in a stimulating chapter of his *Companion to the Study of Virgil* suggests that the Roman, the governor, is as much to be pitied as his victim, his defeated enemy, and Saint Augustine thought it natural to weep over the death of Turnus. Yet I do not believe that Shakespeare's *Antony and Cleopatra* would have been well received by Augustus.

It is certain that Augustus placed a heavy burden on the shoulders of his poet, and yet evident that Virgil erected a polite fence around his privacy and the freedom that he worked in. There are times when we can see his personal feelings were out of line with the momentum of his story. Virgil's closest patron and friend had been and still was Maecenas, and I have no doubt that somewhere lurking among the tribal leaders of the Etruscans must be the founder of that line of kings Horace says Maecenas was descended from. The descent of Caesar from 'Iulus', the Ascanius of the Aeneid, was a claim about two hundred years old, but the claim of Maecenas was no doubt older.

Virgil gained greatly by his splendid commission: it made him rich, and gave him a chance to write poetry on a scale it would be hard to surpass. He was publicly lectured on in his lifetime, and the walls of Pompeii have preserved an amazing wealth of graffiti that quote the Aeneid (not all by schoolchildren). When he had nearly finished his poem, he must have been exhausted. He had composed at a rate of more than a book a year, and he wanted a holiday before he undertook his final revision. So he set off to Greece for a few years, thinking of the pursuit of philosophy, which really he had never abandoned, or which had never let go of him. He had been to Greece before apparently, and he seems to have known Lerna and Pheneus, the north-east Peloponnese, and possibly Mycenae, perhaps even Kalavryta and Mount Kyllene in the north-west, a day's ride behind Patras.

Virgil had always been a scholar and a critic, his reading was wide, and his decisions about Homer and about the Aeneid were magisterial. It is interesting that what the earliest ancient critics notice in him, a skill at using ordinary words in new collocations, is the other side of the coin from that 'new kind of affectation' of which Maecenas was accused. We have no reason to think very highly of Maecenas's verse, but there is a circle which he brought together and which Horace celebrated early in his career (Sat. 1, 5). Souls more sincere and free / Earth never bore, nor closer tied to me, was his verdict. (I have treated that circle as far as we know anything about it in my Horace, published in 1997.) They were intensely respectful of Virgil, and two of them were the literary executors to whom we owe the Aeneid in the authentic form in which we have it. Virgil must have lived a withdrawn life, even in his house on the Esquiline, because he got through so much work, but also he was shy of his fame, and did not enjoy public readings (at which he might be sharply criticised in the niggling manner of those days). Among poets his closest friend and deepest admirer was Horace, whose *Carmen Saeculare* rehandles national and Virgilian themes with notable loyalty.

Among the many sources adapted by Virgil in the Aeneid, the most frequent is Homer, but he is as liable to do the opposite to what Homer did as to translate him, and his sources are often multiple. Lucretius, the glossy poet Apollonius of

Rhodes, Ennius and Theocritus all contribute. Among places, the gardener who I have always hoped was a retired pirate near Tarentum, and the poor Arcadian fisherman from the rivers around Lerna, both seem to indicate personal knowledge and affection. He is said to have owned land in Sicily. The part of Italy he knew least was the East coast around Rimini and Ancona.

Italian folk-tales affect Virgil, such as the tree where Sleep has roosted, and every leaf shelters a dream, and the curiously persistent legend of the sow and her litter. I had thought that was a Greek legend, because I had come across a mysterious secret sow of gold with a dozen golden piglets in Peloponnesian villages where antiquities had been found: only once it was a golden duck with a dozen golden ducklings. But a similar belief existed in the Greek towns of Asia Minor, where the number was seven: it is possible that this bizarre superstition dated from the Roman Empire, certainly the people of Laurentum claimed it for their own, as the Romans claimed the she-wolf. No one thought to classify such stories in the ancient world. Where did Virgil see or hear of a shepherd burning a forest in the mountains? Come to that, where did he really get the strange tale of the regeneration of bees in the fourth Georgic? I do not think the antiquarian Varro can always be the answer to such questions.

We have seen Virgil's homosexual sympathies at work in book five, and then with Nisus and Euryalus, with Paris and Lausus: even Turnus is called 'young' more often in book twelve as we begin to half-like him. In real life, Virgil like Horace was in no position to marry the kind of Roman lady he mixed with, because although his case was less extreme than Horace's, he was still not a nobleman by birth. Anyway, he seems to have been tranquilly homosexual. Maecenas or Pollio gave him a boy he fancied whom he trained up to be his secretary: he owned another boy who was a poet (Cebes). If Horace had eight or ten slaves, Virgil must have had a dozen or twenty, though it is true that the Epicureans disregarded or abolished slavery among themselves, so it may well be that in Siro's villa he had none and felt more at ease. That in the end was where he asked to be buried. He was rumoured to have had an affair with a woman called Plotia, the wife of Varius and a kinswoman of Plotius, but we know even less about this entanglement that we do about the land in Sicily (in which I scarcely believe).

Stones crumble and even Virgil's monument is lost, probably swallowed by the sea: the west coast of Italy has altered very much. In Rome the forum of Augustus contained the statues of a number of Virgilian heroes, but whether Virgil inspired them is not clear; a monument that has survived nearly complete and does seem to reflect his ideas is the calm and beautiful *Ara Pacis Augusti*, the Altar of Peace, still in the shed where Mussolini put it beside the Tiber. A small inner frieze above the altar is an imitation of the Parthenon frieze with its cattle, and on the tall outer screen there is a very beautiful woman; perhaps she is Mother Earth, but I have always thought she was Italy. She sits among the reeds of a lake, looking very like Italy as Virgil would have imagined her. The procession on the way to sacrifice includes the imperial family, including Augustus and Agrippa. Among the magnificent garlands of flowers, marble bees are buzzing. It is as memorable as any Roman work of art that has survived, and as deeply Greek as it is Augustan.

If we want to date the death of Virgil, which was in September of 19 BC, more accurately in terms of art history, then he died in the year the Pont du Gard was finished, that stunning, unpretentious aqueduct. It is even possible there was once a head of Virgil that derived from the antique in Mantua, but that was lost in the renaissance. A gold medal was struck in Paris to commemorate Napoleon's conquest of Mantua, and one was sold in London in 1997.

At the time of his death Virgil had been in Athens on his way east, since his three years of revision were to be spent in Greece and in Asia Minor, but Augustus also had been in the east, bargaining with the Parthians over Roman control of Armenia, and on his way home he swept up Virgil in his train. It may easily be that Virgil was already unwell: he was after all nearly fifty-six. He fell ill of the disease that killed him at Megara, a small town west of Athens that retains to this day a simplicity and a dignity, and a few impressive monuments not often visited. September was a bad month in the ancient world, and Horace at least was always careful of it, but apart from Virgil's general ill-health, bad stomach and tendency to sore throat, he had been spitting blood, so it sounds as if he was tubercular. The Esquiline might have suited him better: his house there overlooked the gardens of Maecenas, and it was that estate that Augustus himself used as a sanatorium for his maladies. Whether or not the invitation to travel with Augustus was kindly intended, it killed Virgil. When he got to Brindisi he was seriously ill; there is a suggestion that he delayed there because he wanted to see Metapontum, where temples are still standing, but in a few days he was dead.

He divided his comfortable fortune into twelve, leaving a twelfth to Maecenas, the same to Varius and to Plotius Tucca, a quarter to Augustus, and the remaining half to his half brother by his mother's second marriage, Valerius Proculus. His body was burnt and his ashes and his bones taken home to the villa that was once Siro's, where they were buried 'this side of the second mile-stone towards Pozzuoli' from Naples. On the monument a simple couplet was carved, said to have been written by Virgil himself, but I doubt that, under the circumstances, and hazard the conjecture that the two lines might be by Horace.

IX. ASHES

Mantua made me, Calabria unmade,
The Siren holds me idle in her shade:
Who sang the crown, the shepherd's crook, the spade.

Whether they are by one friend or another, the Siren is Parthenope, the city of Naples, and they recall the end of the fourth Georgic. Possibly no one was familiar yet with the Aeneid, but one is glad to see the loyalty to Virgil's earlier poetry.

This couplet raises in its way the question that is more insistently raised by the main provision of Virgil's will: his attempt to have the Aeneid burnt, which was frustrated by Augustus who insisted on full publication and instructed the literary executors. It was not the mere unpolishedness of the Aeneid that was worrying Virgil, the half-lines he could supplement impromptu in his wonderful voice. The poem itself had not driven him to desperation, no one tells us he was feverish, and his financial arrangements were clear.

Can it have been the whole commission, some philosophic scruple about the whole idea of the Aeneid, some resentment of pressure from Augustus that worried Virgil? Why else would he allow three years for the revision?

The first answer is that they were years to be spent travelling, and refilling the exhausted cisterns of his imagination. Secondly one must remember that he was essentially a Hellenistic poet to the marrow of his bones, a stylist who had learnt to apply his dazzling ability to a long narrative: though never again as perfectly as in the fourth Georgic. This element in his character as a poet, which was so extreme one can almost think of him as a Greek poet who just happened to write in Latin, determines much about the Aeneid that might otherwise puzzle us: including its Homeric influence in structure as in phrasing, its episodic character and tendency to romance or fairy-tale, and the decline of obituary ironies into a style like the gentle falling of a leaf, which is precisely that of Hellenistic epitaphs. Did he mind Horace's superiority?

Virgil was not concerned to criticise the spirit and momentum of his entire Aeneid, or of the Roman empire under Augustus. These are modern scruples. One notes that he lied shamelessly about the battle of Actium, which fills an important position at the end of book eight. In particular he reverses the roles of Augustus and Agrippa, and suppresses the importance of the cavalry which swung the land battle by changing sides. It is possible that he did not know anything about what happened at Actium and did not care: but he certainly could easily have found out, and I feel sure he did know, and that covering it up with a massive and baroque presentation piece was the best he felt could be done.

As for the subjected peoples on the shield of Aeneas in book eight, they die away quickly into rivers, and mere distance. The last men on earth, the Morini (8, 727) are the furthest North-Germans Tacitus knew anything about: they occur in his *Germania* at the point where it is dying out into the legendary distances of Herodotus or the Hereford Mappa Mundi, and the same catalogue of imperial conquests in the Aeneid that ends with them has begun a few lines earlier with the naked nomads of inner Africa. All these peoples are distant and vague and exotic. If Virgil had revised them he would have done so merely as a Hellenistic stylist. My own view is that he ought to have abandoned his Shield, which does not really rival Homer's. Nonetheless, it is an astonishing, utterly unexpected episode composed with a particular brilliance of its own, though it is surpassed at the end of book six in the underworld.

Virgil can be as neat as he can be baroque, and as reverent to antiquarian religion as he is to legendary history, though if one compares him with Homer he shows less delight in the gods. What surfaces in his Aeneid of purely Roman religion is deeply gloomy, and centres on such characters as Allecto and the Dirae. If we had to rely on Cicero, we would think of the Dirae only as omens of evil whom it was fatal to neglect (the coup by which Virgil produces them at the end of the Aeneid as living creatures probably takes colour from some Greek equivalent).

Virgil seems to have manipulated his gods with almost too much coolness, and one notices that Juno has resort to an oath by the river Styx (12, 816) as 'the only superstition that remains to the gods', using the word *superstitio*, which has the same meaning that it has in English: Cicero knew precisely what it meant. The truth is that Virgil did not believe in the gods, he simply picked through them somewhat fastidiously, and employed only those he would need for his Homeric poem. But he no more believed in the malice of Juno than in the power of Faunus over his tree at the death of Turnus. If he has made Jove a rather woolly figure who changes his mind, that is because fate, the fact of what happens, is not easy to predict. Fate is not personified, and may well represent something in which he does believe. I do not for a moment suppose that he believed in the ingenious metaphysics of his remarkable underworld. He spoke of man as being more decent, more religious than the gods (12, 839), that is excelling their gods in piety.

Virgil's influence was vast, his victory was immediate, and Augustus lived on long enough to make him famous. That had been his bargain after all, or his bet. Augustus was thrilled by his determination to celebrate Rome as Homer had celebrated Troy or Greece, and the link between Rome and Troy must have seemed, did seem, undeniable. It is important that when Augustus in Spain wrote to Virgil asking for a prose outline of the unwritten poem, he was sent nothing, and he was only read the Aeneid by the poet himself in that enviable voice, as each book was finished: first of all we are told books two, four and six: Troy, Dido and the underworld. Virgil's was the master of the individual line, and more quoted than any other Roman poet. As late as the fifth century AD it was possible to learn one's trade as a poet in Latin by knowing the poetry of Virgil, as Ausonius did, and to write lines in as it were Virgilian ink, memorable to this day.

NOTES

Introduction

1. *Agenda*, Vol. 23, nos. 3-4, pp. 180-201.
2. At the bottom of this inspiring muddle there may lie a mistake about Virgil's fourth Eclogue – which will be dealt with in Chapter 2.
3. Louise Adams Holland (1979).
4. R.G. Austin (1971), p. xiii.
5. If Dido, in her suicide, which is certainly heightened by theatrical influence, and later in her rejection of Aeneas in the underworld, embodies a protest, a woman's protest against gods and male ambitions, then she raises Virgil's height in my estimation. But alas I do not think this is the case.
6. Quoted by R.G. Austin (1971), p. xii.
7. If the earlier and far better though less full version of it attributed to Wyatt (Muir, *Unpublished Poems of Wyatt and His Circle*, n. xxiii; see p. xvi, n. 5) should be really be Wyatt, as I think it is, then may be he had a less full text.
8. E. Courtney (1993), pp. 83-5.

I. The Youth of Virgil

1. These art works now fill regional museums.
2. That alone would make him lord of a forty acre field in the distribution of land in any new colony.
3. Ocnus is (thought to be) a version of the Etruscan name Aucnus.
4. Edward Courtney in his *Fragmentary Latin Poets* (p. 189-91) points out that 80 lines about Lydia were wantonly stuck onto the end of the Curses because the name Lydia occurs in both poems, but he does not believe any of the muddle is by Valerius Cato.
5. I could never remember the reference, which Pauline Tennant kindly found for me in an essay by her grandmother Pamela Grey. I had previously referred to this bit of brilliant versification in a lecture on Theocritus, given at a Texas conference on Hellenistic Poetry later published by California, but for ten years I forgot who wrote it, I am sorry to say, causing much distress and annoyance to editors of the conference papers.

II. Country Singing

1. 'Hellenistic' a pre-Roman process of man being made divine.
2. The idea that the Aeneid was an image of the life of man – which is an offshoot of Christianizing Virgil – freakishly recurs in my cousin Ronald Knox's autobiography, *A Spiritual Aeneid*.

III. Virgil's Italy

1. Fraenkel's *Horace* makes this point very clearly, pp. 287-8.

2. Chilver, *Cisalpine Gaul*, 193.
3. Ms D'Orville 77, f. 100r., Published in *A Continental Shelf* (1994).
4. It seems a shame to study him without fighting one's way blow by blow through Housman's long forgotten battles. This makes a lengthy task for an apparently small reward; personally I never got beyond volume one of four or five, having halted enthralled at the influence of the constellations on the starting mechanism for horse races as described by Pausanias at Olympia.
5. *Ancient Book Illumination* (1959) pl. xvi.
6. Meiggs *Trees* (1982) App. 6.
7. Marc. gr. 479, f. 21.

IV. Transformation Scene

1. But once it has gone beyond your field of vision you no longer in England have a legal right to reclaim it, so it is vital to be beforehand with a swarm.
2. Among birds (Geo. 1, 415-16) Virgil was less optimistic.
3. This used in my beekeeping days in the early fifties to be supplied free by the government, under some old wartime regulation I imagine.

V. The March of Time

1. 'I often made war by land and sea and as conqueror I pardoned all citizens who asked pardon. I preferred to preserve those outside peoples who could safely be forgiven and not to exterminate them. About five hundred thousand Roman citizens were bound to me by oath. Of these I settled in colonies or brought home to their towns a little more than three hundred thousand with the money they had earned, and I gave them land or money as the reward of service. I took six hundred ships of or above the size of triremes. I triumphed twice on horseback and three times in a chariot ...'
2. We do not know when it was that he refused an offer of the goods of an exiled man, but probably earlier.
3. C. Hardie, *Vitae* p. xxi.
4. *CIL4*, 3072.
5. *Antiquity* Sept. (1945), p. 125. [[no EN in text]]
6. Jackson Knight (1944) drew attention to some valuable remarks by L.R. Palmer (*Latin Language*,1954), which will make sense to readers with little or no Latin, and although I have tried not to discuss or to quote the Latin language, I cannot refrain from noting where (apart from commentaries) wisdom is to be found.
7. *Studies on Homer*, Vol. 3, 527, cited by Conington in his Introduction to the Aeneid.

VII. Sand

1. Nine days are also standard for a funeral in Roman ritual (cf. Aen. 5, 645).

VIII. Italian Earth

1. Literally *illustrem fore*, a brilliant future.
2. One curious piece of Roman antiquarianism will serve to illustrate the rest. The ancient Roman word for money was *pecunia*, which comes from the word for cattle, *pecus* meaning a herd, because in the old Roman economy you paid your debts in animals, only latter in lumps of metal. The Romans were slow to feel the need for coinage of their own, but they were in close contact with Pyrrhus, king of Epirus, and the Greeks of south Italy, who already commanded resources for striking the finest coinage. The first Roman

mint was in the temple of Juno Moneta, which gives us the word money. This was after the period of the Roman kings, and was a typical achievement of the republic. Yet Suetonius says that Augustus at his dinner parties used to give away small presents of ancient coins, 'even the coins of kings'. Since those coins never existed (either Augustus minted a private coinage of apparent antiquity, which might fool Suetonius a century of more later, or Suetonius is mistaken in some other way. No doubt the mistake was inglorious, but we know that the coins of the consuls might allude to ancient events in their family histories, though their heads must not appear. So we are left with the guests of Augustus, poring over legendary or real Roman history, minted on antique coins. It seems to have been through this kind of study that Augustus become so interested in the obscure hero Cossus therefore mentions (Aen. 6, 841). I must admit that Ogilvie on Livy 4, 30 offers a smoother and more probable solution.

3. Though not attestations of the pun, cf. Geo. 1, 375 and Iliad 3, 7.

4. Cf. the Penguin edition.

5. K.W. Gransden, Intro. to book eight.

INDEX

Publisher's note: as italics have been kept to a minimum in the book, the style in the index may differ.

233

INDEX

Revelation, Book of, 50, 187
Rhadamanthus, ruler of part of the
  underworld, 185
Rhamnes, first to be killed in war of
  Latium, 207
Rhea, mother of Aventinus, 197
Rhesus, Thracian prince, 149
Rhine, 16, 69
Rhodes, Rhodians, 110, 154
Rhodope, range of mountains in Thrace, 81
Rhoetus, killed by Euryalus, 207
Rhone 16
Riace, town in south-east Calabria, 159
Rimini 13, 225
Robigo, included in Varro's list of gods, 74,
  78
Rome passim
Romulus, mythical co-founder of Rome,
  83, 128-30, 134, 146, 186, 194,
  201-202
Rubicon, river marking boundary between
  Italy and Cisalpine Gaul, 34, 124
Rufus, Varius, poet, 64
Rutuli, nation of Turnus, 129-30, 158, 192,
  195, 203, 206, 214, 219

Sabine, of tribe from north-east of Rome,
  86, 89-90, 92, 194, 198, 204
Sabaeans, mentioned in first Georgic, 76
Sabelli, tribe which took over Cumae, 180
Salamis, island near Athens, 133, 201
Salassi, Alpine tribe, 17
Salii, dancing priests, 201
Salius, Arcadian follower of Aeneas, 176
Sallust, Roman historian, 16
Salmoneus of Elis, inhabitant of
  underworld, 185
Saloniki, modern Thesaloniki in north-east
  Greece, 110
Salvidienus Rufus, associate of Augustus
  who later betrayed him, 30
Samians, founders of Puteoli, 26
Samos, island off western Asia Minor, 142
Samothrace, island in north-east Aegean,
  130, 195
Sandys, George, translator of Virgil, 11
Sappho, Greek poet, 208
Sardinia, 142, 144
Sarpedon, Trojan warrior killed by
  Patroclus in the Iliad, 211
Saturn, Greek Kronos, ruled over golden
  age in Italy, 52, 78, 81, 86, 91, 192,
  194-95, 202
Saturnia Iuno, term used of Hera, 142, 178
Saturnius, term used of Neptune, 178
Satyr, spirit of wild life with traits of goat,
  28, 56-57

Saxanus, god of stone-cutters, 75
Scaevola, Quintus Mucius, friend of Cicero,
  7
Scales, constellation, 79
Scipio, family of prominent generals, 149,
  187
Scorpion, constellation, 69, 75
Scribonia, marriage of important for fourth
  Eclogue, 54
Scriptores Erotici, until recently considered
  unsuitable for general access, 25
Scybale, slave descrived in Moretum, 20
Scylla, daughter of Nisus, king of Megara,
  20, 59, 81,
Scylla, sea-monster, living opposite
  Charybdis, 145, 163-64
Scythia, south Russian plains, 43, 93, 109
Sele, rivers marking boundaries of
  Campania, 101
Selinus, city in west Sicily, 164
Seneca, philosopher and historian, 209
Seneca, tragic dramatist, 154, 219,
Sergeaunt, commentator on Virgil, 151
Sergestus, captain in boat race of Aeneid bk
  5, 175-76
Servius, grammarian and commentator, 33,
  36, 57, 96, 124, 128, 139, 158
Severn, river, 18
Shakespeare, 3, 9, 19, 28, 48, 82, 87, 104,
  138, 141, 154, 169, 223
Shylock 115
Sibyl, originally priestess and clairvoyant,
  later minor deities associated with
  oracles, 27, 31, 50, 53, 111, 131,
  135-36, 161, 163, 172, 178, 180-85,
  193-94
Sidon, Phoenician city near Tyre, 151
Sila, mountain chain in toe of Italy, 92
Silarus, river Sele in south Italy, 85, 92, 110
Silenus, central character of sixth Eclogue,
  57-58, 62, 111
Silvanus, god of woodland, 13, 75, 90,
  204-205
Silvia, daughter of peasant Tyrrhus, 196
Silver Goose, in Aeneid bk 8, 205
Silvius, Aeneas's posthumous son, 186
Simois, river on plain of Troy, 150
Sinon, traditional captive figure in Aeneid
  bk 2, 154
Sirens, maidens whose beautiful song lured
  sailors on to reef, 117, 118, 179, 227
Sirmio, town on south of Lake Garda, 13
Siro the Epicurean, mentor and friend to
  Virgil, 22, 24, 33, 90, 124, 225-26
Skyros, Greek island, 92
Smyrna, city on west coast of Asia Minor,
  121

246